BUILDING THE
AWESOME
ORGANIZATION

BUILDING THE
AWESOME
ORGANIZATION

SIX ESSENTIAL

COMPONENTS

THAT DRIVE

ENTREPRENEURIAL

GROWTH

KATHERINE CATLIN
& JANA MATTHEWS

SECOND IN A SERIES OF BOOKS ON MANAGING GROWTH
FROM THE
KAUFFMAN CENTER FOR ENTREPRENEURIAL LEADERSHIP

Hungry Minds, Inc.
Cleveland, OH • Indianapolis, IN • New York, NY

Hungry Minds, Inc.

909 Third Avenue
New York, NY 10022

Library of Congress Control Number: 2001099315

ISBN 0-7645-5400-X

Editor: Pamela Sourelis
Production Editor: Heather Wilcox
Designer: Michael Rutkowski
Production by Hungry Minds Indianapolis Production Services

Special Sales

For general information on Hungry Minds' products and services please contact our Customer Care department: within the U.S. at 800-762-2974, outside the U.S. at 317-572-3993 or fax 317-572-4002. For sales inquiries and reseller information, including discounts, bulk sales, customized editions, and premium sales, please contact our Customer Care department at 800-434-3422.

Manufactured in the United States of America

5 4 3 2 1

"BAO has all the elements needed to help build a great company — a recipe book of great ideas and practices. The depth and detail make this a very actionable book, and a must-read for any entrepreneur serious about building a real company."

— Jeff Behrens, President, The Telluride Group, Inc.

"One of the most practical guides to the nuts and bolts of building an organization that I have ever read. Any executive will find substantive insights that will make their companies more effective."

— Patrick Lencioni, author of *The Five Temptations of a CEO* and *The Four Obsessions of an Extraordinary Executive*

"This book spoke to me, both to all the familiar challenges of working with teams in high-growth environments, as well as to the core steps that I've seen really work in a real company with real leaders. This is the right stuff for CEOs to lead with."

— Joanne C. Conrad, Principal, The Conrad Nelson Group

"Practical, incisive, and well-written. No more excuses for CEOs who lament their lousy corporate cultures. Get going and fix it!"

— Dan Schimmel, CEO, OneSource Information Services

"These authors know what it takes. They walk the talk — even dance it sometimes. Every entrepreneur and potential one needs this tremendous and valuable work of art and science!"

— Jean Hollands, CEO, Growth & Leadership Center

"This book is an absolute must-read for any growing, entrepreneurial business. After reading dozens of the best business books, this easily makes my top five of required reading books for any business leader or CEO. It has made a profound impact on my thought process and approach to the business."

— Dan Gould, President & CEO, Synergy Investments

"If you only have time to read two business books this year, read Building the Awesome Organization . . . twice! Essential reading for the entrepreneur."

— Tod Loofbourrow, President & CEO, Authoria

"With wit and wisdom gained from practical experience and relevant research, Jana Matthews has fashioned a must-read book for any entrepreneur who wants to build and lead an organization fueled by passion, fired by vision, and filled with achievement."

— Ray Smilor, President, Foundation for Enterprise

"Being a first time-entrepreneur leading a fast-growth company is like running full speed through the dark over unfamiliar terrain. Catlin and Matthews cast light on the path ahead, which allows you to take advantage of hidden opportunities and dramatically reduce the risk of stumbling."

— Aaron Kennedy, President & Founder, Noodles & Company

"Finally — a book that provides practical, actionable advice to entrepreneurs and CEOs on how to develop an organization to support growth. This book is a 'must read' for anyone trying to accelerate the growth of a company."

— Pat Cloherty, Chairman, The U.S. Russia Investment Fund

"Building the Awesome Organization provides leaders and entrepreneurs with valuable tools for navigating the storms of growth. There is no harder part of the company-building process than dealing with the rapid growth that often comes with success. This book has real tools and techniques that can help anyone in any type of enterprise."

— Gary Hoover, author, Hoover's Vision: Original Thinking for Business Success

"I read a lot of business articles and books looking for a few good nuggets I can use to build and improve our company. When I finished reading this book, I got more than a few nuggets. I got an entire gold mine."

— Jack Stack, author of *The Great Game of Business* and
A Stake in the Outcome: Building a Culture of Ownership

"What these two entrepreneurial thought leaders have done is 'awesome.' They have taken things that many of us have sensed, felt or known intuitively and expertly crafted these principles into a turnkey execution plan. This is truly a 'design for entrepreneurial success.'"

— W.R. "Max" Carey, Jr., author of *The Superman Complex*

"Matthews and Catlin illuminate why building the awesome organization is the key to growth. But they go far beyond concepts and provide hands-on tools that will help entrepreneurs — in fact, leaders of all kinds of organizations — create success. I can't wait to implement these ideas within Babson College."

— Mark Rice, Murata Dean, F.W. Olin Graduate School of Business

"A quick, concise entrepreneurial guide that yields real-world solutions for both start-ups and established businesses. This book lays the foundation for any business success!"

— Bob Nelson, Ph.D., author of *1001 Ways to Reward Employees* and
co-author of *Managing For Dummies*

"Matthews and Catlin have created the blueprint for a successful organization. Essential reading for entrepreneurs and venture capitalists everywhere!"

— Guy Kawasaki, CEO, Garage Technology Ventures

THE KAUFFMAN CENTER SERIES ON MANAGING GROWTH

What does it take to grow a company? The Kauffman Center for Entrepreneurial Leadership has identified three bodies of knowledge that entrepreneurs need to know "cold" in order to manage growth:

- How to build an awesome organization

- How to finance growth

- How to make the necessary leadership changes as their companies transform through growth

Few resources exist to help entrepreneurs master these critical areas, so the Kauffman Center and publisher Hungry Minds have joined to create a unique series of books to fill this information void. The mission of the Kauffman Center Series on Managing Growth is to enable entrepreneurs to manage and accelerate the growth of their companies.

Presented in a concise, lively format, the books in this series are designed to match the needs of busy entrepreneurs who are short on time and want quick access to ideas that will help them build stronger organizations. Key points are augmented with stories from successful entrepreneurs, by boxes highlighting vital signs, by red flags indicating problems that need action, and by summaries of your role as leader and of big lessons learned by successful entrepreneurs.

Building the Awesome Organization is the second book in the Kauffman Center Series on Managing Growth. *Leading at the Speed of Growth* is the first. Each book is a major building block in any entrepreneur's knowledge base of how to grow a successful company. For more information on this series, visit www.entreworld.org or www.hungry minds.com.

MISSION

The Mission of *Building the Awesome Organization* is to enable entrepreneurial leaders to build the foundation for growth.

ABOUT THE AUTHORS

KATHERINE CATLIN

For the past 15 years, Katherine Catlin has helped CEOs and their executive teams manage the challenges of fast-paced growth. As founding partner of The Catlin Group, a consulting firm in Hingham, Massachusetts, that works with entrepreneurial companies nationwide, she created and leads High Growth CEO Forums, where CEOs regularly meet to exchange ideas, challenges, and best practices for growth. Catlin also developed Building the Profit Spiral™, a proven growth-planning process that enables CEOs not only to avoid typical pitfalls, but also to define winning strategies, build a cohesive management team, and gain companywide commitment to growth goals. Her firm has established a Web site for CEOs, www.ceoexchange.com, which provides ideas and information on growth issues.

JANA MATTHEWS

Jana Matthews, President and CEO of Boulder Quantum Ventures, is an expert on entrepreneurial leadership and business growth. A member of the original senior staff of the Kauffman Center for Entrepreneurial Leadership, Jana was the architect of the Center's world-renowned programs designed to teach entrepreneurs how to manage growth. She has authored or co-authored six books and founded three companies. Boulder Quantum Ventures (www.BoulderQuantumVentures.com) provides leadership and management education and consulting to CEOs and their top teams to enable them to unlock their company's growth potential. She enjoys writing books, helping entrepreneurs build successful companies, and fly-fishing in New Zealand.

CONTENTS

FOREWORD

Ewing Marion Kauffman was a true entrepreneurial leader. Born into a modest home near Kansas City in 1916, he left as a young man to serve in the U.S. Navy. After returning to his hometown he took a job to provide for his family. He believed that hard work, dedication to principles, and respect for others created the path to success. When he wasn't treated fairly by his employer, he quit.

With an initial investment of $5,000, Mr. Kauffman started a pharmaceutical company in the basement of his house in 1950. First-year sales reached $36,000, and the company made a net profit of $1,000. Over the years, he assembled a team and built Marion Laboratories, Inc., into a diversified health-care colossus. In 1989, when it merged with Merrell Dow, Marion Laboratories had 3,200 employees, annual sales of approximately $1 billion, and a value of more than $6 billion. The company operates today as part of Aventis, one of the world's leading life science companies focused on pharmaceuticals and agriculture. Aventis has 92,500 employees worldwide and revenues of approximately $22 billion.

"Mr. K," as he was called, used his entrepreneurial skills to create several other successful organizations. For example, he brought major league baseball back to his community by purchasing the Kansas City Royals. In typical entrepreneurial fashion, Mr. K developed the Royals into a championship team that won six divisional titles, two American League pennants, and the 1985 World Series. Mr. K's Royals boosted the city's economic base, profile, and civic pride. He also created the Ewing Marion Kauffman Foundation as an "uncommon philanthropy" and endowed it with more than $1 billion.

In 1992, a year before his death, Mr. K created the Kauffman Center for Entrepreneurial Leadership at the Kauffman Foundation. He recognized that the health of our economy is dependent on the ability of entrepreneurs to grow companies and was convinced that the best way to help entrepreneurs is to identify and teach the knowledge, skills, and values that contribute to entrepreneurial success. If entrepreneurs could learn how to develop successful companies, jobs would be created and the economy would be strengthened. This, he believed, would help the Kauffman Foundation achieve its mission of "self-sufficient people in healthy communities."

The Kauffman Center for Entrepreneurial Leadership is the largest organization in the world with the sole purpose of encouraging entrepreneurial success at all ages and levels, from elementary-school students to entrepreneurs leading high-growth companies.

Mr. Kauffman is one of those few founding entrepreneurs who stayed with his company for more than 40 years. His ability to learn from experience and his reflections about what is required to be a successful entrepreneur have provided us with a rich legacy of knowledge about entrepreneurial leadership, the importance of continual learning, and the spirit of discovery. This book is a distillation of what we have learned from him — and from many other successful entrepreneurs — about what is required to build an awesome organization.

This book is part of the Kauffman Center Series on Managing Growth and one of the learning resources the Kauffman Center has created for entrepreneurs. The Kauffman Center's Web site (www.entreworld.org) was specifically designed for entrepreneurs. Check the Web site for information on Kauffman Gatherings of Entrepreneurs, diagnostic surveys to identify "what you know and what you don't know you don't know," the Kauffman Business EKG on-line benchmarking system, CD-ROMs, audiotapes, and other products and services. All are designed to help entrepreneurs pilot their companies through growth. These resources have been developed by and with hundreds of successful entrepreneurs who have shared their knowledge, insights, and stories so that others might learn from them. We hope you find them useful as you work to write your own entrepreneurial success story.

Katherine Catlin, Partner
The Catlin Group

Jana Matthews, President
Boulder Quantum Ventures
High Growth Expert
Kauffman Center for Entrepreneurial Leadership

DEDICATION

This book is dedicated to:

Katherine Catlin's parents:
John Raymond Cummings, for his inspiration and creative drive.
Jean McNeer McCurry, for her compassion and courage.
Both for giving me the spirit of adventure.

Jana Matthews's parents:
Carolyn Markey Beauchamp, for sharing her wisdom about managing people.
L. Emmet Beauchamp, for teaching me about markets and customers.
Both for encouraging me to pursue my dreams.

ACKNOWLEDGMENTS

Over the past few years we've worked with hundreds of remarkable entrepreneurial leaders. Their willingness to talk about their experiences and share personal insights and lessons learned has enabled us to discover the critical stages and challenges of growth. The Kauffman Center's Gatherings of Entrepreneurs, The Catlin Group's High Growth CEO Forums, our own consulting projects, workshops for software and Internet councils, and in-depth discussions with entrepreneurs have provided many opportunities for us to learn about the evolution of growth companies. The leadership changes required to meet the challenges of growth are especially significant. The commitment and energy required to build an awesome organization, the foundation for growth, is enormous. We thank all these entrepreneurs for sharing their knowledge and experiences, and for helping us help other entrepreneurs.

We also want to thank our families, in particular Chip and Chuck. They believed in us and encouraged us at every step along the way. Likewise, we want to thank the following people for sharing their knowledge and supporting us in this endeavor: Dan Grace, Ray Smilor, Brad Feld, Sue Hesse, Mike Herman, Michie Slaughter, Bill Payne, Gary Marple, Kate Pope Hodel, John Tyler, and other colleagues at the Kauffman Center. We also want to thank members of The Catlin Group and of Boulder Quantum Ventures, as well as Jeanne Yocum, Kathy Duncan, Judy Farren, and Pat Mullaly for all their help. Finally, we want to acknowledge the contributions of our agent, Jim Levine, as well as Mark Butler, Pam Sourelis, Heather Wilcox, and the team at Hungry Minds. They have helped us develop the roadmap that entrepreneurs can use to build great companies.

CHAPTER 1

WHY BUILD AN AWESOME ORGANIZATION?

"Typically a business doesn't move in a straight line; there are lots of turns in the road, lots of unexpected obstacles that you come up against. It's the awesome organization that can navigate around those obstacles to reach success. In a lot of early-stage companies, leaders spend all their time on building the product and then when you get internal conflicts or changes in the market, you spiral down and lose momentum because you haven't built the organization."

The United States is filled with entrepreneurs. Everywhere, people with ideas, daring, and ambition are starting and building companies. But, many would-be tycoons find that growing a business is the hardest thing they've ever tried to do. And, along the way, many don't make it.

What's the secret of those who succeed? Successful entrepreneurs know that innovation drives growth. They also know it takes people with a shared passion for problem solving and turning ideas into reality to produce innovation. Innovative companies invent and reinvent new markets, products, services, and business models, all of which lead to growth. If you build an awesome organization that attracts, retains, and inspires people to create and innovate, your company will grow. If you don't, your company will decline. It's that simple.

The mission of this book is to help entrepreneurial leaders build awesome organizations that achieve entrepreneurial growth. Whether you're a first-time entrepreneur or a serial entrepreneur with several successful start-ups under your belt, this book will be a valuable resource. Use the organizational framework and the assessment tools in this book to strengthen your organization, improve your company's ability to compete, and manage the growth that drives marketplace success.

DEFINING AN AWESOME ORGANIZATION

Here's how two successful entrepreneurs describe an awesome organization:

> "An awesome organization is where the entire organization shares the same intensity and clarity of vision that the entrepreneur brought to the company on the first day it opened its doors."

> "We've finally put the elements of an awesome organization in place, and we've never had this kind of performance. The environment crackles with excitement, purpose, intensity, change, and innovation. But the reverse was true before we were able to put the right things in place. When we are performing at an awesome level, it's physically and emotionally tangible at every meeting, every interaction."

People love working in an awesome organization; they tell their family, friends, and customers what a great place it is to work. Customers love doing business with an awesome organization, and they spread the word, too. The company's culture and its people become part of its brand and contribute to its competitive edge in the marketplace.

The following box, "Vital Signs: Characteristics of an Awesome Organization," defines the chief qualities of a great organization. Think about how your company stacks up against this checklist.

VITAL SIGNS: CHARACTERISTICS OF AN AWESOME ORGANIZATION

An awesome organization:

- Is a market leader, has highly valued products and services and good profit margins.

- Has high-quality leadership and a workforce that is extremely talented, self-motivated, and highly productive.

- Has a shared vision and core values that everyone understands and embraces.

- Has a plan that everyone uses as the road map for setting priorities, making decisions, and taking action.

- Has a culture that rewards people for their ideas and contributions, and fosters great teamwork at all levels.

- Has people who are dedicated to learning and helping each other learn.

- Has streamlined processes to assure maximum efficiency in all areas of operation.

- Focuses continually on innovation and improvement, with new ideas constantly bubbling up and being implemented.

- Anticipates change and continually redefines every part of the business to ensure that its competitive edge is always sharp and distinctive.

- Capitalizes on new market opportunities; considers the needs and wants of the customers and prospects before making decisions.

UNDERSTANDING WHY THERE AREN'T MORE AWESOME ORGANIZATIONS

Why do so few entrepreneurs succeed in building awesome organizations? Most don't realize how important it is. Some hire people as fast as they can and focus on sales and revenues. Some are great technical or market experts but don't know what constitutes a great organization or how to manage people. Others get so wrapped up in getting a product out the door or raising the next round of financing that they pay no attention to building an organization that will sustain growth. But, when the company "hits the wall" and stops growing, they come face-to-face with a complicated set of organizational problems that could have been avoided — if they'd only known which building blocks to put in place — from the beginning.

Entrepreneurs who don't know what they don't know can lead their companies into dangerous territory. Beware of these common pitfalls.

Thinking awesome organizations "just happen." They don't! Building the organization is your primary responsibility, and you have to work at it, every single day, throughout the life of the company. Truly great organizations are carefully constructed, one building block at a time. You lay the foundation of a great company when you hire outstanding people, create a culture that inspires innovation, develop and implement a solid growth plan, have a top team that is a role model for all teams, and develop fine-tuned systems and processes. You provide the kind of leadership that awesome people want when you guide, coach, and encourage them to help you build an organization that can be a market leader. If you don't make a conscious effort to build a great organization, it will develop haphazardly and the results will be very disappointing — to you and your employees.

> "Adrenaline can get your first product out the door, but if you're going to build a multi-product company, you need organizational tools and processes to surmount the complexity. A few years down the road, adrenaline just doesn't do it any more. Having these organizational tools and processes in place enables the company to keep working on existing products while senior management focuses on the future."

Bottom line: Building the organization must be a top priority. You must make a conscious, concerted effort to develop each of the building blocks, as well as the organizational tools and processes needed to support growth.

Developing plans by yourself and expecting other people to execute them. Awesome people won't stay at a company whose leader tells them to put their heads down and implement plans they've had no role in creating. They want to be active participants in planning the company's future, be challenged, and gain new skills. They want to work in an organization that encourages them to learn, grow, create, innovate, and excel.

"People take a job for the challenge, for their ego, and for the money. They stay because of their peers, their successes, what they learn, a chance to help shape the future of the company, and the opportunity to keep growing."

Hiring "bodies for slots." Entrepreneurs often don't think hard enough about what kinds of people are needed to build a great organization, and most don't search long enough to find the right people. They are so busy trying to hire people for all the open positions that they end up hiring employees who are less than awesome. Listen to one CEO describe the kinds of people he wants to hire into his company:

"We want awesome people who will roll up their sleeves and get their hands dirty. They can lead by example and pull other people along, but not do their work for them. An awesome person can take constructive criticism, is able to learn and change, and is open-minded enough to say, 'Tell me what the organization needs; I'm willing to do whatever it takes.' Even if this particular job isn't going to stretch them at this time, they'll take it on because it needs to be done, and they'll expect to get rewarded with a big opportunity. An awesome person clearly has the brains and skills to do the job but probably more importantly has the ability to work within the structure and culture of the organization. He or she will embody that culture — live that culture, and those are the kinds of people we're looking for."

Not understanding what awesome people want. Sometimes entrepreneurs fail to attract or retain awesome people because they don't understand what these people want. At the Kauffman Center for Entrepreneurial Leadership, successful entrepreneurs were asked to identify their most outstanding people. We then interviewed some of these great employees and asked them to describe their ideal workplace — the kind of company they would want to join and help grow, over the long term.

These awesome people told us they want to work for an organization with a compelling vision, people-oriented values, and a culture of trust that stimulates risk-taking and encourages creative ideas. They expect lots of two-way communications about the company's strategic direction and financial performance. It's important to them to work with peers they can respect and enjoy in a dynamic, fun, participatory environment. They want leaders who mentor, provide feedback, empower, and give them opportunities to learn and grow. They want to have a sense of ownership about their work and a chance to make a difference in the world. They want to be sure they have challenging work, autonomy, flexibility, and rewards and recognition for their high performance.

If you want to attract and keep the kinds of people you need to grow the company, you have to build the kind of organization they want to join.

Not understanding how the organization will change — and your role as leader will change. In the early stages, your company was small enough for you to manage everything, make all the decisions, plan "on the fly," and respond to opportunities as you saw fit. But in order for the company to grow, you must consciously build an organization that will support growth. You cannot do it all yourself, and you will not be able to pursue all the opportunities that come your way. You must make some choices, chart a direction, and develop a plan for growth. Over time your role as leader will change as you begin to institutionalize the culture, standardize the hiring processes, develop planning and budgeting processes, and share leadership with your top team. If you don't do this, your company will not be able to grow and you will become the bottleneck or worse, the cement boots that drag your company down.

The first book in the Kauffman Center Series on Managing Growth, *Leading at the Speed of Growth: Journey from Entrepreneur to CEO,* describes how and why the entrepreneur's role must change as the company moves from start-up to initial growth, change again when it moves into rapid growth, and change yet again in order to move the company into continuous growth. (See appendix B, "Stages of Growth and the Leader's Roles," for a brief description of these three stages of growth.) The creativity, drive, and will to succeed that made you an entrepreneur in the first place will help you to adapt to the changing leadership roles and responsibilities required to build an organization that will support growth. Your experience, insights, and problem-solving skills will enable you to deal with the tough challenges every CEO of a growing company faces. Regardless of whether your current organization is awesome — or not — you *can* develop a great company *if* you are willing to change your role as leader as your company grows, and *if* you are willing to focus your time and attention on building an awesome organization.

RECOGNIZING SIX COMPONENTS OF AN AWESOME ORGANIZATION

This book will help you overcome the pitfalls described earlier in the chapter and serve as your "map" to building a great company. Our framework describes the six building blocks, or components of an awesome organization. Each of them is equally important; none can be ignored. Each component must be consciously built and continuously strengthened if you want your company to grow. If any single component or building block is weak, the company's growth and performance will be at risk. The six components of an awesome organization, described in chapters 3 through 9, are:

- **Culture for growth.** An awesome organization has an empowering, motivating environment that attracts awesome people and then retains them because it enables them to thrive and perform at their best.

- **Awesome people.** The know-how, skills, insight, imagination, and ideas of your people are the intangible assets that give your company its distinct competitive edge.

- **Plan for growth.** Every awesome organization has a written — yet flexible — plan that defines both the long-term and short-term requirements for growth and innovation. The plan helps guide decision making and enables everyone to focus on projects, tasks, and activities that lead to achievement of the vision and goals.

- **Top team as leaders of growth.** The CEO can't do it alone. Each member of the top team needs to share the vision and fully understand his or her functional and cross-functional roles and responsibilities for implementing the plans and achieving the mission.

- **Infrastructure for growth.** The organizational structure and three sets of processes (finding and leading people, planning and alignment, and management and control) comprise the infrastructure for growth. The infrastructure enables you to institutionalize the organization's mission, vision, and values, and makes the work flow easily and efficiently.

- **You, the awesome leader of growth.** As the company grows, your ability to communicate a powerful sense of purpose and direction will help align everyone with the mission, vision, and values. That will be one of the keys to your success. And, one of the outcomes of building an awesome organization will be an environment that stimulates, encourages, and enables people to achieve extraordinary results.

Very few entrepreneurs have mastered all six components. Some entrepreneurs know they have to hire great people, but they don't know how to create a culture that will help them retain these people. Some know they have to do a better job with planning, but they don't develop the infrastructure that enables plans to be implemented. Others hire and fire top team members without knowing how to build a cohesive top team, what roles team members need to play, and how their own role will change as the team matures and/or the company moves into a new stage of development. This book will enable you to put it all together and will show you what you need to do as the leader to build each component of an awesome organization.

Building an organization capable of competing and thriving in today's business climate is challenging, to say the least. So in addition to providing the framework and describing the six components of an awesome organization, we have included a number of tools and resources that will help you assess, and then strengthen, each component in your own company.

USE THE LEARNING TOOLS WE'VE PROVIDED

We've discovered that great leaders are great learners, and that the most successful entrepreneurs are constantly learning. This book will help you learn what you need to know to develop an awesome organization, assess how awesome your own organization is — and determine where you need to make improvements. The learning tools in this book include:

- **Lessons from Fellow CEOs**

Entrepreneurs prefer to learn from their peers, so we've included a large number of stories from entrepreneurial leaders who have faced the same tough issues you struggle with daily — entrepreneurs who have figured out how to build great organizations. Their companies range in size from 10 to 800 employees and from $1 million to $150 million in revenue. They have experienced significant annual growth rates of 20 percent, 50 percent, or more. We've provided the framework and context, and then used their stories to illustrate the points. Their stories are set off by quotation marks.

Since some of the entrepreneurs were not willing to share confidential stories and candid insights unless they could remain anonymous, the entrepreneurs telling the stories are not identified. But, you'll read about their mistakes, hear them tell what they did — or wished they had done — to develop their organizations, and what lessons they learned. In several places, you'll also hear from the people these entrepreneurs identified as awesome employees.

- **Overview Quiz and *BAO SCANs***

In addition to learning from peers and mentors, entrepreneurs learn by immediately applying what they have learned to their own situations. They like to assess themselves and their organizations, ask probing questions, find answers, take action, and achieve quick results. That's why we have included an Overview Quiz in chapter 2, "Take the Quiz: How Awesome Is Your Organization?", and *Building the Awesome Organization (BAO) SCANs* at the ends of chapters 3 through 9. These assessment tools are designed to help you, your leadership team, and your employees evaluate how well your company is performing in each of the six components or building blocks of an awesome organization.

The Overview Quiz and the *BAO SCANs* can also be downloaded from www.entreworld.org, the Web site of the Kauffman Center for Entrepreneurial Leadership. The Center's Web site is a rich and comprehensive resource of useful information and best practices for entrepreneurial leaders who want to grow their companies. Whenever you see the symbol shown in the accompanying figure, you can download that tool from the Managing Growth Book Series section at www.entreworld.org.

If you want to stay healthy, you need to have periodic checkups. If you want to have a healthy organization, you need to check on its health at regular intervals, as well. The Overview Quiz will enable you to assess the overall health of your company, and the seven *BAO SCANs* will provide you with a more detailed assessment in each of the book's components. With that information you can develop a "fitness profile" for your organization. We encourage you to have your top team take the Overview Quiz as well as the *BAO SCANs*. Once you and they understand where the problems are, be sure to read the appropriate chapters, and then develop an action plan for needed improvements.

You might also want to have some of your awesome people take the Overview Quiz and the *BAO SCANs*. This is a great way to involve employees in identifying problem areas and helping shape the future of the company. Asking employees for feedback will encourage them to contribute new ideas to help move the organization forward and will demonstrate that you are focused on learning and improving, and are trying create an open culture.

The *BAO SCANs* are not intended to be scientific benchmarking tools. They were not designed to provide comparative data between or among companies but rather to enable you to identify (1) areas of strength and weakness and (2) any areas where you, the top team, and/or your employees have different perceptions of the company's strengths or weaknesses. Based on the results of the *SCANs* and the Action Plans, you'll be able to determine where you need to focus time and resources to strengthen your organization.

Every organization has good points and bad points that often reflect the founding entrepreneur's or CEO's strengths and weaknesses. The *BAO SCANs* will enable you to hold up a mirror to the organization — and to yourself. Acknowledging areas that need work can be painful, but every company, and every person, can benefit from such assessment.

Setting priorities is often a challenge for entrepreneurs, especially if it appears that many issues need to be addressed at once. The Overview Quiz and the *BAO SCANs* will help you focus on the changes that can have the greatest impact on the development of your organization and will improve its ability to sustain growth.

● Vital Signs, Your Role as Leader, and Big Lessons

The Vital Signs boxes found throughout the book contain some of the most important information in each chapter. Sections at the end of each chapter address your role as leader and summarize key ideas or Big Lessons. These sections serve as recaps for rapid learning and quick review. Use them to refresh your memory when you're working on a specific component of the awesome organization.

● Red Flags

Each chapter includes boxes with warning signs, called Red Flags. Read through them and think about whether they apply to your company. Do not ignore the Red Flags. Use the *BAO SCANs* at the end of chapters 3 through 9 to help you identify specific problems and develop action plans in response to the Red Flags.

● Appendixes

We've developed a series of appendixes to provide additional information and tools:

> A: Glossary of Growth and Organization-Building Terms
>
> B: Stages of Growth and the Leader's Roles
>
> C: Creating a Core Values Statement for Growth
>
> D: Model for Creative Problem Solving
>
> E: Examples of Mission, Values, and Vision Statements
>
> F: Helping Build Your Company's Profit Spiral™

USING THIS BOOK AS YOUR MAP

This book provides you with a description of the organization you need to build to support and accelerate growth — and a "map" to help you get there. Maps are powerful learning tools. They indicate that someone has figured out the route to success. They present alternative ways to get to the desired goal and show which routes are dead-ends. Maps identify rivers, valleys, mountains, and deserts so you can be prepared for what lies ahead. Some entrepreneurs don't like to use maps and prefer, instead, to make their own way. But in today's speed-driven world, the prize goes to those who get there first. Why waste valuable time and resources learning lessons that others have already learned and are willing to share? Read this book, benefit from the wisdom of experienced entrepreneurs, discover the quickest path through the woods, and shorten your journey to success.

As you read this book, you may find you're already doing what we recommend — and that's good! Confirmation that you're on the right track is as important as warnings that you're on the wrong one. Use the Overview Quiz and the *BAO SCANs* to identify where your company is doing well, and what areas need further improvement. The information in each chapter should get you headed in the right direction, and continued use of the Overview Quiz and the *BAO SCANs* can help you chart your progress, over time.

We've designed this book as a resource that you can use again and again, year after year. Share it with your top team and with your board of directors or advisors. Share it with other entrepreneurs. Consider it your trusted resource, guidebook, and map as you build your awesome organization. Don't put it on the shelf. Use it!

Your first step to building an awesome organization is to turn the page and take the Overview Quiz in chapter 2. Ask your top team to take it as well. Use the results to frame a discussion of two key questions:

- "What do we need to do to make sure our company is constantly improving, innovating, and growing?"

- "What do we need to do to build our own awesome organization?

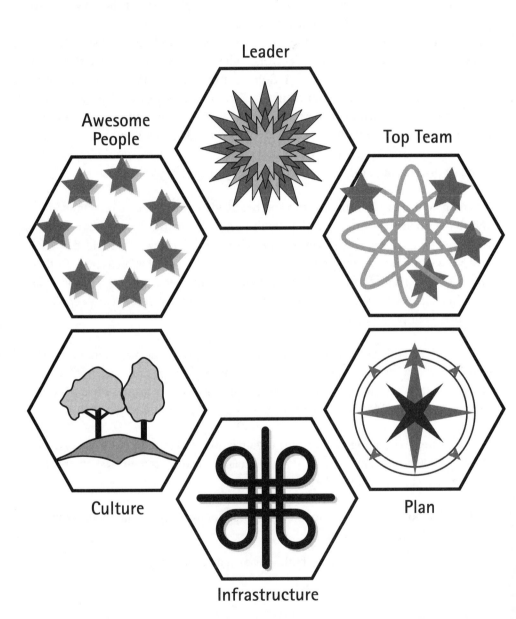

Leader

Awesome
People

Top Team

Culture

Infrastructure

Plan

Six Essential Components that Drive Entrepreneurial Growth

CHAPTER **2**

TAKE THE QUIZ:
HOW AWESOME IS
YOUR ORGANIZATION?

The most successful entrepreneurial leaders are constantly seeking an edge — a way to improve the company's performance and growth so it can be even better tomorrow than it is today. This chapter gives you a tool — the *Building the Awesome Organization Overview Quiz* — for assessing how awesome your company is. Use the Overview Quiz to establish a baseline regarding how well your organization is operating; work with your top team and create an action plan to address problems, and then track improvements.

You can also use the results of the *Overview Quiz* to help chart your path through this book. Although we've organized the chapters in a sequence that makes sense to us, we've written each chapter to stand on its own, so it's not necessary for you to read the chapters in order. If your company's *Overview Quiz* scores are lowest in the Top Team component, for instance, you can go directly to chapter 7, "Prime Your Top Team for Growth." If they are lowest in Planning, then the first chapter you might want to read is chapter 6, "Create Your Plan for Growth." Keep in mind, though, that all the components or building blocks of an awesome organization are interconnected; each one is part of a total system. So eventually you will need to read all the chapters and take all seven *BAO SCANs* in order to get an accurate reading on the "awesomeness" of your organization. As you review the results of each of the *BAO SCANs,* think about what changes you need to make to capitalize on the strengths of your organization and shore up its weaknesses.

THE BUILDING THE AWESOME ORGANIZATION OVERVIEW QUIZ

The *Overview Quiz* will provide information about your organization's current strengths and weaknesses and will help you determine what areas are most in need of improvement. In addition to taking the *Overview Quiz* yourself, have your top team and other key people complete it. Compare your responses and perceptions with theirs. Work together to identify innovative ways to solve problems and come up with new ideas to strengthen your organization.

RATING SCALE

Use this scale to respond to each rating question

1 - - - - - 2 - - - - - 3 - - - - - 4 - - - - - 5 - - - - - 6 - - - - - 7
NEVER   *SOMETIMES*   *ALWAYS*

CULTURE FOR GROWTH

An awesome organization has an empowering, motivating culture that attracts awesome people and retains them. It enables them to thrive and perform at their best. Awesome people look for:

1. A work environment that is supportive, creative, fun, and challenging.

2. Autonomy and flexibility to produce awesome results.

3. Big challenges, high expectations, and fair rewards for great performance.

4. A team of great peers to respect, enjoy, and learn from.

5. Managers who are accessible, who are good listeners and communicators, who respect, trust, and value their people, and who show sincere appreciation.

6. Opportunities to be involved in planning, decision making, and problem solving.

7. Opportunities for growth and learning, mentoring, and feedback.

8. Fair compensation, rewards, and recognition, and an opportunity to share in the company's success.

9. A meaningful vision and core values that provide focus and clarity for everyone in the company.

1 0. Open, honest, and frequent communication about strategy, goals, issues, and financial performance.

1 1. Encouragement to contribute new ideas and take risks that will make a difference for the company.

A. We have an awesome corporate culture.　　　　　Rating: _____

B. Which statements describe our culture's strengths?　　Statement #s _____

C. Which statements describe areas in which
our culture is weak?　　　　　　　　　　　　　Statement #s _____

AWESOME PEOPLE WHO DRIVE GROWTH

Awesome people have the talents, skills, and expertise your company needs. They share the company's values and are able to handle company growth. They have four basic sets of characteristics:

1. They are self-motivated and committed to the mission; they keep the customer first; and they do whatever it takes to get the job done.

2. They respect and help others; they are team-oriented; they model company values; and they influence, even inspire, others to achieve great things.

3. They are creative problem solvers who take risks, learn from successes and failures, and have great ideas that help the company innovate and grow.

4. They are learners, who are able to grow faster than the company and adapt quickly to change.

A. We attract and retain awesome people.　　　　　Rating: _____

B. Which characteristics best match our people's
strengths?　　　　　　　　　　　　　　　　　Statement #s _____

C. Which characteristics describe situations
where our people are less than awesome?　　　　Statement #s _____

CLEAR PLAN FOR GROWTH

A written plan provides a long-term and short-term framework for growth and innovation. The plan helps guide decision making and enables everyone to focus on projects, tasks, and activities that lead to achievement of the vision and goals. The plan needs to be developed with input from all levels of the organization so everyone feels ownership and is vested in the success of the plan. It needs to be tracked continuously, adjusted to changing market conditions, and updated annually (at minimum). An effective plan has six parts:

1. **Market and Customer Focus:** We understand what's going on in our market(s) and are meeting our customers' needs effectively.

2. **Mission and Values:** We know what business we are in and what our company is trying to achieve.

3. **Vision and Objectives:** Our company's objectives are well defined.

4. **Strategies and Action Plans:** We know what to do to reach those objectives.

5. **Infrastructure and Resources:** Our structure and resources are adequate to implement our plans effectively.

6. **Culture:** Our cultural environment supports implementation of our plans.

A. Our planning process results in a written plan that describes where we want to go and how the company is going to get there.   Rating: _____

B. Which parts of an effective plan from the above list best describe our plan's strengths?   Statement #s _____

C. Which parts of an effective plan from the above list best describe where our plan needs the most work?   Statement #s _____

A TOP TEAM THAT LEADS GROWTH

Each top team member has responsibilities in a functional area. But together, the top team must share the leadership of the company with the CEO. They must fully embrace the company's vision and plan, understand how their roles and functions are integrated, and coordinate their activities across functions to support company growth.

The top team has six major responsibilities for leading growth. The team must:

1. Create and update the company's plan for growth.

2. Communicate so everyone in the company is on the same page and aligned with the plan.

3. Develop and protect the company's values and culture.

4. Attract and retain awesome people.

5. Manage the top team's dynamics and pitfalls as a model for all teams.

6. Learn from each other and help each other to succeed.

A. Our top team is very effective in leading the company. Rating: _____

B. Which major areas from the above list best describe our top team's strengths?   Statement #s _____

C. Which major areas from the above list best describe the areas in which our top team needs to improve?   Statement #s _____

INFRASTRUCTURE WITH ORGANIZATIONAL STRUCTURE AND PROCESSES FOR GROWTH

Successful companies carefully design their organizational structure and develop processes to support growth, embed the mission, vision, and values of the company into the organization, and make it easier to get work done. In order to have an awesome organization, the following four issues regarding organizational structure and process development need to be addressed:

1. **The organizational structure is designed to be customer-centric, efficient, and effective.** It supports the company's plan for growth and clearly defines people's roles, responsibilities, accountabilities, and cross-functional interdependencies.

2. **Processes for Managing and Leading People:** Processes are well established for attracting, recruiting, selecting, and hiring people; orienting and integrating them into the company; managing and reviewing performance; developing people by providing opportunities for continuous learning; fostering team development; developing compensation systems that reinforce

the culture (salary, benefits, rewards, and recognition); and developing succession plans as well as policies and procedures for termination.

3. **Processes for Planning and Alignment:** Processes are effectively used for planning; for tracking and disseminating market and customer information; for communication; for continuous innovation and improvement; for measurement of performance to objectives; and for policy development.

4. **Processes for Management and Control:** Processes are developed and used for budgeting and tracking revenues and expenditures, financial management and raising capital, information technology and support, and facilities management.

A. Our infrastructure supports our company's growth.　　Rating: _____

B. Which statements best describe the areas of our
infrastructure that are the strongest?　　　　Statement #s_____

C. Which statements best describe the areas of our
infrastructure that need the most work?　　　Statement #s _____

You, THE AWESOME LEADER OF GROWTH

Remember, if you are the CEO, you will be evaluating your own performance!

Leadership Tasks: As company leader, the CEO:

1. Sets the company's direction with a mission, vision, values, and strategic plan.

2. Talks about and makes sure everyone in the company understands and is involved, committed to, and aligned with the mission, vision, values, and strategic plan.

3. Cultivates a high-performance, high-involvement culture.

4. Builds and leads the top management team as a model for all other teams.

5. Manages corporate resources to sustain healthy performance.

6. Designs the organizational structure and processes to fit the culture and strategy.

7. Engages in continuous learning for self- and company-improvement.

8. Anticipates, initiates, and leads the transitions required for the company's growth.

A. The CEO's performance is consistent with these eight leadership responsibilities.   Rating: _____

B. Which statements best describe areas in which the CEO is strongest?   Statement #s_____

C. Which statements best describe areas in which the CEO needs to improve his or her effectiveness?   Statement #s_____

Leadership Style: Awesome people expect that the CEO, as the company leader:

1. Is a thoughtful listener and open, honest communicator.

2. Has integrity, does not compromise values, and behaves consistently with values.

3. Actively seeks new ideas and is comfortable with change.

4. Trusts and respects employees — and shows it.

5. Is accessible and promotes rapport.

6. Is energetic, optimistic, and excited about the company and its future.

7. Genuinely cares for other people and helps them to reach their goals and dreams.

8. Fosters teamwork.

9. Is a practical visionary, with ambitious but realistic goals.

10. Provides opportunities, freedom, and mechanisms for employees to grow and be creative.

A. The CEO exemplifies these leadership style qualities.   Rating: _____

B. Which statements best describe areas in which the CEO is strongest?   Statement #s _____

C. Which statements best describe areas in which the CEO needs to improve his or her leadership style?   Statement #s _____

SCORE SUMMARY AND INTERPRETATION

A Rating Score of **7** in any area indicates this is a prime area of strength that will facilitate and support the company's growth. Scores of **5** and **6** indicate considerable strength in these areas, but you will want to consider making incremental improvements to increase the score. A score of **4** is a cause for worry. A rating of "Sometimes" indicates a lack of consistency that sends conflicting signals to employees and inhibits growth; thus, significant improvements will be needed. Scores of **3 or below** are big red flags indicating areas or behaviors that hinder the company's growth and require your immediate attention.

RESULTS ANALYSIS

Look back over the *Building the Awesome Organization Overview Quiz:*

1. List three statements that you rated the highest. Choose those you feel are key strengths and contribute most to the success of the company.

   A. _____

   B. _____

   C. _____

2. List three statements that received the lowest rating. Choose those you feel are the most critical weaknesses and should be targeted for improvement.

   A. _____

   B. _____

   C. _____

3. Write three statements that define your priorities for change (for example, how can we capitalize on the strengths or improve the weaknesses?).

   A. _____

   B. _____

   C. _____

4. List three things our company could do to implement these changes.

A. _____

B. _____

C. _____

ACTION PLAN

Recognize what you and your company are doing well and celebrate! Think about what you have done that enabled you to achieve these great results and how that can be applied to your weaknesses. But, do not overlook areas that need improvement or think they will improve on their own over time. Use these steps to develop your Action Plan for Improvement:

1. Ask your top team to complete the *Building the Awesome Organization Overview Quiz* and the Results Analysis. You may also want others in the company to complete the *Quiz* to get more comprehensive feedback.

2. Meet with your top team to:

• Compare and contrast your ratings on various statements with their ratings, as well as areas you have identified as strengths with those needing work.

• If applicable, discuss the reasons why their responses are different from yours.

• Agree on areas for improvement or change; be as specific as possible.

3. Prioritize those areas that must be addressed and will make the biggest difference. Develop them into Action Plans for Improvement.

4. Get consensus on the Action Plans and the resources and budgets needed to make the necessary changes.

• For each Action Plan, specify the goal, desired outcomes, steps to take, team members responsible for implementation, resources required, key measures of success, and the time frames for achieving the goal and tracking results.

• Assign a cross-functional team to implement each Action Plan. Include members from different departments who will be affected by the changes. Members should have the necessary skills and insights to accomplish the plan. Identify a team leader and/or executive sponsor who will be held accountable for managing the team, tracking progress, and achieving the desired goal.

5. Communicate the Action Plans for Improvement to everyone in the company. Get involvement, input, and feedback.

6. Hold yourself and others accountable for achieving the new goals and milestones.

7. After a designated period of time (three to six months), evaluate progress, identify new or emerging problems or opportunities, set new goals, make new team assignments (if appropriate), and take action. In a year, retake the *Building the Awesome Organization Overview Quiz* and repeat Steps 1 through 6 as required. Remember that continuous assessment, action, and improvement are essential to building an awesome organization that is strong enough to support continuous growth.

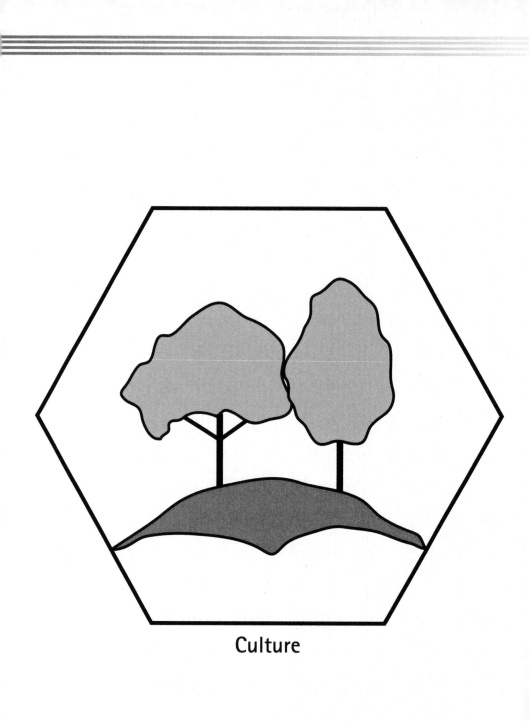

Culture

CHAPTER 3

DEVELOP AN INNOVATIVE CULTURE FOR GROWTH

"In the early days of our company, we didn't understand how to set up the culture at all. We tried hard to be nice to everyone, but we weren't really being honest with each other. There were conflicts under the surface. No one was happy. Rumors were everywhere. Backstabbings and insults flew around. The culture really sucked. Then we learned to define and write down our values. We learned what it really meant to use honesty and candor as we tried to resolve conflicts. We learned how to identify and solve problems. We were then able to create the culture we really wanted. In fact, now I see culture as my main priority."

Culture is the first of the six elements of an awesome organization that we address in this book because an empowering, supportive culture is the bedrock of every great company. Building a highly participatory, people-oriented environment that reflects and reinforces the company's core values will stimulate creative ideas, high standards of performance, fun, and excitement. This, in turn, will enable you to attract and retain the awesome people your company needs to grow and to innovate. Because companies with cultures that foster innovation are clear winners in the marketplace, culture is truly a bottom-line issue.

A positive culture empowers people, holds an organization together, and supports forward motion. A negative culture is debilitating because it obstructs the energy, innovation, and creativity that are at the heart of every growing enterprise. Companies with negative cultures lose their speed, agility, and flexibility, and are unable to accommodate the demands of growth. Review the Red Flags in the following box, "Red Flags: Warnings That All Is Not Right with Your Culture." If any of these Red Flags apply to your company, keep reading to learn what to do about these problems.

RED FLAGS: WARNINGS THAT ALL IS NOT RIGHT WITH YOUR CULTURE

You know there are problems with the culture when:

 You hear many more problems and gripes than ideas and solutions.

 There's a sudden increase in turnover.

There's a lot of activity and meetings, but not much is getting done.

You're worried that your culture is being diluted by new people coming from other organizations with different values.

The original excitement and passion have been replaced by tension and frustration.

You hear more complaints than usual about money — salaries, raises, and bonuses.

New people don't feel welcomed by the people who were "there at the start."

Nobody knows what's going on.

People don't offer ideas, and you're beginning to wonder how to tap into their brainpower.

You have no idea if people feel motivated by their work, and you doubt that people are working at their full potential.

You haven't defined your core values; people don't know the values; or they aren't acting in accordance with the values.

> 🚩 People aren't happy; they say it isn't fun to work here any more.
>
> 🚩 There's very little genuine teamwork.
>
> 🚩 Departments have an "us versus them" mentality about other parts of the company, and sometimes even toward customers.

The most important message in this chapter is this: Don't leave culture to chance or relegate it to the staff in Human Resources.

Some entrepreneurs recognize the importance of having a great culture but think it's touchy-feely, intangible, and hard to influence.

> "Culture *is* touchy-feely, but that doesn't mean it shouldn't be a top priority. If you read all the articles about the learning organization and worker empowerment, you realize American industry pays a tremendous price for not paying attention to culture. I think CEOs today understand the importance of these issues. If they don't, their companies are just not going to make it."

> "If you keep culture and structure too loose, it can backfire and actually hurt growth. Eventually, your culture will fall apart if you don't put something in place to support it as you undergo rapid growth. In a way, it's like helping a teenager put in place the framework to guide them as an adult. We have a very autonomous, open environment that I desperately want to protect. We have a magical culture here, and I want to keep that while growing rapidly. But I figured out some time ago that we needed to add some structure, plans, and processes if we wanted to have the framework for growth."

The reality is that your culture has specific components that you and your top leadership team must explicitly define and develop to ensure maximum innovation and growth. If you continuously assess and strengthen your company's culture, you have a good chance of creating the kind of place where awesome people want to work and can thrive. (See the following box, "Vital Signs: The Culture Awesome People Want," for descriptions of the kind of culture awesome people want in companies they join.)

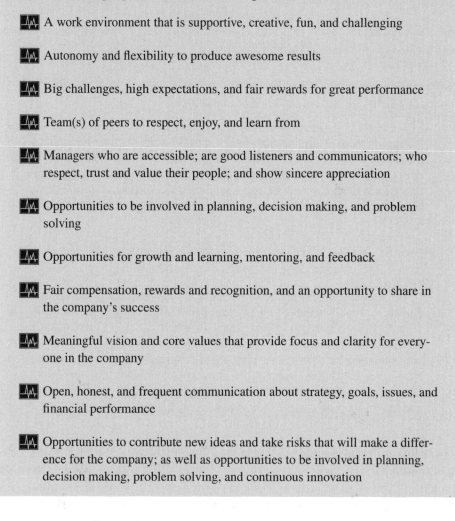

VITAL SIGNS: THE CULTURE AWESOME PEOPLE WANT

People whose CEOs identified them as awesome said they would join and stay with a company that had the following kind of culture:

- A work environment that is supportive, creative, fun, and challenging

- Autonomy and flexibility to produce awesome results

- Big challenges, high expectations, and fair rewards for great performance

- Team(s) of peers to respect, enjoy, and learn from

- Managers who are accessible; are good listeners and communicators; who respect, trust and value their people; and show sincere appreciation

- Opportunities to be involved in planning, decision making, and problem solving

- Opportunities for growth and learning, mentoring, and feedback

- Fair compensation, rewards and recognition, and an opportunity to share in the company's success

- Meaningful vision and core values that provide focus and clarity for everyone in the company

- Open, honest, and frequent communication about strategy, goals, issues, and financial performance

- Opportunities to contribute new ideas and take risks that will make a difference for the company; as well as opportunities to be involved in planning, decision making, problem solving, and continuous innovation

Many companies are competing for awesome people. If you have the kind of culture they're looking for, they'll choose your company. An empowering culture can be your competitive edge when it comes to hiring and keeping awesome people.

"If you look at the legacy that you leave behind as an entrepreneur, it's not the products, customers, brand names, or technologies. In 30 to 50 years, our products will be obsolete, the technologies we use today will be obsolete, and the employee set at that point will be retired. We hope the brand will survive. But the real legacy you'll leave is a set of values or culture, a way of doing things that allows new people to come in, learn, grow, and be better than they ever could be before — or alone — and then go on to do bigger and better things within our company, to create new and better ways to 'wow' our customers."

"I believe that your only competitive advantage is your people and their shared values. The one thing your competition can't have is your people. So what you do to build a culture should be a big deal."

GETTING CULTURE RIGHT FROM THE START

Building a great culture with all the elements described in the preceding Vital Signs box is not easy. And, it's difficult to maintain the company's original entrepreneurial culture during growth. But if you work at it, you *can* define and then keep alive the parts of your culture — especially the creativity and passion — that helped you build a successful organization in its early stages.

Many entrepreneurs in growth companies don't think they can spare the time to work on culture because they need to focus on getting a product out the door, finding customers, raising capital, and generating revenue. They figure they can work on culture-related issues down the road when everything else is running smoothly. But, if you don't focus on building the right culture from the very beginning, you will lose great people and/or hire the wrong ones. Then you'll have to spend time weeding out people who don't belong, hiring new people, and getting everyone re-focused — all of which will certainly put the brakes on growth.

Some entrepreneurs have a hard time defining the kind of culture they want, can't articulate what is needed, or can't figure out how to get their managers to transmit key messages about the importance of culture to the whole organization. When new people are added but aren't told what kind of culture the CEO is trying to create, it becomes much more difficult to keep everyone on the same track. But if you define the values and behavior that are important to you and your company, then communicate that to everyone, you've taken an important step toward creating a culture that will support growth. Core values help unify the organization. They help create a feeling of belonging to something that people can be proud of.

> "One of our values is to work together like a family. One of our salesmen loves to barbecue. When he had a good sales day, he would cook lunch for everyone in his area. Then he started to do it on a regular basis. The next thing you know, people started saying, 'I've got a special recipe; next week is my turn,' and spouses were saying, 'Maybe I should come by for lunch that day.' Every company has to decide whether to foster things like this or nip them in the bud. In our case, it turned out to be a great opportunity for us to socialize, enjoy each other's company, and a great way to reinforce our family-oriented values."

CULTURE STARTS WITH CORE VALUES

Experienced entrepreneurs know it is not easy to stay entrepreneurial and innovative as the company grows. Some first-time entrepreneurs will not specify values, develop plans, or create processes because they believe that doing so will move them toward corporate bureaucracy. But, if you don't articulate your core values, you won't be able to hire people who share those same values, trust them, or hold them accountable for achieving the results you want for your company — in short, you won't be able to grow. Creating the culture for growth requires that you articulate and live the values, hold others accountable, and not allow people who don't live the values to remain in the company.

ARTICULATE AND LIVE THE VALUES

How do you create a culture that draws awesome people to your company? You start with a set of core values that you and your top team articulate, and then you demonstrate them every single day. The core values of your organization must come from you. These values are the guiding principles that reflect *your* deeply held beliefs about how people need to work with each other to achieve outstanding performance. You must clearly articulate the standards that guide you in life and that you want to guide your employees as you all work together to build a successful company.

Although the values ultimately come from you, don't try to define them by yourself. Seek input from others, and think about what kinds of behaviors those values produce. This input will help you clarify your own values and beliefs, will build employee commitment to those values, and will help you identify the set of fundamental principles that you want to guide everyone's daily interactions. These will then become your values statement. (See appendix C, "Creating a Core Values Statement for Growth," for an exercise in creating a core values statement to support growth.)

"Every entrepreneur who starts a business has some feelings about how to manage, develop, and grow the business. But as a corporation grows, it's important to turn those feelings into words on paper, to have a single set of guiding principles that are known, understood, and practiced by everybody."

✧

"Before we developed our values statement, when I sensed a misalignment in decisions or behaviors, it seemed sort of diffuse. I couldn't pinpoint or articulate the problem. But now that the values are written down, we're recognizing people for living by them. Now, when people go off track, it's much easier to discuss the behaviors I expect from people, and to keep everyone aligned with the values."

✧

"These are our values. They're very simple, but getting them down on paper and sharing them with everyone has had a big impact. Unwavering accountability to these guidelines and their definitions has really helped in making decisions and initiating actions.
- **Customer-focused**—To help our customers succeed and win.
- **Flexible**—To be nimble and agile in responding to feedback, both positive and negative.
- **Honorable**—To act with integrity; to do what is right.
- **Innovative**—To create new, useful, easy-to-use, cool products and processes.
- **Open**—To be open and honest; to be approachable by others on difficult matters, professionally and personally.
- **Passionate**—To work hard, play hard, and live hard; to care enough to give yourself to your tasks.
- **Persistent**—To not give up, and to treat all feedback as an opportunity to do better.

- **Results-oriented**—To be driven by achieving concrete results; to measure success by external variables.
- **Team-oriented**—To work and think well in groups of people; to respect, listen, and value the opinions of others as a critical means for the organization to succeed and function well.
- **Winning**—To create win-win-win situations."

HOLD PEOPLE ACCOUNTABLE TO THE VALUES

Your core values show what you will tolerate and what you won't. Once they're written down, and the behaviors and actions that demonstrate them are described, the core values become the code of conduct throughout the organization that defines how people treat each other and how they treat customers, vendors, and everyone the organization touches. Everyone should know these values and live by them.

> "I have a basic mantra that expresses my values, and I talk about it all the time. It's that I have high expectations, but I'm also extremely flexible. I think everybody starts out having high expectations for their business but most are very rigid on the back end in terms of the flexibility they show employees. We don't really have a start time or closing time at work; people come as early as 4:30 in the morning and some as late as 11:00 AM. Some work until 10:00 PM. I generally don't believe in having to count sick days or get a lot of permissions to take time to go to the dentist. You just need to have coverage and get your work done. Our values include work hard/play hard. People manage their own time. The theory is pretty easy to understand, but it's very difficult for some managers to accept. However, we've gotten unbelievable work out of the entire group of people as a result of setting the expectations very high and letting people enjoy their jobs and have some flexibility about doing their work."

Make sure your core values are not just presented as motherhood and apple pie. They need to have real meaning. People need to have examples of behavior that are consistent with your values. Ewing Kauffman built a very profitable, multi-billion-dollar company where people were highly productive, morale was high, and turnover was low. One of his values was "Treat others as you want to be treated." For him that meant providing information ahead of time so people could prepare for meetings, answering phone calls on the first or second ring, returning phone calls within a few hours, arriving at work and at meetings on time, striking deals with partners that were win-win for both parties, and being thoughtful and considerate in conversations and actions.

When you have a set of values, but people don't behave in accordance with those values, they need to be made aware that they are falling short. If they continue to ignore the values, you must move them out of the organization. You can't capitulate or compromise on values; if you do, your culture will suffer irreparable damage, just as it will if you fail to adhere to the values yourself. Mr. Kauffman had a brilliant VP who did not treat his people the way Mr. K expected him to do. He called meetings at the last minute, was late to meetings, and was generally inconsiderate of others. Mr. K tried to mentor and coach him and provide feedback on his behavior. But, as Mr. K said, "He didn't change, so he had to go." Mr. K knew that if he tolerated this behavior and kept the VP, regardless of how brilliant he was, employees would question Mr. K and his values, and that would begin to destroy the culture he was trying to build.

> "You're on display all the time, whether you like it or not. And if you do something, it must be acceptable behavior. For example, too many entrepreneurs say, 'I'm paying for performance,' but what they're really paying for is results. If you send the message that all you care about is results, you'll get in trouble. If you pay for results and you don't care how people get them, don't be surprised if your employees begin to cut corners, not tell customers the whole truth, or make promises they can't keep. Ultimately, that comes back to haunt you."

> "When someone doesn't match the values, that's a big test. Many companies go too far by saying, 'We'll keep this person because we have a people-oriented culture.' They think 'people-oriented' means automatically keeping everyone. Actually, they're destroying the culture because everyone else wonders why this person is still there."

Do Not Allow People Who Don't Live the Values to Remain in the Company

Don't hesitate to ask others to help you evaluate how effectively people are adhering to your core values. Violations of your core values are red flags that you haven't selected people who share your values or that you haven't done a good job defining and communicating the beliefs you hold dear. If you allow the values to be violated, no one will take them seriously. Whatever the problem, you have to fix it immediately. If you don't take action, the awesome people who were attracted by your company's values will become disillusioned and leave.

If you have defined your values and selected people who match the values, any hiring "mistakes" will become readily apparent. The hiring manager needs to talk with the person and provide specific examples of how their behavior does not match the values of the company. Sometimes your employees will help the person understand why and how they need to modify their behavior. If the person continues to behave inappropriately, you — or the hiring manager — will need to talk with that person and discuss specific changes they will need to make (within a specific time frame) if they want to remain in the company. Once in a while the person will recognize that he or she is a misfit in this culture and will leave.

"We had a technical writer who was the best technical writer we ever had. Unfortunately, she ended up engaging in 'I'm better than you are' games via e-mail and in hallway conversations. In cross-functional team meetings, she was always blaming issues on other people. Finally, three or four people from her team suggested that she find another job because her behavior wasn't in sync with our culture. In her exit interview, she said, 'I do things differently than you do.' We were glad to see her go because she just didn't fit with our culture."

"I hired a new manager for engineering when we desperately needed a great new manager. He seemed friendly and likable during his interviews, but it turned out that he intimidated people. He was a dictator, and he didn't listen to others. He ignored their efforts and didn't give any positive recognition or feedback. The entire engineering team grew to hate him. Engineers are the lifeblood of our business, and I realized pretty quickly that I had to fire him even though he was very competent technically. His values weren't right; he just didn't fit our culture of openness, teamwork, recognition, integrity, and leadership."

"Once, against my advice, some of my managers went ahead and built a product that didn't meet our standards. Twenty-eight out of 30 pieces blew up in the field, and the customer was furious. My managers said, 'We gave them what they wanted. We met their specs.' I said, 'That's not how we do business. Go back and make it right.' It cost us $85,000, but we did the right thing. That sent a very powerful message to everyone about how we do business and what our value system is. The managers who did not share that value system are no longer with us. I think that sent a powerful message to our people as well."

You Must Walk the Talk

A final brief but critical point about core values: A company without clear core values is a company in trouble. And, when your organization does have clear core values, you must put them into action in every part of the business. (See the box, "Vital Signs: Using Core Values.") It all starts with you, the leader. Here's how Mr. K described the leader's role in building culture:

> "A leader is one who has the attributes that he 'walks' the 'talk.' You can tell people that you are going to do certain things, that you are going to be honest with them, that you have integrity, but talk doesn't mean anything unless you really put it into action. In other words, your actions mean much more than your words. You must live what you preach, and do it right, and do it often, day after day."

> "I think the way you run the organization says it all. If you say you're something, but you're something else, people see that. If you say you're going to do one thing but you do something else, they get it. People aren't dumb."

VITAL SIGNS: USING CORE VALUES

Here are ways to use the core values throughout the organization to create the culture you want in your company:

- Include core values in the job profiles you develop prior to recruiting; develop interview questions that will help you identify past behaviors that match (or don't match) these core values. (See chapter 4, "Attract Awesome People for Growth," for more information on job profiles and interviewing.)

- Include values in all planning and goal-setting activities so they are part of annual company, department, and individual plans.

- Incorporate the core values into orientation and all training sessions. For example, if open, two-way communication and teamwork are core values, train people in active listening and how to be effective team members.

continues

-continued

Ask people to rate how well the organization adheres to the values, ask for ideas on how things can be improved, and then respond to their suggestions.

Teach the values. After everyone knows them, display them prominently on walls, hand out values wallet cards, and feature values prominently in the employee handbook.

Use the values in performance feedback; evaluate not just the work people are doing but the way they do their work, how they exhibit the values, and then adjust their compensation and rewards accordingly.

Make values the basis of all communication. For example, say, "Because our values include X, we are going to do Y."

Establish a reward system that recognizes individuals whose behavior exemplifies the values. Give awards, prizes, bonuses, raises, promotions, and written recognition to the individuals who live the values; publicly hold up these people as models.

THE TIE BETWEEN CULTURE AND RECOGNITION

Rewarding people for the values-related behavior you're trying to foster is a critical but often-overlooked part of building a strong culture. Employees who live by the company's values and achieve the results that lead to its success should receive meaningful rewards that demonstrate how important the right kind of behavior is to the organization's overall performance.

Profit sharing, stock options, phantom stock, or other forms of equity or equity-like compensation produce a sense of ownership and can be very important in maintaining commitment. You also need to use a variety of nonmonetary ways to recognize the contributions of individuals and teams. Employee awards for achievement, parties that honor successes, and other celebrations create heroes and rituals that become the visible embodiment of your culture. All these are important mechanisms for fostering the culture you want.

"We have over 80 employee awards, lots of parties, lots of teamwork, and a very special spirit here. People really care because I really care about them. I go out of my way to find things I can do for my people. We also have a very special annual award for the employee who represents the spirit of our company, which is an award for teamwork and cooperation, contributing to the whole, dedication to doing the job, making the company proud, taking the initiative to be helpful, keeping his/her own spirits high, and raising the spirits of others. All different kinds of employees have won the award. Sometimes it's somebody in the service department; sometimes it's someone in the office; sometimes it's someone in the stores. We ask people to nominate someone who's doing the kinds of things that make us proud, that make us smile, the kind of employee who's a model for everybody."

"After we defined our values and corresponding guidelines, I wanted to inculcate them in a fun and meaningful way. As CEO, I can't be the only one watching people do something right and patting them on the back for it, so I sent our five values around and asked everyone to send e-mails to someone they noticed fulfilling a particular value, along with a copy to everyone else. People are really enjoying this acknowledgment of each other's efforts."

"We value high performance, so we celebrate accomplishments. We take everybody out to the amusement park once a year. And every once in a while, we just take off at noon on Friday and go have a blast."

THE 7 C'S OF CULTURE

In addition to the foundation of core values, seven critical elements must be built to form your company's innovative culture. When these elements are developed within your company, they become organizational competencies that you can count on to be powerful drivers of growth and to give your organization a strong, compelling competitive advantage. We call these the 7 C's of Culture.* Here's what they are, along with descriptions of the culture they produce:

*The 7 C's of Culture, ©2001, The Catlin Group.

1. Customer and Market Focus

Everyone must constantly listen to and fully understand the customer, make appropriate decisions, and take effective action to meet the current and future needs of customers and target markets. In addition to providing critical information, this customer-centric listening and decision making also builds positive relationships with customers.

> "At the end of every meeting, I ask 'Have we accomplished something today that adds value to our customers?' Asking that question at the end of every meeting, no matter what kind of meeting, has become routine. It has become the norm within our culture."

There are several ways you can bring the customer's perspective into the organization. Before you make decisions, ask for sales and service data or data from customer interviews or surveys of random samples of customers. Encourage your product or service development group to test their new ideas on prospective customers, to analyze the data, and share the results broadly. Ask for data from focus group discussions with customers or potential customers and share that information broadly as well. Customer and market information sometimes gets isolated in the sales, marketing, or customer service departments and isn't shared with other parts of the company. To encourage everyone to keep the customer "front and center," figure out an approach that fits with your culture and will enable your employees to have access to the customer and market information that gets collected. For instance, you could designate an individual or a cross-functional team to develop mechanisms for this information to be broadly disseminated in a variety of ways, such as develop formats for short written reports, five-minute presentations, one-page summaries, or e-mails to all employees. Or, you could set up a database of customer information and make it accessible to anyone who wants to use it. Or, you might schedule quarterly meetings to discuss the question, "What are the changing needs and wants of our customers?"

Maintaining a customer and market focus will help you avoid the problem of employees thinking they already know what customers want. Some people cling to their own ideas about what customers need and don't want to hear information that might refute that. A lot of product failures grow out of "we-know-what's-best-for-them" thinking.

But, make sure you also focus on what the customers will need tomorrow, not just what they want today. Explore their future needs and anticipate the challenges they will face from competitors. Often, this is where true innovation and growth opportunities are found. Make sure your people spend time learning about the problems customers are having difficulty solving, the challenges they face now, and those they are anticipating in the future. This will help your company to create and develop exciting new solutions that nobody has thought of, including your customers.

> "Our most critical success factor is our desire and ability to listen carefully and respond to our customers. We constantly solicit feedback from customers and require sales and service managers to submit monthly reports that are distributed to 12 people who analyze them; then we discuss them in monthly meetings. We base our decisions for all our products and product improvements on that feedback."

2. COMMUNICATION

Open, two-way communication channels — up, down, and across the organization — are designed to ensure that everyone knows what is happening within the company and what is expected of them. Everyone should know the company's vision, mission, values, and strategies, and understand how those apply to his or her job. People must have enough information to make good decisions, provide feedback, and develop new ideas. Verbal and written communication must be constant and cross functional so people's efforts can be coordinated and focused on the same goals. It takes time, but it's critical to use a variety of communication methods and to encourage dialogue, interaction, and feedback.

> "If you assume that everyone thinks like you do, you will misread a lot of situations and miscommunicate. Once you realize that people think differently, you have to understand that they can think differently from you without being wrong. Some people love details, and if you don't give them detailed reasons and explanations, they may think you haven't really thought through your idea. Other people can't stand the details and will be bored if you don't stay at a high enough level. Until you understand that people's brains are wired differently, you are going to be frustrated and you will frustrate them with your communications."

> "Anything that elicits feedback and people's opinions in a structured way is really helpful because it drives communication across lines. Driving communication up through the organization is one of the hardest things to do.

Structured tools like surveys and open meetings with two-way dialogues are critical; they help a company think with one brain. Until a company can think with one brain, it can't move with one body."

3. COLLABORATION

Functional and cross-functional teams must operate effectively to accomplish mutual goals, solve problems, and move the company toward its vision. People should enjoy working together on teams, tackling important priorities, and accomplishing results. Effective collaboration builds cooperation and trust, enables people to learn from each other, and promotes the continuous innovation required for the company's growth.

Having diverse people work together to approach problems and generate ideas leads to solutions that are unique and creative, yet balanced and viable. But team leaders need to be skilled in managing this diversity. Different thinking styles and skill levels are fertile ground for miscommunication and personality conflicts. To overcome these potential pitfalls, get agreement on the team's mission and deliverables (as well as each member's roles and responsibilities), and develop operating guidelines for meetings, problem solving, decision making, and communication.

"A recent experience showed me how good collaboration is here. About 2 weeks ahead of a major sales call with a million-dollar sales opportunity, we had many people coming up with ideas about how to present our proposal to this client. Everyone got involved in developing the battle plan. Having all those heads involved in creating a winning presentation was very powerful."

"Our whole company is a network of teams working on critical projects and plans. We set up teams to run what we call 'key business areas.' Their job is planning and implementing in their areas so their work fits with our overall company mission, vision, and plan. Each of those teams has a cross-functional advisory team that offers ideas and ensures coordination with other parts of the company. We are thriving because these teams work so well."

4. CREATIVITY AND PROACTIVE PROBLEM SOLVING

When people are focused on the vision and plan and asked to define new opportunities and problems, challenge established practices, or brainstorm options, they generate fresh, innovative, and viable solutions with energy and buzz.

In a truly innovative culture, everyone in the company is a member of at least one team whose charter is to discover new ideas to move the company forward. Some of the teams are asked to identify problem areas, determine what isn't working, and then find and implement answers that will improve the situation. Other teams are established to discover and develop longer-term opportunities — new products, new processes, new approaches to the market, new partnerships — that will keep the company on the cutting edge as a leader. People and teams are regularly recognized and rewarded for being problem solvers, opportunity creators, risk takers, and innovators. (See appendix D, "Model for Creative Problem Solving," for a creative problem-solving model that can be used to spur creativity around all types of issues.)

> "The key to our innovation is creativity, giving ourselves the freedom to think. We have regular brainstorming meetings to play 'what if.' We're constantly looking for new ways to provide extraordinary service and new products."

> "We constantly search for new ideas and are willing to accept and develop ideas from any source — from customers to employees to the board of directors to our own fantasies. We manage ideas by finding what's most valuable in them and then modify them to make them work. In this way, we act as angel's advocates, rather than devil's advocates, which is so much more productive . . . and innovative."

> "The only way to encourage innovation is to reward it and recognize it and to hire and retain for it. Those are the kinds of things we try to spend our time on. We give awards for innovation at our quarterly meetings. We encourage people to learn to think out of the box and to get training that will support innovation."

5. CONSTRUCTIVE LEADERS AND LEADERSHIP

The CEO and leadership team must align everyone with the mission, values, and goals; develop talent; build relationships; and provide a motivating, challenging, and fun environment that rewards high performance. Leaders need to be held accountable for hiring the right people, developing them, and delegating responsibility to them appropriately. They need to reward behavior by establishing a variety of recognition and reward programs, including fair compensation, bonus and awards programs for teams and individual winners, and celebrations of milestones. On the other hand, they also need to make the tough decisions to let people go who don't fit the culture or don't meet the company's performance expectations.

Great leaders know how to communicate, delegate, and coach people to achieve outstanding results. They encourage calculated risk taking and give people enough autonomy and flexibility to try new ideas without having to worry about being punished for failure. And, they're willing to admit mistakes and reach out to their team to help solve problems.

> "I went to visit a customer who was never one to pull punches and someone I'd known for years. After the demo and discussion of where we were going, he looked me square in the eye and said, 'You're going to get killed,' and I said, 'What are you talking about?' I went to him thinking we had built a very cool product, but he said it would be a maintenance and administrative nightmare that he and other customers didn't want. So with that one piece of feedback, I went back and looked at all the customer feedback that we had. All of a sudden, I felt like I took the filters off and realized we were going in the wrong direction. As the leader and CEO of the organization, I knew no one else was going to make that tough decision. So I sat down with my co-founder and our executive team and said, 'This isn't right, we're going down the wrong path — we need to change.' My fear, lying awake at night — I didn't get a lot of sleep during this period — was that these folks would all bolt and say, 'We're going to go somewhere else.' But instead what happened was a real defining moment for the company. Our team shared this feedback very openly and engaged all our people in looking at the solution to the problem. What happened over the period of about a month was remarkable. People really wrestled with the problem, and in the end everybody came to the same decision, and everybody was aligned. We had more momentum a month later than we'd had going into this, and we were a team."

In describing what he felt constructive leadership was all about, Mr. K said:

> "Our corporate culture came about because of our philosophy of sharing with those who produce, which created a trust and a confidence with our associates.

It came about because of our philosophy of treating others the way you would like to be treated, because of the various programs we put in place that gave stock ownership to every individual, and because of our profit sharing retirement program. All this created a feeling among all associates that the company was more than just a company; it almost had a personality of its own. This was enhanced by leaders who listened to our associates, set an example, tried to be leaders and not managers, and used the appreciation factor as much as possible. It's all the little things that you do, day by day, week by week, month by month that enable you, over a period of time, to build an extraordinary culture."

6. CONTINUOUS LEARNING

Exchange of knowledge, information, experiences, and feedback builds people's skills and increases the effectiveness of individual and corporate performance. People need to have lots of opportunities, inside and outside the company, to learn from each other, take courses, develop their skills, develop themselves, try new projects, and prepare for a great future.

> "We have a wide variety of workshops inside the company. We prefer these to sending people to training and seminars outside the company because they can learn together and apply what they learn immediately on the job with others who understand what they're trying to do. In our company we encourage all kinds of 'learning for action'."

> "People who go to outside seminars come back and make presentations to their teams so everyone can benefit. This helps spread the learning throughout the organization and leverages the resources we devote to outside training."

Encourage people to mentor others as well. Coach people to develop skills in leadership, communication, effective teamwork, creative thinking, and problem solving. This will help people do their jobs better and will also strengthen the culture.

> "We have a comprehensive mentoring process. Everyone on our top team is responsible for mentoring high potential individuals. We hold ourselves accountable for being good mentors by having the mentees evaluate our performance. Over the past few years, we've learned a lot from these evaluations, and our mentoring skills are getting better and better, which, of course, means our mentees are benefiting even more from these relationships."

Finally, use tools such as the *BAO SCAN* at the end of this chapter and other chapters as mechanisms for organization-wide learning.

7. CHANGE MANAGEMENT

Continuous growth requires constant change. Change offers opportunities to try new things and learn new skills. Encourage experimentation and initiate change as appropriate. Be thoughtful about what needs changing, establish a plan for the change, and communicate both the *why* and the *how* of any changes. The way you and your top team embrace change will serve as a model to others in the company, enabling the company to stay nimble and entrepreneurial, act quickly to overcome barriers and capture opportunities, and stay on the leading edge.

> "It isn't change that bothers people so much; it is not knowing what the change might be. If people understand the values of the organization and they trust the top team to always work within those values, they find it easier to go through change. If they don't trust the people leading the changes, then they will be more worried about the outcome of the change."

> "As the leader you have two choices. Either your people must continue to learn and grow or you will have to change the people, because nothing will be the same tomorrow as it was yesterday."

THE DEVIL IS IN THE DETAILS

Does the culture we just described sound like a tall order? Well, it is, but you *can* build systematic processes that enable your organization to excel at each of these elements. Keep in mind that the 7 C's are very closely intertwined, so working on one will impact the others. Collaboration and teamwork, for example, is dependent on excellent communication. When information flows freely, people talk and listen, ideas develop, and teamwork flourishes. Good teamwork starts at the top with constructive leaders who model the kind of collaborative behavior and creative output they expect from all teams. Bringing the "voice of the customer" into the company encourages change, because customer's needs and wants are always changing. And expecting teams to come up with creative and innovative solutions requires them to learn from each other and build on the knowledge of the group.

Recognize that the little things do matter. Every new person you hire, every action, decision, policy, communication, incentive, and reward counts. Even the physical environment of your facility counts. The reverse is also true: Every time you hire the wrong person, decide not to communicate important information, or don't bother to maintain the cleanliness or appearance of your building, you send a message about your culture.

> "Think of culture as a reflection of the physical environment of your company. You can walk into a place and pick up its culture and values from physical cues very quickly: what's in the waiting room, what gets recognition via plaques and trophies, how clean is the place, what about the presence or absence of customers, the books lying around. It just goes on and on. Think about what you want to have in the physical environment, in the workplace that is culture-related. Think about how you express your culture in tangible ways."

> "We care about individuality and creativity, so we invited everyone to paint and decorate their offices any way they wanted. We had a lot of fun seeing what everyone came up with."

Some companies set up Culture Teams to propose the best ways to use input from employees about how to improve the culture. This cross-functional team can serve as a model for how all teams in the organization should work together. It can serve as a living example of an innovative culture: involving its members in new responsibilities, seeking new ideas, collaborating across departments, experimenting and taking some risks, communicating well, and completing an important task that produces positive change.

> "We had awesome people, but they were all working far too hard and were beginning to say this wasn't fun any more. We began to realize we needed to change the culture to one that encourages hard work but is also enjoyable. We set up a Culture Team that was led by a senior manager and included people from all levels and functions. They took a culture survey out into the organization, got input, and made recommendations. We took action and evaluated things again in six months. It made a big difference, and this is now an ongoing process for us."

WHEN THE CULTURE IS BROKEN

Sometimes you need to change or "fix" your culture. This is difficult, but it can be done. When you have to fix your culture, turn it into a creative learning process. You and your people must search for new perspectives, challenge assumptions, take risks, and be willing to redefine or eliminate habitual ways of doing things in order to create a whole new environment.

> "I used to say there was some sort of disease in this company. We had good people. We had a worthy cause, and our strategies were on target. But for some reason, we couldn't execute those strategies. Everybody was unhappy and antagonistic, and the results were terrible. Basically, the culture was broken. We learned that we weren't providing a steady guiding hand for our people and weren't giving them ways to succeed. So we provided those things, and then, perhaps the biggest lesson of all, we got out of their way and let them do it their way."

To repair a broken culture, follow the steps outlined in the following box, "Vital Signs: Six Steps to Fix a Broken Culture."

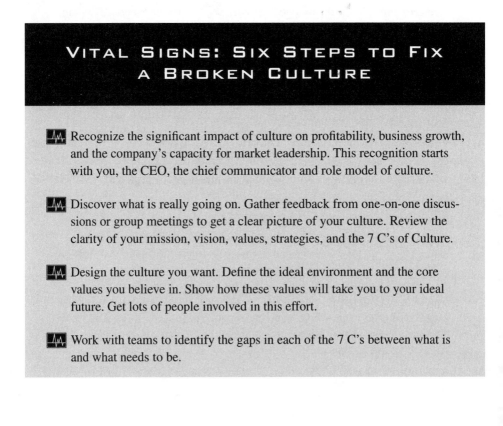

VITAL SIGNS: SIX STEPS TO FIX A BROKEN CULTURE

Recognize the significant impact of culture on profitability, business growth, and the company's capacity for market leadership. This recognition starts with you, the CEO, the chief communicator and role model of culture.

Discover what is really going on. Gather feedback from one-on-one discussions or group meetings to get a clear picture of your culture. Review the clarity of your mission, vision, values, strategies, and the 7 C's of Culture.

Design the culture you want. Define the ideal environment and the core values you believe in. Show how these values will take you to your ideal future. Get lots of people involved in this effort.

Work with teams to identify the gaps in each of the 7 C's between what is and what needs to be.

■ Define an Action Plan that includes ways to make your values an integral part of your business strategies and decisions. The plan should also include ways to help people develop the skills they'll need to flourish in the new culture.

■ Get results. Hold people accountable for the core values and changes you've defined and recognize their achievements in visible, concrete ways. Make sure you hire, promote, and reward people who exhibit your values and fire those who don't. Constantly test decisions against the mission, vision, and values. And, celebrate successes.

PERCEPTION IS REALITY

Your perceptions and those of your leadership team about the culture may differ from the reality that the rest of the people in your organization experience. It's easy to fall into the trap of believing that your perception of the culture is the real one because you have a vested interest in the success of the culture you've been trying to create. But don't dismiss the perceptions and opinions of others as "wrong." Don't ignore negative comments about the company's culture and think it's just a few bad apples griping about the environment. Acknowledge the possibility that there may be a gap between what you and your top team think your culture is and what everyone else thinks it is.

> "We think of culture in our office as conversation. So if you want your culture to change, you have to change your conversations. In the past, our conversations weren't as positive as I wanted them to be. We went through a trying period, but now everyone is excited and working together and doing incredible things that I would never have imagined could be possible."

To help you determine whether your perception matches the reality of others in the company, we suggest you take the *BAO SCAN,* "Develop an Innovative Culture for Growth," at the end of this chapter yourself, then have your top team and other key people, especially your awesome people, complete it as well. Use the *BAO SCAN* to check reality. Depending on the size of your organization, you can also use the questions in the *BAO SCAN* in one-on-one or small group discussions or interviews with a cross-section of people in the organization. If you have a large number of employees, use a mix of techniques, including one-on-one interviews and focus groups, and ask a larger cross-section of people to complete the *BAO SCAN.* Be sure to keep the scores from the various groups separate so you can readily compare and contrast the responses of different groups. When you seek feedback on the culture, you provide a powerful example of behavior that's consistent with a core value of an awesome organization: open, two-way communication.

YOUR ROLE AS LEADER

To be an effective leader of a culture that fosters innovation and growth, you must:

- Define the culture you want; envision your ideal, write it down, and then share it with others.

- Get feedback and try to incorporate other people's ideas so they also have ownership in the values and culture you are trying to create.

- Develop new ideas about how to make that culture real.

- Focus on and constantly communicate the mission, values, and vision of your company and embody the values in your every action.

- Hold yourself and the top team accountable for extremely high standards of performance as leaders and builders of the culture.

- Listen to what people have to say about how to improve the culture.

- Be persistent and strive to succeed, even when others say it can't be done.

- Recognize and reward people creatively and generously, and celebrate success!

BIG LESSONS

1. Recognize that core values are the foundation of culture. A company's core values and the CEO's belief system must match.

2. Be proactive about building your culture. Define your core values, build the 7 C's of Culture, and establish appropriate rewards and recognition programs.

3. Pay attention to culture. Ignoring it can stifle your company's growth!

4. Realize that awesome people will join a company because of its positive culture, and they will leave a company with a negative culture or a culture that is incompatible with their own values.

5. Understand that ignoring breaches of the core values will break your culture.

BAO SCAN: DEVELOP AN INNOVATIVE CULTURE FOR GROWTH

Use this *SCAN* to assess your culture. Take this *BAO SCAN* yourself, and then have your top team and other key people complete it as well. Compare your responses and perceptions with theirs. Work together to identify innovative ways to strengthen your culture.

RATING SCALE

Use this scale to respond to each rating question

1 - - - - - 2 - - - - - 3 - - - - - 4 - - - - - 5 - - - - - 6 - - - - - 7
NEVER   *SOMETIMES*   *ALWAYS*

PART A: RATE YOUR OVERALL CULTURE AND CORE VALUES

Culture is the intangible element that enables people to perform at their best (or can trip up companies that aren't paying attention to it). It can include everything from overall values to personality and environment.

1. Our company's culture enables people to be innovative, achieve extraordinary performance, and make continuous improvements.   Rating: _____

2. What words best describe your culture? _____

_____

_____

_____

Core Values are deeply held beliefs about how people need to treat each other and work together.

3. Our company's core values serve as guidelines
for my behavior.   Rating: _____

4. List your company's core values. Rate how often each is demonstrated throughout the company.

_____   Rating: _____

_____   Rating: _____

_____   Rating: _____

_____   Rating: _____

PART B: RATE THE 10 KEY FACTORS OF AN INNOVATIVE CULTURE FOR GROWTH

1. My work environment is

    a. Supportive   Rating: _____

    b. Creative   Rating: _____

    c. Fun   Rating: _____

    d. Challenging   Rating: _____

2. I am expected to produce awesome results and am given

    a. Guidance   Rating: _____

    b. Autonomy   Rating: _____

    c. Flexibility   Rating: _____

3. I have opportunities for

    a. Growth   Rating: _____

    b. Learning   Rating: _____

    c. Mentoring   Rating: _____

    d. Feedback   Rating: _____

4. I work with people that I

    a. Respect   Rating: _____

    b. Enjoy   Rating: _____

    c. Learn from   Rating: _____

5. Our company's leaders

    a. Respect and trust employees   Rating: _____

    b. Show sincere appreciation for our efforts   Rating: _____

    c. Exhibit people-oriented values   Rating: _____

    d. Make themselves accessible to all employees   Rating: _____

    e. Communicate well   Rating: _____

    f. Actively listen   Rating: _____

6. This company offers

    a. Fair compensation   Rating: _____

    b. Rewards for performance   Rating: _____

    c. Recognition for performance   Rating: _____

    d. Opportunities for sharing in the company's success   Rating: _____

7. We have companywide focus and clarity on

    a. A vision that is meaningful to me   Rating: _____

    b. Core values that are clear   Rating: _____

    c. Making decisions that help us achieve our vision   Rating: _____

    d. Making decisions that are consistent with our values   Rating: _____

8. I have an opportunity to be involved in

    a. Planning   Rating: _____

    b. Decision making   Rating: _____

    c. Problem solving   Rating: _____

    d. Continuous innovation   Rating: _____

9. Communications in this company

    a. Are open   Rating: _____

    b. Are frequent   Rating: _____

    c. Are consistent   Rating: _____

    d. Clarify what is expected of me   Rating: _____

    e. Provide information about strategy.   Rating: _____

    f. Provide information about goals   Rating: _____

    g. Provide information about issues facing the company   Rating: _____

    h. Provide information about the company's financials   Rating: _____

10. I have opportunities to

    a. Contribute new ideas   Rating: _____

    b. Take calculated risks   Rating: _____

    c. Be a proactive problem solver   Rating: _____

SCORE SUMMARY AND INTERPRETATION

A Rating Score of **7** in any area indicates this is a prime area of strength that will facilitate and support the company's growth. Scores of **5** and **6** indicate considerable strength in these areas, but you will want to consider making incremental improvements to increase the score. A score of **4** is a cause for worry. A rating of "Sometimes" indicates a lack of consistency that sends conflicting signals to employees and inhibits growth; thus significant improvements will be needed. Scores of **3 or below** are big red flags indicating areas or behaviors that hinder the company's growth and require your immediate attention.

RESULTS ANALYSIS

Look back over the *BAO SCAN: Develop an Innovative Culture for Growth:*

1. List three statements that you rated the highest. Choose those you feel are key strengths and contribute most to the success of the company.

A. _____

B. _____

C. _____

2. List three statements that received the lowest rating. Choose those you feel are the most critical weaknesses and should be targeted for improvement.

A. _____

B. _____

C. _____

3. Write three statements that define your priorities for change (for example, capitalize on the strengths or improve the weaknesses).

A. _____

B. _____

C. _____

4. List three things our company could do to implement these changes.

A. _____

B. _____

C. _____

ACTION PLAN

Recognize what you and your company are doing well and celebrate! Think about what you have done that enabled you to achieve these great results and how that can be applied to your weaknesses. But, do not overlook areas that need improvement or think they will improve on their own over time. Use these steps to develop your Action Plan for Improvement:

1. Ask your top team to complete the *BAO SCAN: Develop an Innovative Culture for Growth* and the Results Analysis. You may also want others in the company to complete the *SCAN* to get more comprehensive feedback.

2. Meet with your top team to:

   - Compare and contrast your ratings on various statements with their ratings, as well as areas you have identified as strengths with those needing work.

   - If applicable, discuss the reasons why their responses are different from yours.

   - Agree on areas for improvement or change; be as specific as possible.

3. Prioritize those areas that must be addressed and will make the biggest difference. Develop them into Action Plans for Improvement.

4. Get consensus on the Action Plans and the resources and budgets needed to make the necessary changes.

   - For each Action Plan, specify the goal, desired outcomes, steps to take, team members responsible for implementation, resources required, key measures of success, and time frames for achieving the goal and tracking results.

   - Assign a cross-functional team to implement each Action Plan. Include members from different departments who will be affected by the changes. Members should have the necessary skills and insights to accomplish the plan. Identify a team leader and/or executive sponsor who will be held accountable for managing the team, tracking progress, and achieving the desired goal.

5. Communicate the Action Plans for Improvement to everyone in the company. Get involvement, input, and feedback.

6. Hold yourself and others accountable for achieving the new goals and milestones.

7. After a designated period of time (three to six months), evaluate progress, identify new or emerging problems or opportunities, set new goals, make new team assignments (if appropriate), and take action. In a year, retake the *BAO SCAN: Develop an Innovative Culture for Growth* and repeat Steps 1 through 6 as required. Remember: Continuous assessment, action, and improvement are essential to building an awesome organization that is strong enough to support continuous growth.

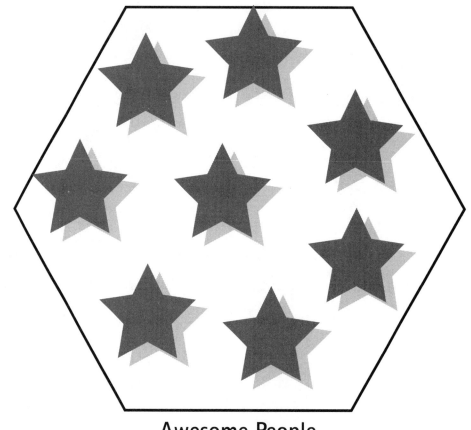

Awesome People

CHAPTER 4

ATTRACT AWESOME PEOPLE FOR GROWTH

"I want people willing to do whatever it takes to win. The guy who was supposed to be doing our mechanical engineering took over research and marketing. Then he became our first trainer. Then he became our first salesperson. He didn't care about the position. He didn't care about anything but helping the company be totally successful. He was awesome."

Who are the awesome people in your organization? Do certain names come instantly to mind? In this chapter, we're going to discuss what makes someone an awesome employee, how to attract him or her to your company, and what to do to get that person to accept your offer. If you don't know what makes an employee awesome, you need to read this chapter — because they are the people who will accelerate your company's growth.

Awesome people have the talents, skills, and expertise you need to grow your company; their values match your core values. In addition, they are able to grow as fast — or faster — than the company grows. Jot down the names of some people you consider awesome. Next to each name, write three reasons why you chose that person. If your list is short, you'd better make some changes quickly.

RED FLAGS: YOU DON'T HAVE ENOUGH AWESOME PEOPLE WHEN . . .

If you find yourself agreeing with many of the statements below, you probably have a shortage of awesome people:

- The list of people you immediately identify as awesome is short.

- You can think of several awesome people who didn't accept your job offers.

- You can think of awesome people who used to be with your company but left.

- People are constantly bringing problems to your doorstep, but no one offers solutions.

- People don't suggest ideas for innovation or change.

- People don't appear to be learning from their mistakes and keep making them over and over.

- People aren't adapting well as their jobs grow and expand during company growth.

Note: Some of these Red Flags could be due to problems in your culture. If you haven't defined your core values, you may be hiring the wrong people. Be sure to read chapter 3, "Develop an Innovative Culture for Growth," for more information on creating the right culture.

Awesome people radiate an inner energy that is contagious. They are team players who thrive on working with others to accomplish results and are willing to run through walls, if necessary, to do so.

Awesome people don't just identify problems or opportunities; they find and implement solutions. They pull together teams to fix what needs fixing. They take a broad view of the company and look beyond their own jobs and departments. They are always seeking new information and adding new skills to their repertoire. They are creative and see the big picture. Awesome people are able to anticipate problems that may cause bumps down the road and take action to avert such problems.

VITAL SIGNS: WHAT MAKES PEOPLE AWESOME

The Kauffman Center for Entrepreneurial Leadership asked dozens of CEOs of high-growth companies to identify the characteristics of the awesome people in their organizations. Based on their responses, we identified four key characteristics:

 Awesome people are self-motivated.

- They have a personal mission, they want to make a difference, and they have set personal goals for themselves.

- They are committed to the company's mission and vision and understand the need to be customer focused; their values are consistent with the company's values.

- They take ownership and responsibility for doing whatever it takes to get the job done.

 Awesome people are respectful and respected.

- They ask other people for advice and ideas; they respect others' opinions.

- They know how to work well in teams and enjoy the team process.

- They influence and inspire others to achieve great things.

 Awesome people are creative problem solvers.

- They challenge the status quo and like to conceptualize and articulate new possibilities.

- They take risks and learn from their successes and failures.

- They have great ideas that help the company innovate, grow, and become more profitable.

 Awesome people are learners.

- They are able to stay ahead of the curve and match or exceed the company's growth.

- They never stop learning; they learn from every experience and share knowledge with others.

- They adapt quickly and are not afraid of change.

"We like wide thinkers. We want somebody who uses inductive reasoning rather than deductive reasoning, somebody who can take a couple of events over here and link them to an event over there. Another way you might put it is somebody who is flexible, who doesn't have to own the right decision, who is willing to change his or her mind and willing to take a new approach to old problems."

Awesome people are able to work cross-functionally. They seek information from other parts of the company and the outside world that enables them to do their jobs better. They stay on top of what's going on in the market and what's happening to customers. They are continual learners and enjoy helping others learn as well.

"We set project milestones and when we reach them, we take time to debrief and talk about what is working and what isn't, so we can make midcourse corrections. A lot of companies only do this if something goes wrong and they want to find someone to blame. But our awesome people look at debriefings as a very powerful learning tool to identify successes as well as things that need fixing, so people really learn what worked and didn't work, and why."

Change does not bother awesome people; in fact, they thrive on change and adapt to it with speed and agility. Highly flexible, they are innovators who are always looking for new, better ways to do things and for new ways to support the company's vision and mission, which they thoroughly understand and embrace.

"We recently took twenty of our up-and-coming people off site to think 'out of the box' about new projects the company could undertake to boost our growth. We came away with a long list of ideas to pursue, four teams with assignments to gather more information and make proposals — and a ton of excitement."

HOW AWESOME PEOPLE DESCRIBE THEMSELVES

The preceding Vital Signs box identifies the characteristics of awesome people. Now listen to awesome employees as they describe their company's culture and why they work there:

"What motivates me is the challenge. I'm not wealthy by any means, but if you asked me the first five things that would make me stay with the company, money would not be on the list. What I am really looking for in a company is to feel challenged, respected, and when I do a good job I want to be recognized for it. That's what this company is doing, and that's why I'm here."

❀

"The thing that probably motivates me the most is the drive to learn, and the subtle encouragement to do better. I read a lot. I like to take as many classes as I can each year. I like to learn new things — whether it's about computers or whatever I'm interested in — and just explore that topic and read as much as I can about it. This company encourages me to do that."

❀

"I believe an awesome employee is the product of a cooperative effort. I don't think you can just wander into a company and become an awesome employee. In fact, people who are awesome employees in one context may not be in another. I know that I'd be considered a problem employee in another kind of company. If there's not a good fit with a company's culture, an awesome employee could be considered a real pain — always bringing up problems, always wanting to change the way we do business, always thinking of new and better ways to do things. Some managers don't like that; they don't want to hear that."

❀

"Our CEO always says he wants to keep it fun, fast, and fulfilling. He does that in different ways. We have a hot air balloon team, and going ballooning is one of the most fun things we do. On a Saturday afternoon you might get a call saying, 'Hey, today we're going to go fly the balloon. Want to come?' Okay, cool, and so you go out and spend the day with people you work with, who are also your friends. You go out and have a good time, fly the balloon, then go out for dinner and you make a day of it. That's one of the things I enjoy about working here."

Awesome people tell us they want to work in an organization where they can learn, be respected, be rewarded, think outside the box, and work with great managers who trust them. They want a company that has a vision, a direction, and a plan, and a company that includes ethics and values as part of the culture. They want to work for winners — entrepreneurs they believe in — and they want to have fun. All of this is consistent with the descriptions of culture we discussed in chapter 3.

HOW TO TRANSFORM SERIAL EMPLOYEES INTO COMMITTED EMPLOYEES

Many awesome people are "serial employees," moving from company to company, seeking positions where they can keep learning and remain fully engaged. This behavior pattern means you have to work hard to hire awesome employees and then work equally hard to retain them after they sign on. You need to convince them that they never need to leave your organization for greener pastures, that they can have the great career they want in your company. But in order to do this, you have to design your organization in ways that will help them excel and meet their personal career goals.

To attract and retain great people, you must build an awesome organization that has strength in all six components described in this book: innovative culture, awesome people, a plan for growth, well-functioning executive team, solid infrastructure, and great leadership. The best of the best are *not* going to join a company where their hard work and fresh ideas are not appreciated, they are not rewarded for high performance, they don't have a lot of opportunities to grow and keep learning, and they aren't involved in important projects (planning, decision making, problem solving) that help the company grow and succeed.

FOUR AREAS TO MASTER

To build the awesome-people component of your company, you have to master four areas:

1. **Attracting and Hiring Awesome People.** Identify the right people to hire, develop a winning offer, and convince them to join your company.

2. **Leading and Managing Awesome People.** Lead and manage in ways that meet the needs of awesome people so they don't leave your company out of frustration.

3. **Providing Growth Opportunities.** Give awesome people opportunities to learn and grow into new positions. Recognize their achievements and reward them in ways that are meaningful to them.

4. **Dealing with the Fits and Misfits.** Monitor performance and be willing to promote those who perform and deal with those who don't.

We'll discuss the first area — Attracting and Hiring Awesome People — in this chapter, and address the other three areas in chapter 5, "Retain Awesome People for Growth."

YOUR KEY RESPONSIBILITY: ATTRACT AND HIRE AWESOME PEOPLE

Successful entrepreneurs have told us that their awesome people are their competitive advantage, that recruiting and hiring awesome people is critical to the success of their companies. For this reason, hiring awesome people is one of the most important responsibilities you and your managers have. But many companies, especially when they need to hire a large number of people in periods of high growth, fall into the trap of hiring bodies for slots, which inevitably causes problems down the road. Remember, you always need to be recruiting good people. Keep the pipeline full of great prospects, people you think would be a good fit with your company. Don't wait until you need to fill a position to start looking.

> "When someone gives me great service — when they are friendly, prompt, courteous, and solve my problem — I tell them so. I say, 'Thank you for your great service. Here's my business card. If you're ever looking for a new opportunity, please call my number and tell my assistant I gave you this card. We'll interview you within 24 hours because you're the kind of person we're looking for in our company.'"

Finding candidates who are a good match with the requirements of the position *and* your culture is not easy. You and your hiring managers will need to use your networks to identify good people. Awesome people are likely to know other awesome people, so ask your employees to help you with recruiting and reward them for their efforts.

It takes more time to hire the right people in the beginning, but it is far less costly in the long run. Hiring mistakes damage individuals, their units, and the whole organization; and, it takes valuable time to address the problem and deal with the individual. Entrepreneurs often underestimate the time, money, and psychological cost of hiring the wrong person. So take the time on the front end and hire smarter, rather than faster.

> "Good people beget good people. If you have a strong organization, and you have good people in the organization, then hiring the next good person is a whole lot easier than if you don't. The corollary is also true."

> "One lesson I've learned is to spend more time and effort on recruiting and getting the right people. Basically, you are only as good as the people you hire. Our work on designing a real recruiting process has been worth its weight in gold."

> "Remember that great people want to work with other great people; never let down your guard when you are recruiting and hiring."

SIX STEPS TO RECRUITING AWESOME PEOPLE

Everyone who is in a position to hire people should understand the following six steps to recruiting awesome people.

STEP 1: CREATE A JOB PROFILE

Job profiles are critical tools of recruiting. They make you think in advance about the skills and values of the person you're seeking. Operating without job profiles opens the door to ad hoc recruiting where people are hired because they have winning personalities or great track records — though their skills and/or values don't really match your needs.

Job profiles aren't the same as "job descriptions," which are more narrowly focused on a job's tasks. A job profile is a broader list of responsibilities and values. It defines how the job contributes to company goals, and it includes roles, responsibilities, skills, educational, and cultural requirements for the job.

To develop a job profile, describe the person you are looking for in terms of values, skills, experience, education, achievements, and characteristics (for example, a team player, a people developer). One technique for doing this is to create a composite profile of your awesome people and then add the job skills and background needed for the specific position you're filling. Think about how this job is linked

VITAL SIGNS: WHAT'S IN A GOOD JOB PROFILE

Creating a detailed job profile may seem time-consuming on the front end, but the benefits are well worth it. When designing a job profile, include the following information:

- A description of what the company does, as well as its mission, vision, values, and culture. This reminds everyone, including the candidate, that you are looking for someone who matches the values and the culture, who can relate to your mission and vision — as well as someone who has the right knowledge and skills.

- A summary or outline of the responsibilities of the position, the person to whom the position reports or the position's place in the organizational structure, and ways the person in this position is expected to contribute to the company's goals.

- The educational requirements and types of prior experience that might be useful for someone to bring to the job.

- A description of the cross-functional responsibilities or priorities that are inherent in this job. This is important to include because people often ignore or pay scant attention to these responsibilities.

- The opportunities for career growth if the person performs well in this job.

to other jobs — whether you expect the job to expand or the person to grow enough to be promoted into another job. (See the preceding box, "Vital Signs: What's in a Good Job Profile.")

Inexperienced managers, under pressure to hire a lot of people, often don't take the time to develop job profiles. Some don't have a clue about hiring, job profiling, the skills required, or how various jobs need to be linked. They just hire their friends — or people they like — and assume everybody will work hard and get the job done. Sometimes entrepreneurs leave hiring to the managers. They abdicate responsibility and say, "I'm confident our managers know what we're looking for and can spot it when they see it." Both of these approaches will lead you and your managers to hire the wrong people, and that will stifle growth.

Hiring mistakes occur when there are no job profiles. In addition, a new hire without a job profile will find it hard to know what's expected of him or her after starting work — and nobody else will know what the new hire's supposed to do either! All of this wastes time, talent, and energy — at a time when you need every-one to be focused and maximize effort.

Take time to develop and review the job specifications with some of the awesome people who will be working with the new employee. Involving them in develop-ing the job profile engages them in the process and helps them understand the kind of person you'd like to recruit. Consequently, they'll be more likely to help you hire the right person and be more committed to helping the new hire succeed.

STEP 2: USE THE BEST SOURCES TO FIND GOOD CANDIDATES, AND THEN DECIDE WHOM TO INTERVIEW

Hire from within when possible; hire from outside when necessary. If no internal candidates fit the job's requirements, use other sources to recruit candidates, including employee referral programs, advertising, personal networking, job fairs, on-line resume services, or external recruiters. The number and types of recruiting processes you use should depend on the size of the pool of candidates you think you need, the job level, and the difficulty of finding candidates with the values and skills required.

Review resumes, compare them to the job profile, and decide which candidates to invite in for interviews. Determine which four to six existing employees are most appropriate to interview candidates and ask them to help you. Contact the candidates and set up a schedule of interviews.

STEP 3: DEVELOP AND FOLLOW AN EFFECTIVE INTERVIEW PROCESS

Unfortunately, many entrepreneurs of growth companies don't take the time to develop an interview process or don't insist that it be used consistently with all candidates. Instead, they allow each interviewer to make up processes, and use "personal chemistry" as the determinant when making hiring decisions. There is no substitute for a structured interview process; it has a much higher probability of attracting awesome people than ad hoc processes do.

Your role as chief of hiring is to champion the development of an effective interview process. This is the only way you can be sure that the right kinds of people are being hired without having to interview everyone yourself. You also need to participate in sessions in which managers are trained to do the interviewing. Talk with them about why it's important to have an interview process and to do behavioral interviewing (described below). Show them how you communicate the mission, vision, and values of the company when you yourself hire people — for example, when you hire members of your executive team — and describe how you check out whether people you are interviewing share your values. Then, walk the talk and make sure your managers do as well.

Effective interviews allow you to find out about the whole person and determine whether she or he can contribute long-term to the organization — not just whether the person has the skills to do the job. A good interviewer can judge whether a candidate has the right values, experience, and capabilities to do the job.

USE BEHAVIORAL INTERVIEWING

Behavioral interviewing, a technique that helps you judge future performance based on past performance, is the most effective interviewing method. Behavioral interviewing is based on the premise that people will behave the same way in the future as they have behaved in the past. You need to find out whether a person will fit with your company's culture (team oriented, creative, risk taker, able to learn from mistakes, and so on). So you need to ask for real-life examples of how she or he behaved in the past.

For instance, if you want to know how the candidate might respond to pressure or deal with failure, you could pose a hypothetical question such as, "How would you deal with a setback?" But if you do behavioral interviewing, you will say, "Think about a time when something you worked for, and counted on, didn't work out. Talk a little bit about that situation and how you dealt with it." This requires the candidate to speak from experience and gives you a glimpse into the candidate's past behavior. You can then probe for more information by asking, "What did you do next?" and then "Why did you choose that course of action?"

Here's another example of behavioral interviewing. Say you want to explore the person's experience with teamwork. You could ask a question such as, "Tell me about a time when you were leading a team and the team was not hitting its goals and deadlines." After the person describes the experience, follow up with questions like, "What did you do then?" Probe more by asking "Why?" and "What did you learn from that experience?" Behavioral interviewing provides opportunities for candidates to share experiences, explain what they did, why they did it, and what they've learned. This, in turn, provides you with many insights about whether a candidate shares your values, is motivated, respectful, a creative problem solver, and a learner.

REMEMBER, YOU'RE BUYING AND SELLING

When you're interviewing candidates, be sure to ask them questions, listen carefully to their answers, and respond to their questions, but don't try to close the sale during the interview. The hiring process is an interesting mix of buying and selling. On the one hand, candidates want to know what kind of company they'll be joining and your expectations regarding their roles, responsibilities, and performance. On the other hand, you want to know more about the person you're thinking of hiring and whether they're a good fit with your company. Most candidates will try to sell you on the notion that they're right for the job, and you'll be tempted to sell the candidate on the job and your company. But, be careful not to sell too hard. It's very easy to get caught up in the thrill of the chase and end up hiring less than awesome people because you spend more time selling than exploring whether the person is a good fit for the job. Instead, share your vision, talk about the company's mission, values, and culture, and answer the candidate's questions as honestly as you can. Then, make sure the candidate has a chance to interview some of your awesome people and ask them why they chose to work in your company.

> "I've come to realize that I don't make good hiring decisions. I start out the interview telling the candidates about the company, its mission, my vision and dreams, and pretty soon I'm selling them on the company and what a great place it is to work — because I really believe it is a great company and a great place to work. I get excited, and they get excited — and it has nothing

to do with the job or their fit with the job. I'm just a great salesman! So they'd leave the interview all charged up, and I'd feel good about them. We'd hire them, and in 90 days we'd realize — or they'd realize — that they weren't the right person for the job, and we'd have a real mess. So now we've developed a process and a system, and I don't do the interviewing anymore. We have other people do the interviewing — and they do a much better job hiring people than I did."

The interviewing process should include a series of interviews in which you gradually narrow down the candidate list. If possible, invite prime candidates to spend a whole day at the company, perhaps even work with a team on problem solving or a similar activity. At the end of the day, ask them for their impressions and what they learned about the company. This is an especially good technique to use when hiring members of the top team who will be critical to the success of the company.

LOOK FOR PEOPLE WHO CAN GROW TWO LEVELS

The people you want must be able to grow at least two levels in your organization and know more about their functional area (finance, marketing, product development, technology, and so on) than you do.

"We never hire anyone who can't be promoted at least two levels. That way, I have to hire three times fewer people. If I hire someone who can be promoted two or three times, I can spend tomorrow's energy finding the next person who can be promoted rather than replacing the one who can't."

"A key thing I always try to do is to get people better than me. If you hire people worse than you, then the organization averages down. What you want to do is find people that average you up and average the whole organization up. Then what you want to do is delegate and share responsibility. If the founder holds on to all the responsibilities, you ruin your organization."

Ewing Kauffman built a highly profitable, multi-billion-dollar company where people were highly productive, morale was high, and turnover was low — a company that was the darling of Wall Street. He advised entrepreneurs to hire people "smarter than you." Doing so will enable you to grow the capabilities of the organization rather than limit it to the level of your own ability. " If you hire people you consider smarter than you, you are more likely to listen to their thoughts and ideas. This is the best way to expand your own capabilities and build the strength of your company."

"The key is having awesome managers who know how to hire awesome people. If you have mediocre managers, they will always hire mediocre people. 'B' players will not hire 'A' players; they will hire more 'B' or even 'C' players. So if you want to grow, it's critical to have awesome managers who will hire the talented people you really need."

STEP 4: SELECT THE BEST CANDIDATES AND CHECK THEIR REFERENCES

Make sure everyone involved in the interviewing process provides feedback to the hiring manager on the candidates' strengths, weaknesses, and cultural fit, and any red flags. While the decision to hire someone is the hiring manager's, everyone involved in the hiring process is responsible for providing feedback on all the candidates.

The hiring manager should select the person or persons who are the best fit with the requirements of the position and the company's culture. Be willing to turn down candidates who are less than awesome. Extensive reference checks with those candidates' past managers, peers, and staff should be a critical part of the hiring process because past behavior and performance are the best predictors of future behavior and performance. Remember to check educational records and do credit checks on company officers and others who will have the authority to sign requisitions or checks above a certain dollar amount. Do not skip this process just because someone seems like a fantastic prospect.

STEP 5: MAKE THE OFFER

Once you've completed the series of interviews, received feedback from all the interviewers, and completed the necessary due diligence to confirm the individual's educational and career credentials, you need to structure a killer offer that will ensure that the awesome person accepts the job. But before you make a formal offer, talk with the candidate about what issues are important to him or her, for example, compensation, flex time, current and deferred compensation, vacation time, opportunities to grow and develop, and so forth. Then develop a written offer. This process helps you avoid last-minute misunderstandings about what the candidate was expecting versus what your company is prepared to offer.

"To go after awesome people, you need to know what really motivates them. What stirs their soul? How can you tie into something important to them? Often they come up with some very creative things that you wouldn't think of because you're thinking about what would be motivating to you. We recruited one person whose goal was to write a book. She signed on when I said we could make that happen."

❁

"I learned that people are motivated by a lot more than money. One strong motivation is the freedom to be able to grow something. That's how we were able to hire two internationally known people from another company. We used the analogy of going from a tanker to a rowboat. We offered them the ability to really direct which way their rowboat was going."

PEOPLE WANT MORE THAN MONEY

As we noted earlier, great people are looking for a stimulating environment where they can build their skills, learn new things, and contribute to the growth of a thriving organization. You'll need to offer such people many things beyond salary to attract them to your company. You'll need to make it clear that this is a place where they can make a difference; be part of and even lead teams that are working on important issues; and have a chance to experiment, take risks, and be innovative.

Awesome people want to have a chance to take charge of their own careers. They value programs that help them assess their abilities, training options to build their skills, and courses that will prepare them for new responsibilities. Mentoring programs, team building, career planning, and opportunities to change jobs and switch departments will not only make your company more attractive to awesome people but will make it easier to retain them once they do come on board. Programs such as these send signals to prospective job candidates that your company is committed to helping employees develop themselves, that they really are valuable resources, and that the company won't just use them up and spit them out.

Awesome people also value the flexibility to create balance between their personal and professional lives. Offering flex schedules, job sharing, telecommuting, reduced summer hours, or similar plans can improve your company's ability to attract great people.

Many first-time entrepreneurs assume they can't afford awesome people. They don't understand that some people are willing to take a cut in pay for a share in the upside. Awesome people will often accept a job at a lower salary if they are given a chance to share the rewards (profits and equity) they helped create. Not everyone is willing to do this, and sometimes people's financial obligations dampen their appetite for risk. But, you should test this concept with candidates you really want to hire but can't afford at their current salaries. Many candidates have been persuaded to take pay cuts and join companies that commit to sharing the rewards with people whose performance makes a real difference.

DEVELOP A COMPENSATION SYSTEM BASED ON RISK AND REWARD

Ewing Kauffman recruited people to Marion Labs who were willing to take some risk — for a share in the rewards. The base salaries for managers, directors, and officers were set a bit below traditional levels, but compensation packages always included big opportunities for profit sharing and stock options if the company did well. Mr. K. wanted people who were risk takers, who would work hard and develop creative ideas to help the company be more competitive because they had something to gain if the company was successful. And, he made good on his stated core value that "those who produce should share in the rewards." When the company merged with Merrell Dow, almost everyone had stock options; more than 10 percent of the employees became multi-millionaires, and many more became near millionaires.

When negotiating with chosen candidates, describe your risk-reward compensation strategy. Talk with them about their goals and priorities in life, and find out what's important to them. Then, structure an offer that takes all that into consideration — for example, opportunities to work at home if children are sick, opportunities to travel, stock options, bonuses, profit sharing, lower salary with an extra week of vacation, education, or training that builds their skills in areas that interest them.

> "One of the things we did was try to get people at the mid- to low end of the salary scale because we wanted people who were willing to take a risk. Then we compensated them handsomely with equity, bonuses, and so forth. The issue is not what you pay, but what you offer to attract the people you want. You've got to offer something more than just money, or they'll leave the first time someone else offers them more money. So it has to be a combination of your culture, your product, your passion, your vision, the team they're working with, and/or a share of the future opportunity that you're all building."

STEP 6: OUTLINE WHAT WILL HAPPEN AFTER THE CANDIDATE ACCEPTS THE JOB

Sometimes it's a matter of days, other times it may be weeks or months from the time you make a job offer until the new hire actually joins the company. Your goal is to keep new hires excited about their new jobs, reinforce their decision to accept the employment offer, get through all the personal changes they will need to make (for example, moving, relocating families, and spousal job change), and help them prepare for the job. After candidates accept a job offer, send the new hires and their families a "welcome aboard" gift basket. Schedule weekly phone calls during which you update new hires on issues of significance. Send them copies of reports, plans, and new policies. Offer them a consulting contract for a day or two a week so you can tap into their knowledge and expertise while they are making the job transition. Remember to talk with them and get their input before you make decisions that will impact the areas or projects they will be responsible for after they arrive.

YOUR ROLE AS LEADER

In summary, these are your responsibilities, as chief of hiring, when it comes to attracting awesome people to your company:

- Champion the development of a recruiting process specifically designed to identify and attract awesome people.

- Be sure job profiles and behavioral interviewing are mainstays of the recruiting process and that your awesome people have opportunities to participate in recruiting and interviewing candidates.

- Stay involved; make sure people follow the hiring process.

- Make sure that job offers address all the issues of importance to the awesome person being recruited, including opportunities to keep learning; and, remember that those who produce should share in the rewards.

- Make hiring awesome people an important priority for all managers, hold them accountable for doing it, and make it one of the factors in their performance reviews.

> "I think you can never put too much time or too much work into hiring the right people because the cost of getting it wrong is so high that you can't afford it."

In chapter 5, we'll talk more about what you need to do to retain awesome people. You and your top team may first want to check on how well you're attracting awesome people by taking the following *BAO SCAN: Attract Awesome People for Growth*.

BIG LESSONS

1. Remember that awesome people are the essential ingredients in your company's success.

2. Watch for the red flags that signal you don't have enough awesome people or that you're losing the ones you do have.

3. Understand what awesome people look for in a company, what issues are important, and then structure your recruiting and hiring processes to attract them.

4. Make cultural fit a criterion for hiring — or not hiring — a candidate.

5. Make sure all managers follow the six steps to recruiting awesome people.

www.entreworld.org

BAO SCAN: ATTRACT AWESOME PEOPLE FOR GROWTH

Use this *SCAN* to assess your organization's current strengths and weaknesses in attracting awesome people. Take this *BAO SCAN* yourself, and then have your top team and other key people complete it as well. Compare your responses and perceptions with theirs. Work together to identify innovative ways to solve problems and come up with new ideas about how to attract the kinds of people you need to sustain — and accelerate — your growth.

PART A: ASSESSING YOUR AWESOME PEOPLE

1. How many of your employees are awesome people?

    a. Almost all

    b. Most

    c. Almost half

    d. Some

    e. Only a few

2. List three employees you consider awesome.

a. _____

b. _____

c. _____

A. List several characteristics that make each one an awesome employee.

_____

_____

_____

B. How did you attract each of them to the company?

_____

_____

_____

C. Why did each one want to come to work for your company?

_____

_____

_____

D. Why have they stayed with your company?

_____

_____

_____

PART B: RATING YOUR COMPANY'S ABILITY TO ATTRACT AWESOME PEOPLE

RATING SCALE

Use this scale to respond to each rating question

1 - - - - - 2 - - - - - 3 - - - - - 4 - - - - - 5 - - - - - 6 - - - - - 7

NEVER   SOMETIMES   ALWAYS

1. We attract awesome people.   Rating: _____

2. We are known inside and out as an awesome organization.   Rating: _____

Questions to consider:

- What makes our company an awesome organization?

- What are our core values?

- How do we make them real?

- What is our value proposition for employees?

- Why would the best and brightest want to work here?

3. We recruit, interview, and select people who are the
right fit for us.   Rating: _____

Questions to consider:

- What are our criteria for identifying people who fit with our culture?

- Are we capitalizing on our awesome people's ability to attract other awesome people?

- Are we seeing enough of the right candidates?

- If not, what can we do to improve?

- Have we developed good job profiles and a structured interviewing process?

- Are people following the process?

- Are we making the right kinds of offers to the right kinds of people?

- Are we losing candidates we want? If so, why?

- What works best about our hiring process?

- What improvements do we need to make?

4. The CEO is the champion of the process for finding,
interviewing, and selecting awesome people.   Rating: _____

5. The CEO holds managers accountable for finding,
interviewing, and selecting awesome people.   Rating: _____

6. We follow our plan for attracting more awesome people
to our company.   Rating: _____

SCORE SUMMARY AND INTERPRETATION

A Rating Score of **7** in any area indicates this is a prime area of strength that will facilitate and support the company's growth. Scores of **5** and **6** indicate that you have considerable strength in these areas, but you will want to consider making incremental improvements to increase the score. A score of **4** is a cause for worry. A rating of "Sometimes" indicates a lack of consistency that sends conflicting signals to employees and inhibits growth; thus significant improvements will be needed. Scores of **3 or below** are big red flags indicating areas or behaviors that hinder the company's growth and require your immediate attention.

RESULTS ANALYSIS

Look back over the *BAO SCAN: Attract Awesome People for Growth:*

1. List three statements that you rated the highest. Choose those you feel are key strengths and contribute most to the success of the company.

   A. _____

   B. _____

   C. _____

2. List three statements that received the lowest rating. Choose those you feel are the most critical weaknesses and should be targeted for improvement.

   A. _____

   B. _____

   C. _____

3. Write three statements that define your priorities for change (for example, capitalize more on the strengths or improve the weaknesses).

   A. _____

   B. _____

   C. _____

4. List three things our company could do to implement these changes.

A. _____

B. _____

C. _____

ACTION PLAN

Recognize what you and your company are doing well and celebrate! Think about what you have done that enabled you to achieve these great results and how that can be applied to your weaknesses. But, do not overlook areas that need improvement or think they will improve on their own over time. Use these steps to develop your Action Plan for Improvement:

1. Ask your top team to complete the *BAO SCAN: Attract Awesome People for Growth* and the Results Analysis. You may also want others in the company to complete the *SCAN* in order to get more comprehensive feedback.

2. Meet with your top team to:

- Compare and contrast your ratings on various questions with their ratings, as well as areas you have identified as strengths with those needing work.

- If applicable, discuss the reasons why their responses are different from yours.

- Agree on areas for improvement or change; be as specific as possible.

3. Prioritize those areas that must be addressed and will make the biggest difference. Develop them into Action Plans for Improvement.

4. Get consensus on the Action Plans and the resources and budgets needed to make the necessary changes.

- For each Action Plan, specify the goal, desired outcomes, steps to take, team members responsible for implementation, resources required, key measures of success, and time frames for achieving the goal and tracking results.

- Assign a cross-functional team to implement each Action Plan. Include members from different departments who will be affected by the changes. Members should have the necessary skills and insights to accomplish the plan. Identify a team leader and/or executive sponsor who will be held accountable for managing the team, tracking progress, and achieving the desired goal.

5. Communicate the Action Plans for Improvement to everyone in the company. Get involvement, input, and feedback.

6. Hold yourself and others accountable for achieving the new goals and milestones.

7. After a designated period of time (three to six months), evaluate progress, identify new or emerging problems or opportunities, set new goals, make new team assignments (if appropriate), and take action. In a year, retake the *BAO SCAN: Attract Awesome People for Growth* and repeat Steps 1 through 6 as required. Remember: Continuous assessment, action, and improvement are essential to building an awesome organization that is strong enough to support continuous growth.

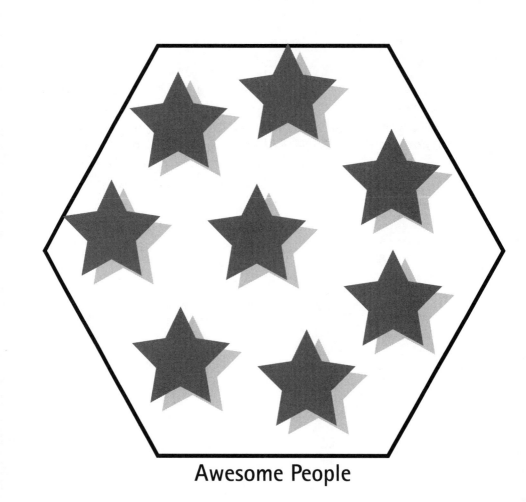

Awesome People

CHAPTER **5**

RETAIN AWESOME PEOPLE FOR GROWTH

"Great people want to do great things. They want to be affiliated with great and noble causes. They want to know that their life, their work, is adding up to something more than just a paycheck or a job, that they're making a difference for the better in the way the world works. So if you want to recruit and keep great people, the way to do it is to make sure they know that you stand for something that's really important and noble in the world, and then give them a chance to work on it."

In chapter 4, "Attract Awesome People for Growth," we described how to find and get awesome people. But if you want to grow, you've got to figure out how to retain the people you've worked so hard to recruit. You and your managers need to know how to lead, manage, and reward them so they'll stick around for the long haul and help you build an awesome organization. There are many benefits to retaining awesome people, some of which are described in the following box, "Vital Signs: Benefits of Retaining Awesome People."

VITAL SIGNS: BENEFITS OF RETAINING AWESOME PEOPLE

The following list highlights some of the benefits your organization will experience when it retains its awesome people:

- Turnover is low among the people you want to keep, so you don't spend time and money replacing them.

- Communication flows easily in all directions throughout the organization as people work in an atmosphere of trust and cooperation.

- Teams are more productive because your awesome people have worked together for a long time and know each other and the issues well.

- The culture is healthy; the values are alive.

- The company moves faster because everyone is in sync.

- The company is known as an awesome organization.

- The company produces great results because your awesome people are constantly coming up with new ideas and working hard to bring them to reality.

- It's much easier to recruit more awesome people.

START RIGHT: THE ORIENTATION PROCESS

Awesome people want to be productive contributors as soon as possible, so you need to lead and manage them effectively from day one. When they walk in the door that first day, awesome people want to know more than details about company benefits, where they will sit, the company cafeteria's hours, and information about the company's products and services. Awesome people have joined your company because they think it stands for something important in the world. They want to learn about the company's core values, vision, and mission, as well as the role you expect them to play in the organization.

For this reason, you need to design the whole orientation process carefully so new hires understand the critical elements that make your company successful and what's required for them to succeed in your work environment. An orientation process that helps people understand the culture and the organization reinforces their decision to dedicate a portion of their lives to helping you build a company. With a little thought, you can get them started on the right foot so that all the hard work of recruiting them pays off as they turn into awesome performers.

COMPANY ORIENTATION

The faster you are growing, the more important orientation is to the stability and alignment of your company. A good orientation program for all new hires ensures that everyone gets the same cultural messages and that no one gets short shrift because their manager is out of town or has other pressing priorities. Nothing is worse for new employees than to be left on their own to make sense of the organization they've just joined. This creates negative first impressions and causes people to wonder whether they made the right job choice.

Because you are the leader, you need to be part of the orientation process. It's important for you to welcome new hires to the company and share your vision and passion with them. When the CEO takes time to talk with new hires and describe the values, mission, and direction, it sends a message to everyone that these new people are important, that preserving your culture is important, and that people really are your most important asset.

"For a long time, our orientation process wasn't formalized. We did the usual employee benefits and signing forms stuff, then introductions in the hallways. We were growing fast, hiring people every week, and they were coming in without getting the message about the big picture of where we want to take this company and how we intend to get there. Finally, we realized we needed some consistency about how people got introduced to the organization. Then, after we developed a real orientation process, we decided to put everybody in the company through it — all 750 employees. It really helped get everyone on the same page about our vision, mission, and values. It was a great reorientation for everyone. Now, when new hires go through the process, it's much more effective in terms of getting them up to speed and acclimated to our culture. And I know that part of my role is to lead the whole process."

> "We have a three-day orientation, and I lead the first day, during which we discuss the company's history, mission, vision, and values. That first day includes some skills training in behaviors and actions that demonstrate those values."

As Mr. Kauffman observed, "You have your dreams for the company. People have dreams and goals of their own. It's your job to show them that helping you reach your goals will enable them to reach their goals." He was involved in the first day of orientation and made a point of calling new hires or chatting with them in the lunchroom at least once during their first six months.

As the value of good orientation programs becomes apparent, more companies are increasing the amount of time they allot to this process. Corporate boot camps, in which new employees go through rigorous orientation programs spanning several days, weeks, or even months, are becoming more common. Companies use these programs to clarify the company's purpose, direction, values, structure, plans, and metrics; and to get new people immediately involved in important work. Innovation and problem-solving exercises that capitalize on the fresh perspectives of new hires are often part of such programs. Orientation might even include the spouses and children of new employees, who are invited in for a tour and perhaps lunch, or their own orientation to the new company.

INDIVIDUAL ORIENTATION

Hiring managers need to think about the best way to orient each new employee to the work of their departments. This individual orientation should include a discussion that sets the stage for performance management by covering:

- What's expected of the new person.
- How performance will be measured and rewarded.
- Criteria for success and consequences of failure.
- Requirements for promotion, including setting goals for enhanced professional skills and knowledge.
- The kinds of investment the company is willing to make in the individual's professional development.

In addition, make the new hire feel welcome and give him or her a taste of what it's like to work in your awesome organization. Here's how one entrepreneur welcomes new people:

"We throw parties for people who retire, so someone suggested to me that we turn the process around. Let's throw a party for new hires their first day on the job! So we get the person's business cards ready and get their T-shirt ready, and when they walk in, everybody welcomes the person to the company. We introduce them to their 'buddy,' and we line up people to take them to lunch the first week or two. We try to make joining the company a great experience, make those first few weeks memorable, and show this person that they are now part of an awesome organization."

It's helpful to find an awesome employee who will serve as a "buddy," someone willing to show the new person the ropes during the first few weeks on the job. You might also want to consider asking an awesome person outside the department to serve as a mentor for the new hire. This will enable the new hire to meet a broader group of people than just immediate coworkers, and will promote a better cross-functional understanding of the company. Awesome people enjoy taking on such roles and can be great sounding boards for new employees.

Schedule appointments for the new hires with people in their department as well as in the other departments they will be working with in the months ahead. When new hires meet with their colleagues, they learn more about the company; hear why others joined, why they stay, and what they do; and can talk about how they will work together in ways that will enable everyone to be successful.

"We hired a new CFO to fill an important gap in our Executive Team. He said the first thing he wanted to do was to talk to each individual he was going to be working with, including all of the executives on the management team, the people on his staff, and people on other staffs that he would be interfacing with. He interviewed people about what they did and how that related to the company's goals. He then brought that information back to the Executive Team along with his observations, and what he had learned about our strengths and weaknesses. Then he outlined some actions he thought we should take. He ended up with a very clear idea of what his job should be — which turned out to be a little different than what we had originally thought when we hired him. But we all found the whole process very valuable. We now use this technique as part of the orientation of all new employees. Their first assignment is to interview the people they're going to be working with and to provide feedback on what they've learned."

Giving new employees time to meet and talk with others in the organization may seem time-consuming at first, but it will pay dividends many times over as your company's growth accelerates. If new employees can develop a rapport early on with the people they'll be working with, they will be able to capitalize on that relationship later, when they need help completing tasks, meeting deadlines, or bringing projects in on budget.

HELP AWESOME PEOPLE ACHIEVE GREAT RESULTS

Orienting your new hires is very important, but some entrepreneurs think that all they need to do is hire and orient awesome people, and then get out of their way. It's not that easy. You need to lead them and make sure their efforts are focused in the direction you want to take the company. Make sure you and your managers understand the difference between delegation and abdication, between effective management and micromanagement. Carefully review the following box, "Red Flags: You're Mismanaging Awesome People If . . . "; think about how you and your top team are leading and managing your people.

RED FLAGS: YOU'RE MISMANAGING AWESOME PEOPLE IF . . .

Be concerned if you hear these kinds of complaints from awesome people:

▰ My boss keeps telling me what to do, how to do it, and keeps checking up to see if I've done it.

▰ I don't really know where this company is going.

▰ Our team isn't working together very well — and we aren't working well with any other teams, either.

▰ Nobody seems to care whether I'm producing or not. And, no one notices how hard I'm working — certainly not my boss.

▰ People who aren't performing and don't live by the values are getting the same raises and perks that "awesome" people are getting — and that's not fair.

▰ My manager isn't giving me any direction, and the only time I hear from him or her is when something's gone wrong.

If you've hired the right kind of people, you won't have to spend a lot of time telling them how to do their job or checking on them to see if they're doing it your way. Instead, describe the results you want, point people in the right direction, agree on how progress will be measured, and then check in with them regularly. When you see that they understand what the job requires and that they are performing well, you can then begin to delegate more. But, make it clear you expect them to report on progress as well as new ideas.

> "It's critical that each individual and his or her manager agree on the outcome — what are we trying to do here? What should be the result of these initiatives? Then agree on measuring sticks. I've always said the difference between a pro and an amateur is that the professional keeps score. Measure effectively and reward extraordinarily."

> "I grow leaders by delegating to people. I make sure they understand the ultimate goal, that they know I'll be there when they need me, and that I will support their decisions. And then I let them do it. I think it's important to let people make mistakes and be comfortable making them. If people are afraid to make mistakes, they won't feel comfortable making decisions."

Manage your awesome people in a way that makes the most of their outstanding characteristics; this means providing them with the type of organization they want, as described in chapter 1, "Why Build an Awesome Organization?", and chapter 3, "Develop an Innovative Culture for Growth." To retain your awesome people, you need to delegate effectively, foster great communication and continuous learning, provide coaching, develop teams, ask people for ideas on how to grow the company, and build trusting relationships.

MASTER EFFECTIVE DELEGATION

Your company can't grow unless you, your top team, and your managers understand how to delegate. The unwritten rule in fast-growth companies is that executives and managers are more likely to be promoted if they have identified and developed people who can step up and replace them. Appropriate delegation helps develop the next generation of company leaders.

Delegating does not mean that the manager abdicates responsibility; it means that the employee is given some level of authority to act on behalf of the manager — and that authority can vary from a little to a lot. The following box, "Vital Signs: Six Levels of Delegation," indicates that delegation is more complex than simply giving someone a task and assuming that they will complete it.

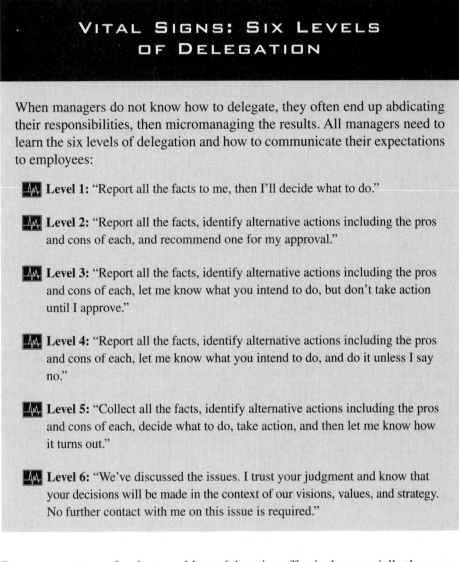

VITAL SIGNS: SIX LEVELS OF DELEGATION

When managers do not know how to delegate, they often end up abdicating their responsibilities, then micromanaging the results. All managers need to learn the six levels of delegation and how to communicate their expectations to employees:

Level 1: "Report all the facts to me, then I'll decide what to do."

Level 2: "Report all the facts, identify alternative actions including the pros and cons of each, and recommend one for my approval."

Level 3: "Report all the facts, identify alternative actions including the pros and cons of each, let me know what you intend to do, but don't take action until I approve."

Level 4: "Report all the facts, identify alternative actions including the pros and cons of each, let me know what you intend to do, and do it unless I say no."

Level 5: "Collect all the facts, identify alternative actions including the pros and cons of each, decide what to do, take action, and then let me know how it turns out."

Level 6: "We've discussed the issues. I trust your judgment and know that your decisions will be made in the context of our visions, values, and strategy. No further contact with me on this issue is required."

Because managers often have problems delegating effectively, especially those new to the managerial ranks, you may need to provide training in effective delegation. For instance, you could take 15 minutes to talk about delegation at a regularly scheduled meeting of your top team and key managers. Or, you might want to develop some exercises in delegation that you could use at a management development day. Another option is for you to take a hands-on approach to coaching individuals on delegation; help them choose the appropriate level of delegation, depending on the type of issue they are dealing with and the level of trust and confidence they have in the individual to whom they are delegating.

FOSTER TWO-WAY COMMUNICATION

Clearly, having communication flowing both ways between awesome people and their leaders is critical to capitalizing on the self-motivation and desire to drive growth that awesome people bring to the organization. Two-way communication helps people feel involved and enables you to tap into their creativity and innovative ideas.

Managers must help their direct reports understand how various jobs and projects support the company's goals. They should involve awesome people in planning and problem solving on big-picture issues, but they also need to learn about the personal goals and needs of their direct reports and really understand what motivates them. This means that managers and their people need to listen to each other, negotiate, and agree on how to work together to help everyone achieve company goals as well as personal objectives. The following stories illustrate the impact of communications on the functioning of the organization and the growth of the company.

"I had a chain of hair salons, and we had really high turnover. So I decided to think of my employees as customers. I sat down with each of them and we talked about their concerns and what I could do about it. I found that most of them worried that they wouldn't make enough to be able to afford to send their kids to college, so I set up a college scholarship fund. They felt they could make more money if they sold some hair products in the stores, but they weren't sure how to sell them, so we did some training around how to sell hair care products. The average salary in our industry is $15,000, but my employees earn up to $35,000 a year, and turnover has dropped to almost zero. All this was the result of my asking 'What's bothering you and what can I do about it?,' then doing things that they suggested."

"We set up a cycle of meetings: 15-minute team huddles every day, 30-minute weekly meetings, and 90-minute monthly meetings, each with well-defined agendas. This rhythm of meetings keeps communication flowing throughout our organization."

"Each member of my top team writes weekly reports based on a 5:15 model; a 5:15 report takes no more than five minutes to read and no longer than 15 minutes to write. It covers the individual's results over the past week and sets goals for the coming week. We use this simple mechanism with all other teams as well, and it has been highly effective in keeping people aligned with our strategy."

Two-way communication is essential to keeping all employees informed about where you are, how well the company is executing its plans, and what changes in the external environment require changes in the plan. Two-way communication is essential in order to assure that everyone stays aligned with the strategy.

PROMOTE CONTINUOUS LEARNING

Fostering a culture of continuous learning to support employee growth and development requires having mechanisms available for people to gain experience, develop new capabilities, and share their learning with others. Continuous learning should address three areas:

- Job learning (specific job skill needs)

- Strategic development (skills needed to support innovation and the company's future, including leadership, teamwork, communication, strategic thinking, and creative problem solving)

- Personal development (improving an individual's skills that may or may not be specifically related to her or his current job)

Develop a coordinated program of mentoring, coaching, on-the-job training, and workshops that build personal, job, and strategic skills. Here are ways to promote continuous learning:

- Determine what training resources are needed to help employees learn the critical job skills and key behaviors that support your company's values, mission, vision, and strategies, as well as leadership skills. In-house training can be designed to support your values and foster team building, and is often more easily and quickly applied to people's jobs than outside training.

- Develop policies about who is eligible to participate in what kinds of training programs (both internal and external), tuition reimbursement, and whether employees will receive time off and/or pay to attend various kinds of educational or developmental programs.

- Develop a mentoring program. Encourage employees to identify a mentor, that is, someone in the company to learn from, in addition to their manager. The mentor should be someone an employee can go to with questions and requests for advice and counsel. Hold mentors accountable through a process in which mentees evaluate their performance.

- Enable people to grow through mechanisms such as job rotation within and outside of departments, emergency fill-in assignments, special one-person projects, and cross-functional team assignments.

- Encourage everyone in the company to take time to discuss questions such as "What have we learned from this experience?" and "How can we do it better next time?" Provide opportunities for people to share their experiences and new knowledge during meetings, at brown-bag lunches, and via the Intranet or e-mail so they can help others learn.

- Develop ways to have awesome people train other people in areas where they have expertise.

> "We have something called the client round table once a week. Client Services leads an open meeting that anyone can come to and learn how we are handling things. We also have a daily meeting from 8:30 to 9:00 A.M. that we call Dissecting the Deal. A sales rep will get up and say, 'Last week I was working a deal and here is what happened.' It gives everyone a chance to learn from the experience of others, and in some cases, the deal is not finished yet so people provide ideas to help move it forward. This process has been hugely valuable."

PROVIDE COACHING

Good managers hold coaching sessions with employees to provide feedback, help them set goals, and encourage them to develop skills and try new challenges. Although Human Resources can train them in effective coaching techniques, the responsibility for good coaching rests with the managers themselves. Managers must first understand the goals and motivations of their direct reports and then provide coaching to help them achieve those goals and become leaders in their own roles. All great athletes talk about the importance of a coach in helping them learn new skills, eliminate bad habits, change their roles, stay balanced, improve their stroke, calm their nerves, and turn in a winning performance.

Awesome employees in young, fast-growing companies often complain that their managers don't give enough feedback or constructive criticism about their performance. This can happen when inexperienced managers are so focused on getting the work done that they neglect coaching. Make it clear to managers that developing and stretching their people is a high priority, provide them with training on how to coach effectively, and make coaching and development of their people part of their performance reviews.

Here are some guidelines you can share with your managers about effective coaching:

- Build a relationship of trust and open communication; this "safe" environment will enable the person to accept constructive criticism.

- Help the person set goals and take action; schedule feedback meetings during which you debrief, critique, review accountability, and set new goals.

- Be objective and talk about what you are observing. Watch, listen, and then describe or provide feedback on what the person did and what effect that had on others. Encourage the person to discover his or her own conclusions and identify the "lessons learned." This is better than spoon-feeding the lessons he or she should have learned from that experience.

- Give objective feedback on your observations as soon as possible. Do not wait too long.

- Teach the person how to critique his or her own behavior; learn to debrief personal experiences, become more aware of the impact of his or her actions on others, and enable them to learn how to coach to others.

SET UP TEAMS

Put your awesome people on teams that are working on high-priority projects that are critical to the company's success. Successful companies know how to develop networks of close-knit teams throughout the company. If you think about your organization from a systems perspective, the whole company can be considered one large team, with employees working in a variety of functional and cross-functional teams.

Develop guidelines for team behavior that apply to all teams, provide training and development in teamwork, and remove bureaucratic processes that interfere with effective teamwork and decision making. (See the following box, "Vital Signs: Setting Up a Team to Succeed.") Make sure everyone on a team understands the

VITAL SIGNS: SETTING UP A TEAM TO SUCCEED

In order for teams to be successful within your organization, you need to set them up correctly:

 Identify a priority that ties directly to achieving the company's vision and strategy.

 Select the team members and the leader. If the team leader is not a member of the Executive Team, name a team sponsor from the Executive Team. The executive sponsor serves as the team's liaison with the top team.

 Review the effective guidelines for all teams with the full team at the first meeting (see the list following this box for more information).

 Develop a partnership chart on which team members identify their individual goals for achieving the team's work, the goals they believe other team members have, what they need from each person on the team to achieve their goals, and what they believe the other people on the team need from them to accomplish their goals.

 Start the work and track progress according to the agreed-on timelines and measurements. Refer to the partnership chart if problems arise.

 Evaluate and reward success.

goals, the parameters within which they'll have to do the work, and the desired outcomes. Agree on timelines and measurements, and then send them off. They'll make some mistakes and may not take the same route you'd use to get to the goal, but let them figure it out for themselves without micromanaging. You'll be amazed at what they produce. Be sure to praise and reward them for their accomplishments.

Effective guidelines for all teams include:

- A common goal with clear deliverables for results to be accomplished that help fulfill the company's strategy.

- Timelines, milestones, and measurements for success.

- Clear roles and responsibilities for the leader and for all team members.

- Defined expectations regarding work to be done during and between meetings.

- Skills in creative problem solving (see appendix D, "Model for Creative Problem Solving").

- Specific mechanisms for communicating between meetings.

- Methods for evaluating the work of the team and for establishing mutual accountability to ensure that everyone is doing what they're supposed to be doing.

When employees are able to participate in one or more teams beyond their functional area, the whole company benefits. Decision making is more consistent and balanced, and conflict resolution becomes easier because employees know and have worked with others outside their functional areas. There is more camaraderie, and people view the company as an open organization versus a closed one. Silos disappear, and there is much more innovation. Working with other awesome people on important or cutting edge projects gives employees a chance to learn, contribute ideas, solve problems, and achieve results — all of which awesome people say they want as part of their jobs.

ASK PEOPLE FOR IDEAS ABOUT HOW TO BUILD THE COMPANY

Solicit the ideas of awesome people and let them know they have an important role to play in helping you build a high-growth company. Awesome people are creative planners and problem solvers. Listen to their ideas. Share what you're thinking — don't assume they can read your mind. Ask them to help you think about how changes in the market will affect your business, describe problems you don't know how to solve, and talk about the new goals you are considering but aren't sure how to pursue. Invite them to help you think through the issues before you make a decision.

Develop brainstorming skills and learn to accept and react to creative ideas without being negative. When someone is presenting a new idea, you need to listen carefully and try to understand the ideas being proposed, ask clarifying questions, focus on the positive aspects of the idea, and then describe the concerns you have about the idea. Using a technique called Creative Reaction Feedback (CRF) will enable you to respond positively to a new idea or piece of information without necessarily agreeing with it.

For example, during a discussion of new market opportunities for the company, you need to listen to the ideas presented, and seek first to understand why the presenter believes it's a new opportunity and why it's a good opportunity for the company. Ask clarifying questions to determine the implications of this idea. For example, what is the impact on current markets, products, services, or the current marketing plan? How would this impact the competition and what financial and staff resources would be required? Then identify the positive aspects of the new market opportunity, as well as those that cause you concern. Move on to the next presenter, and the next, until you get all the ideas out on the table. Then take a look at all the ideas, rather than deal with them one by one. Often several ideas can be combined to create a workable solution to the problem. (See appendix F, "Helping Build Your Company's Profit Spiral™," for more information on CRF.)

Though you may not always agree with the ideas awesome people suggest and may choose not to implement their suggestions, they will know you value them because you have asked for their counsel and advice, have shared your concerns with them, have trusted them with your dreams, and have seriously considered their ideas. More often than not, you'll be able to implement their recommendations, but if not, tell them why. Then, ask for their help in thinking through the direction you have chosen. Keep involving them in finding new solutions, overcoming challenges, and building the elements of an awesome organization.

> "Whenever someone in the company has an important issue they want help with, they ask for people who have an interest in that issue to come to a brainstorming meeting where we plaster the walls with lots of ideas, tap into their creative juices, and get lots of ideas. We especially encourage the crazy ideas and 'what if' scenarios so that we come out with new alternatives we never would have thought of. This is a regular part of how we do business, and it's particularly helpful when problems arise. For instance, we recently were in trouble with a big client, and we brought a roomful of people together to come up with new solutions."

Involving your awesome people in solving company problems and planning for the future provides them with the opportunities to learn and keep growing.

BUILD STRONG RELATIONSHIPS OF TRUST

Be consistent with words and deeds, signal to your employees that they can rely on your support, and let them know you have faith in their abilities. Because awesome people are self-motivated to achieve great things, you don't have to motivate them.

However, you and your managers can easily de-motivate them if you fail to build a trusting environment by micromanaging. Micromanagement sends the message that you lack faith in your employees' abilities to do their jobs, or that you think your way is the only way to do the job. This leaves no room for their creativity and initiative. Compare the two following stories about awesome people, and think about whether and how you're building strong relationships of trust with the awesome people in your company.

> "We lost a great high-level manager with technical expertise we desperately needed, and we thought she had real leadership potential. It was clear in the exit interview that the reason she left was not money but because she didn't feel valued or trusted by a VP with whom she had to work closely. He has been here forever. When she joined us six months ago, he made her feel very unwelcome and tried to tell her how to do her job, despite the fact that she was an expert in her area and he wasn't. Because of the atmosphere he created for her, she didn't feel she could get anything done, so she left."

> "We recently brought in a new VP of sales for a new product line that will be sold into a new market where he has experience and we don't. We shared our vision with him and then turned him loose to create the strategy for that market opportunity. With an understanding of our vision combined with his market knowledge, he was able to come up with a strategy that was much better than what we would have come up with on our own. All of us are excited by the strategy and have real confidence it can be executed."

Some CEOs and managers don't provide enough guidance because they think awesome people can figure things out for themselves. This can cause as many problems as micromanagement. It's easy to make corrections to a project that is a few degrees off center in its early stages. But, if employees continue to move a project in the wrong direction without a correction back to center, they will soon be out of alignment with the company, creating big problems for the organization and others on their team.

This lack of correction and coordination often results in projects with dwindling support and impact, the creation of silos, possible turf wars, unhealthy politics, and other time and energy wasters. You and your managers must be skilled at directing and delegating, and empowering and supporting awesome employees. In addition to developing good communication systems, keeping everyone informed of changes, and asking for regular progress reports, you can also provide guidance and refocus your awesome employees during their performance reviews to make sure that everyone is aligned and focused on company goals.

CONDUCT REGULAR PERFORMANCE REVIEWS

Performance reviews are a good way to communicate with and direct your awesome people. Most entrepreneurs don't give good performance feedback. Sometimes they are going too fast to reflect on how others are performing or to take the time to give feedback. Other times they hope a performance problem will go away if they just ignore it. Others don't want to admit they've made a hiring mistake, so they turn a blind eye to poor performance. A few are misguided and think outstanding people don't need performance feedback.

If your goal is to have awesome people contribute in incredible ways, exceed their own personal best, and move up the ladder quickly, you have to give them feedback — and understand they want feedback — to guide their personal growth and development. There are many different ways to do performance reviews; find one that works well with the culture you're trying to cultivate. Here's how one successful entrepreneur describes his process:

> "We've worked hard in our company to learn how to conduct effective performance reviews. I try to provide informal feedback throughout the year, but once a year I do a formal performance review for everyone who reports to me. First I ask people who've been working with that person to send me an e-mail or voice mail and give me feedback on his or her performance, values, leadership, and areas for development. At the same time, I ask the person to do a self-assessment, a sort of 'year in review.' I read all that and then I write up my own assessment. Then, I sit down with the person, and we talk. I talk about my goals for that position, how that person's work has contributed to the company's achieving its goals, where the person is strong and has performed well, and where he or she needs more development. I take the time to listen to their highs and lows, satisfactions and frustrations — and we talk about the lessons we've all learned this past year. Then we talk about the year ahead, what needs to be done, what the person's goals are, what my goals are, and decide what additional training, education, or professional development is needed for the person to grow in the job and achieve the goals."

Performance review discussions give you an opportunity to coach, recognize achievements, and help your awesome people set new goals and really stretch themselves. Describe new challenges you believe they could tackle, find out what they want to learn, and encourage them to come up with new ideas and proposals. These kinds of discussions serve as checkpoints to make sure your awesome people are tracking with the company and will guide their future growth and development in ways that support the company's growth and development.

Performance feedback helps build a relationship of trust with your awesome people. The very fact that the company takes time to do performance reviews sends a strong signal to everyone that you want to help employees achieve high performance.

> "We do performance reviews once a quarter so we're constantly talking about how things are going. We've normalized the reviews across the whole company so people are being graded fairly and consistently. We do a lot of work to ensure we're talking to our employees, creating a future for them, and understanding their strengths and weaknesses."

During the performance review, get feedback about your own performance and how you can become a more effective leader. Encourage each manager to ask what she or he can do to help employees be more effective in their position. Setting up this mutual feedback process shows you are committed to learning and to improving, and this builds loyalty to you and to the company. Try to get 360° feedback from a representative sample of people who work with the employee, at all levels, for example, the person's manager, cross-functional team leaders, peers, staff, mentor/coach — even customers and vendors. Broad-based feedback is a valuable tool for developing your awesome people.

If an awesome person has personal problems that might be affecting her or his ability to perform, consider providing counseling assistance from an outside source. Such programs can make a significant difference in resolving personal issues that sometimes block even awesome people from achieving their best.

SHARE THE REWARDS WITH THOSE WHO PRODUCE

> "Many entrepreneurial organizations fall apart because of what I call 'I' strain, where the entrepreneur says, 'I did it. I'm responsible. I get all the credit.' Competent people don't want to work for somebody who claims all of the credit, who believes that he did it all. They want to be recognized for what they contributed and produced."

You need to recognize the results awesome people produce and the value of their contributions. Awesome people want to know that you, the leader, are aware of the value they bring to the organization, recognize their contribution, and are willing to share the credit. Celebrate victories; make your awesome people feel like heroes. Public accolades are important, so don't save all your "congratulations on a job well done" remarks for private sessions. Build team spirit with celebrations and widespread recognition of both individual and team performance.

> "We have a recognition program that we call the Rave Program. At every weekly company meeting, we give out raves, which anybody can nominate somebody for. It's recognition for someone going above and beyond the call of duty, and it usually relates to doing something innovative. There might be a dozen people each week who are recognized with raves."

> "It was astonishing how much I underestimated the importance of recognition for employees and appreciation of their work. One reason people leave companies, especially in a creative industry, is to go somewhere where they think they're going to get higher recognition."

FINANCIAL COMPENSATION

Although money may not be the first, or even second, thing that awesome people look for, they do want financial rewards for their hard work. Make sure you develop a compensation system that rewards high performance by individuals and teams. Be sure it reinforces the behavior you want in your organization, and tie it to the results of performance reviews. Don't reward people whose behavior is not consistent with the values or who don't meet performance expectations. Think about your company's compensation when you review the following box, "Vital Signs: Guidelines for Compensation Systems," and decide whether you need to make changes in order to recognize and retain your awesome people.

OTHER KINDS OF REWARDS

In addition to a fair compensation system, you need to recognize great performance in ways that your employees will consider valuable and meaningful and that reinforce desired actions, results, and values. Design creative ways to celebrate individual and team contributions. Be explicit in describing the behavior that is being

VITAL SIGNS: GUIDELINES FOR COMPENSATION SYSTEMS

Although every company needs to develop its own unique compensation formula, here are some guidelines you can use to develop or assess your compensation system:

 Base your pay system on logical formulas that provide fair compensation. Apply them consistently across the organization.

 Develop a formula that includes individual, team, and company performance.

 Understand how to use the three components of compensation: base salary, a performance-based variable, and bonuses. Base salary should be at or slightly below market or what competitors are paying for that position. The performance-based variable will differ, depending on where the employee is in the company; the higher up in the organization, the greater the variable should be as a proportion of the salary. Bonuses are extra incentives and rewards for great performance. Bonuses should never be based just on tenure, but should be tied to performance goals.

 Track the kinds of compensation packages your competition is offering so you're not at a disadvantage when it comes to attracting and retaining awesome people.

 Provide opportunities for stock ownership. If you believe that those who produce should share in the rewards, then you'll want to share a part of the upside with your awesome people.

recognized to encourage similar conduct in others. Mix big and small, formal and spur-of-the-moment rewards. For instance, use "spot awards" such as movie or sports tickets to recognize people who handle a task extremely well on a given day. Or give a significant trip once a year to the employee who refers the highest number of job candidates to your company. Encourage people to send e-mails praising the exceptional efforts of others. Name people who exemplify the company's values as "Employee of the Month" or "Employee of the Year." Give out awards for innovation. Celebrate the success of a project team with a party. All of these are effective ways to recognize, reward, and reinforce high performance and the kinds of behavior that make a great company.

"Daily praise is a good thing. Four words — 'Thank you; good job' — go a long way with employees. That seems to help and motivate them. It's also important to give responsibility, make people feel valued, and let them make decisions. Don't micromanage. Personal notes signed with your first name mean a lot. Mr. Kauffman would write the parents of his associates and say, 'Your son (or daughter) is doing the most wonderful job.' You can imagine the lore this kind of thing builds in a company."

"When you give a gift to a friend or loved one, you take time to really consider who they are. You think about whether to give them a book, or a toy, something you made yourself or something that is mass-produced. Be just as thoughtful when you look at your company and the people in it. Make your rewards unique and customized to your own culture so they really stand out."

Bottom line: Reward high performance, share credit, and celebrate victories in ways that are meaningful to your employees.

DEAL WITH MISFITS, MALCONTENTS, AND NONPERFORMERS

"Why do great people leave companies? They leave because over time there's a breakdown of communication, a breakdown of consistency, and a misperception about competency. And they leave because they don't want to work with the misfits, the malcontents, and the nonperformers."

If you and your managers do what we've outlined in this chapter and build the other components of an awesome organization, you will be able to attract and retain awesome people. But, even the best companies and the most experienced executives make hiring mistakes. When that happens, you need to take quick action.

As we noted earlier, the hiring process provides opportunities for you to explore past performance, past behavior, and determine whether the person has the ability to perform the job and fits with your culture. Then, after people are hired and working in the organization, it's important to continue to assess them on both dimensions, and to provide feedback during formal and informal performance reviews. One way to retain your awesome people is to effectively and promptly address issues of weak performance and poor cultural fit. Great people get discouraged and become disillusioned when misfits, malcontents, and nonperformers aren't dealt with appropriately.

The matrix in the following table, "What to Do about the Fits, Misfits, and Malcontents," can help you assess the employees who fit and those who don't, and determine what action to take regarding each group. Everyone in your organization should be familiar with this matrix, and every manager should use it to guide personnel decisions.

HIGH FIT BETWEEN CULTURE AND PERFORMANCE

People who are a good fit with the culture and are high performers are your most awesome people, your future leaders — the ones who can make your company great. Work hard to retain people who are great cultural models and valuable performers. Make a conscious effort to plan their development as leaders, promote them into increasingly responsible positions, praise them, share stock with them, reward them financially and in other ways, and do your best to keep them.

> "Our company is a meritocracy. You have to perform to be here. And that's what people appreciate about being on this team. They are surrounded by people who have the ability to do their current job and to do that job in the future."

LOW FIT BETWEEN CULTURE AND PERFORMANCE

At the opposite end of the scale from your awesome people are those who don't fit the culture and aren't performing in their jobs. This is a no-brainer; get rid of them — immediately. These people are deadwood. They create more work for everyone. You need to get them out of the organization as soon as possible because they don't contribute; in fact, they are a negative influence. If you keep them, your awesome people will be frustrated and leave; they don't want to work in an organization that keeps nonperformers who don't fit the values.

What to Do About the Fits, Misfits, and Malcontents

		CULTURE FIT		
		HIGH	**MEDIUM**	**LOW**
PERFORMANCE	**HIGH**	Great fit between values and culture. High performer. Future leader of your company. Reward and promote accordingly.	Performance is high but behavior does not always match the values and culture. Coach and mentor. Follow up; reinforce behavior change. No salary increases or promotions until future behavior more closely aligned with the values and culture.	Performance high but behavior does not match values and culture. Provide stern warning, then terminate quickly. High performers are role models and can destroy your culture if their behavior does not fit with your values.
	MEDIUM	Great fit with the values and culture, but disappointing performance. Check current job fit vs. education and skills. Change job or provide training and coaching in current job. Develop performance improvement plan. If no improvement in 3-6 months, terminate.	Fit with values and culture is not great; performance is disappointing. May be in the wrong job or need training. Warn; change jobs, provide coaching. If no improvement in 3 months, terminate.	Behavior does not match the company's values. Warn, then terminate before employee undermines culture and distracts others from high performance.
	LOW	Great fit with values and culture, but performance is marginal. Warn; develop performance improvement plan. If no improvement within 3 months, terminate.	Fit with values and culture is not great and performance is low. Warn. Do not invest time or effort in coaching, education, or job change unless clear potential for improvement. Terminate before others are distracted from high performance.	No fit with culture or values; low performance. Terminate as soon as possible. Their presence will seriously frustrate good performers, and be a drag on company performance.

GOOD CULTURAL FIT AND BELOW-EXPECTATION PERFORMANCE

Some people are good cultural fits but their performance is subpar. They may need more coaching, education, or skills development to do well in their jobs. Because they match your culture, these people are worth investing in, so give them another chance. Talk with them, develop a performance improvement plan, and give them additional support and training to improve their performance.

> "It's essential to place awesome individuals in a situation where they can win, where their contribution can make a difference, and where they can be truly excited about their ability to contribute."

Sometimes an individual who is a good cultural fit may be in the wrong job — either because he or she was hired for the wrong job or because the job has changed significantly and now requires capabilities the person does not have. If such people are good cultural models, try to find other positions within the company where they can succeed. However, if there are no other positions appropriate for them, or if their performance does not improve, they have to go. Be fair about the terms of their departure, and try to make it an amicable (but clear and firm) separation.

> "It has happened here, just as it happens at other companies. Somebody can be the head of Department X, and they were okay heading up Department X three years ago. But now Department X has got a whole bunch of new responsibilities as the company has gotten a lot bigger, and they can't do the job. You have two choices: move them to another job or ask them to leave. That has to happen. Those are not easy decisions. But we make them. And generally, we're better off for making them. The only thing you can do if someone has to leave the company is to try to make it as fair as possible for that person."

> "One of our big problems was what to do with the people who had been with the company since the early days but weren't suitable for promotion. We felt they were still key players and had a lot to contribute. So we gave them project roles rather than management roles. For example, we took four of these people and made them our 'intensive care unit.' If we have a customer problem, we pull them into a special group. They like that; it reminds them of what it was like when we were a smaller company. We let them handle the problems, just like they did in the 'old days,' and so far they've done an outstanding job!"

"I have a project team that reports directly to me and is comprised of people who have been with the company for a while who got 'outgrown' and some new people we've brought in to groom for future roles. When we're not in an active acquisition mode, this project team does enhancements inside the business. They don't do firefighting; they do the kinds of things that take two or three months to get done, but will have an immediate impact on the business. They know how to get around and through the infrastructure and get things done."

LOW OR MARGINAL CULTURAL FIT AND HIGH PERFORMANCE

The most difficult decisions concern people who are outstanding performers but don't fit the culture. Their high performance gives them high visibility, but they are very dangerous and can quickly poison your culture. Because they are high performers, you and others are likely to praise them, reward them for accomplishing their goals, defer to them, and avoid disagreeing with them. This confuses other employees, who hear you talk about the importance of values and culture, yet see you honor and reward those who don't fit the culture at all. Once you recognize a culture mismatch, your natural tendency will be to try to coach these high performers. However, you are unlikely to be able to change their values. If this turns out to be the case, you must move them out of the organization as soon as possible. Give them warnings and develop the appropriate paper trail to support your decision to terminate them.

"We had a VP of sales who was on track to be our COO. He got us on a predictable revenue track and was doing great. But he was also building his own empire and was not communicating with marketing or with our product people. He was upsetting good people, and they were threatening to quit. We also began to notice that our Executive Team was not working well together, and we eventually realized it was because this one guy simply did not fit the culture and was making our entire team dysfunctional. We tried to coach him and give him responsibilities that required cross-functional interaction. But he failed at all those things because his values just weren't the same as ours, so we had to let him go."

"We had a sales unit that turned in their revenue figures before the products were delivered to the customers so the revenue could be counted in the fiscal year in which they were getting their bonuses. When we figured out what had happened, we brought them into a company meeting and fired them in front of everyone. Our legal department, HR department, and everyone advised us against doing so, but we felt it was important to send a message to all the employees that we would not tolerate that kind of behavior in this company, that it was against our values and our culture. We took the risk, and I'm personally glad we did."

We cannot overemphasize how important it is for you to deal quickly with people who do not fit the culture or are not performing. Having such people around affects everyone they come in contact with on their team, in their department, across functions — even customers, suppliers, and vendors. Don't let a misfit become a daily reminder to your awesome people that you are less than totally committed to having an awesome organization.

LEARN FROM EXIT INTERVIEWS

Of course, no matter how hard you try, you can't retain every awesome person. People will leave for reasons that have nothing to do with how much they enjoy their work: They'll move to another city, go to graduate school, or change careers. It's still important to conduct exit interviews with everyone who leaves the company voluntarily, even if they love the company or are leaving because they are moving from the area — or even if you doubt the value of their opinions. Recognize that surprising insights can be gained from the most unexpected sources. Ask questions about what the person found most rewarding and least rewarding about working for your company and what changes they would suggest. Analyze the feedback with managers to try to learn what changes might be necessary to lower unwanted turnover.

YOUR ROLE AS LEADER

When it comes to retaining awesome people in your company, these are your responsibilities:

- Guide the development of — and participate in — an orientation process that devotes a lot of time to the company's mission, values, and vision and sets the tone for a great work experience.

- Pay close attention to your awesome people; talk with them, listen to them, and solicit their ideas.

- Seek feedback from your awesome people about the organization, the direction it's headed, and their role in its future.

- Make sure managers delegate effectively and provide coaching and regular performance feedback to their people.

- Share the rewards and the credit with those who produce great results.

- Weed out misfits, malcontents, and nonperformers as soon as possible.

- Listen carefully to what people say during their exit interviews. Look for patterns and discuss these with your top team.

BIG LESSONS

1. Orientation is not a quick, one-day process; it is an important tool for getting awesome people off to a flying start and fully integrated as contributors to your organization.

2. Awesome people are self-motivated to achieve great results, but they can be de-motivated by bad management practices such as micromanagement or lack of direction.

3. The way to preserve your culture, retain awesome people, and remain a high-performance company is to weed out the deadwood and cultural misfits on an ongoing basis.

www.entreworld.org

BAO SCAN: RETAIN AWESOME PEOPLE FOR GROWTH

Use this *SCAN* to assess your organization's current strengths and weaknesses in retaining awesome people. Take this *BAO SCAN* yourself, and then have your top team and other key people complete it as well. Compare your responses and perceptions with theirs. Work together to identify innovative ways to solve problems and come up with new ideas about how to retain the kinds of people you need to sustain — and accelerate your growth.

PART A. IDENTIFYING YOUR AWESOME PEOPLE

1. List awesome people who have been with the company for a while.

People   Why have they stayed with our company?

1. _____   _____

2. _____   _____

3. _____   _____

2. List awesome people who have left the company in the last year.

People   Why did they leave our company?

1. _____   _____

2. _____   _____

3. _____   _____

PART B: RATING YOUR COMPANY

RATING SCALE

Use this scale to respond to each rating question

1 - - - - - 2 - - - - - 3 - - - - - 4 - - - - - 5 - - - - - 6 - - - - - 7

NEVER   *SOMETIMES*   *ALWAYS*

1. We foster high performance by integrating, inspiring, and involving people.   Rating: _____

Questions to consider:

• What works best in our orientation?

• What needs improvement?

- What works best in communicating clear vision, goals, and expectations?
- Where do we fall short?

2. We listen to and understand our awesome people's goals and interests, and help them see how they can meet those goals by working in our company and helping us achieve our goals.   Rating: _____

Question to consider:

- What else do we need to do?

3. We create opportunities for people to work in teams and make cross-functional connections throughout the company.   Rating: _____

Question to consider:

- What else do we need to do?

4. We lead and manage people to get outstanding results.   Rating: _____

Questions to consider:

- How well do we coach and develop our people?
- What do we need to do better?
- Do we provide regular opportunities for people to receive feedback on their performance?
- Do we have opportunities for people to learn to work in teams?
- Do our managers give the right amount of autonomy? flexibility?
- How well do our managers help people succeed, grow, and develop their potential?
- Do we encourage enough experimentation and solicit enough creative ideas?

5. We retain the people we want.   Rating: _____

Questions to consider:

- Are our awesome people satisfied working in our company? If not, why?
- How satisfied are they with the leadership?

- What recognition, rewards, and incentives do people find most meaningful?

- What is our turnover rate of people we'd like to keep?

- What works best in soliciting people's ideas?

- What works best in building commitment to the awesome organization we are trying to develop?

- Are we providing appropriate compensation, and sharing the rewards with those who produce?

- What else do we need to do?

6. The CEO is the champion of the processes for retaining awesome people.   Rating: _____

7. The CEO holds managers accountable for developing awesome people.   Rating: _____

8. The CEO deals with the misfits, malcontents, and nonperformers. He or she warns, then terminates those who don't share the values, fit the culture, or are underperforming.   Rating: _____

9. The CEO communicates the company's core values.   Rating: _____

Question to Consider:

- How could the CEO be more effective in retaining awesome people?

SCORE SUMMARY AND INTERPRETATION

A Rating Score of **7** in any area indicates this is a prime area of strength that will facilitate and support the company's growth. Scores of **5** and **6** indicate considerable strength in these areas, but you will want to consider making incremental improvements to increase the score. A score of **4** is a cause for worry. A rating of "Sometimes" indicates a lack of consistency that sends conflicting signals to employees and inhibits growth; thus significant improvements will be needed. Scores of **3 or below** are big red flags indicating areas or behaviors that hinder the company's growth and require your immediate attention.

RESULTS ANALYSIS

Look back over the *BAO SCAN: Retain Awesome People for Growth:*

1. List three statements that you rated the highest. Choose those you feel are key strengths and contribute most to the success of the company.

   A. _____

   B. _____

   C. _____

2. List three statements that received the lowest rating. Choose those you feel are the most critical weaknesses and should be targeted for improvement.

   A. _____

   B. _____

   C. _____

3. Write three statements that define your priorities for change (for example, capitalize more on the strengths or improve the weaknesses).

   A. _____

   B. _____

   C. _____

4. List three things our company could do to implement these changes.

   A. _____

   B. _____

   C. _____

ACTION PLAN

Recognize what you and your company are doing well and celebrate! Think about what you have done that enabled you to achieve these great results and how that can be applied to your weaknesses. But, do not overlook areas that need improvement or think they will improve on their own over time. Use these steps to develop your Action Plan for Improvement:

1. Ask your top team to complete the *BAO SCAN: Retain Awesome People for Growth* and the Results Analysis. You may also want others in the company to complete the *SCAN* in order to get more comprehensive feedback.

2. Meet with your top team to:

   • Compare and contrast your ratings on various statements with their ratings, as well as areas you have identified as strengths with those needing work.

   • If applicable, discuss the reasons why their responses are different from yours.

   • Agree on areas for improvement or change; be as specific as possible.

3. Prioritize those areas that must be addressed and will make the biggest difference. Develop them into Action Plans for Improvement.

4. Get consensus on the Action Plans and the resources and budgets needed to make the necessary changes.

   • For each Action Plan, specify the goal, desired outcomes, steps to take, team members responsible for implementation, resources required, key measures of success, and time frames for achieving the goal and tracking results.

   • Assign a cross-functional team to implement each Action Plan. Include members from different departments who will be affected by the changes. Members should have the necessary skills and insights to accomplish the plan. Identify a team leader and/or executive sponsor who will be held accountable for managing the team, tracking progress, and achieving the desired goal.

5. Communicate the Action Plans for Improvement to everyone in the company. Get involvement, input, and feedback.

6. Hold yourself and others accountable for achieving the new goals and milestones.

7. After a designated period of time (three to six months), evaluate progress, identify new or emerging problems or opportunities, set new goals, make new team assignments (if appropriate), and take action. In a year, retake the *BAO SCAN: Retain Awesome People for Growth* and repeat Steps 1 through 6 as required. Remember: Continuous assessment, action, and improvement are essential to building an awesome organization that is strong enough to support continuous growth.

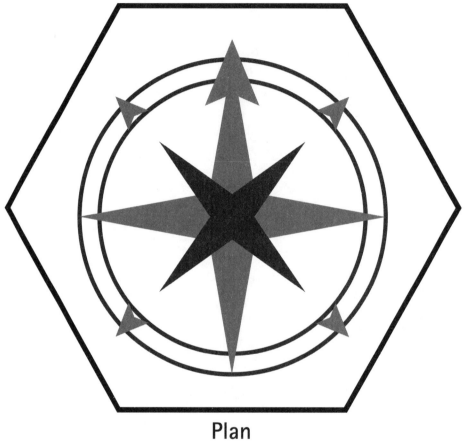

Plan

CHAPTER **6**

CREATE YOUR PLAN FOR GROWTH

> "Prior to the company I now own, I had another company. It was growing too fast. We started opening offices all over the place and did not have enough management teams in place to operate all our facilities. We were still growing, but we hit a wall because we didn't strategically plan how to grow the company. We just started saying, 'This seems like a good place to be,' or 'This is a good customer base.' Then I started a subsidiary, and we opened some stores to be an after-market for our leasing company. Our growth went from 3 percent to 292 percent in one year. We were the fastest-growing company in our state. It was a really rocky ride, and the results were bad because we just didn't think or plan strategically."

As an organization grows, more is added to the mix: more employees, more customers, more ideas for expanding markets and products, and more revenues and earnings. Success itself changes the shape of the market; more competitors are attracted, and customers demand more. Complexity increases as new opportunities and challenges abound. Eventually, this growth fundamentally changes the company.

An organization can easily fall out of alignment as it grows. When a company's purpose and direction become unclear, its structure and processes become strained, communication slips through the cracks, and soon one part of the organization doesn't know what the other is doing. Conflicts flare up because different people have different opinions about what the company's vision and mission should be. It becomes increasingly difficult to set priorities, and people begin to miss key objectives. Some may not understand what the objectives are. Others may not care. Often the measures of success and the consequences of failure become muddled.

All of this happens because growth, no matter what its pace, changes the company. But a plan will help the company stay focused while responding to the myriad of internal and external changes. A plan will enable the company to move through heavy turbulence without falling out of alignment.

> "In the five companies I've run, the biggest challenge was keeping everyone on the same page. People need to share a vision and a strategy, and if you do a good job of communicating your plan, they will be ready to change gears when the ground shifts underneath you."

If you don't have a plan to guide your company through the stages of growth, your company will not be able to sustain growth. Review the following box, "Red Flags: Signals of Poor Planning." If they apply to you and your company, you need to turn your attention to developing a plan and/or improving your planning process.

It is difficult to steer a car that is out of alignment. It is just as difficult to lead and manage a company that is not aligned around a plan for growth, the third element of an awesome organization. The problem may at first appear minor, but the negative consequences caused by misalignment increase significantly over time and create dangerous risks.

In this chapter, we discuss the benefits of planning and identify key questions you must answer as you develop your plan. We also provide a planning model, The Profit Spiral™, and outline a planning process you can follow as you develop your plan.

RED FLAGS: SIGNALS OF POOR PLANNING

The following Red Flags are signals that your company is not effectively planning for future growth:

 You are working off a plan that's only in your head, not written down.

 Your plan is just numbers and doesn't include prioritized initiatives and action items.

 Your plan is a composite of departmental plans that are not based on an overview of the company's mission, vision, values, and strategy, and are not integrated into an overall company plan.

 Outsiders get wildly different answers when they ask your employees to describe your plan and your strategy.

 Instead of engaging in a planning process, you:

- Frequently reorganize the company's structure.

- Hire more VPs with specialized skills without considering how they will impact the team and culture.

- Train everyone in communications skills.

- Change parts of the business model that are the easiest to change — for example, alter pricing, repackage existing products, develop a new corporate message, design a new logo, retrain the sales force, or change the sales commission structure.

THE BENEFITS OF PLANNING

"Finding the time for planning is tough. We're like most growing companies — we spend a lot of time fighting fires. But, I think the fact that planning is a long process is part of its strength. Half of the benefit of planning comes from going through the process."

Even though it takes time, thought, and resources, planning is essential if you want your company to grow and be successful. Too many companies hit the wall because there is no plan behind their rapid growth. If the warnings in the following box, "Red Flags: You're About to Hit the Wall," sound familiar, your company is in the danger zone and is about ready to "hit the wall."

RED FLAGS: YOU'RE ABOUT TO HIT THE WALL

Some of the warning signs that signal your company may be stopped in its tracks are:

- Functional departments are growing and beginning to move in separate directions; silos, and even fiefdoms, are developing.

- It's becoming more difficult to communicate the mission, values, vision, and strategies to people at all levels of the organization as more and more new people join the company.

- Employees are losing sight of the corporate goals.

- Systems and processes are stretched beyond their limits and are no longer efficient.

- You want to address external issues, meet with customers, and talk with industry leaders, but internal matters keep pulling at you, causing frustration and tension.

- Everyone — including you — is preoccupied with fighting fires instead of anticipating and solving problems.

- Industry, market, and technological changes are happening faster than your company can keep up with them.

One way to avoid hitting the wall is to develop and implement a clear plan for the company's successful growth. A well-developed, well-communicated strategic plan guides the whole organization. A written plan allows people throughout the company to make good decisions and take effective action because everyone knows the company's direction and the contribution she or he is expected to make. A good plan encourages managers to take calculated risks because everyone understands the end game. Having a plan helps avoid departmental silos, turf wars, and constant fire fighting, all of which threaten your bottom line.

These positive aspects of planning add up to one huge benefit: A plan creates a road map for success that fosters the continuous reinvention necessary to take the company through all the stages of growth. (See appendix B, "Stages of Growth and the Leader's Roles," for more information about the three stages of growth.) Equally important, the process of planning itself forces you to face the changes that growth brings and helps you move the company from a reactive to a proactive mode that enables the organization to take charge of its own destiny.

> "I realized we would be able to hire stronger people if we had a plan in place and had established clear forward momentum. I didn't want the new people to have to solve the old problems. I also wanted to avoid the possibility that the people coming in might establish their own silos. I thought it was important to define our plan, and to move us away from our silo mentality before bringing in any more new people."

ELEMENTS OF THE PLAN

Let's look at the questions you need to answer as you develop your plan for growth:

- Market and Customers: What's going on in our market? How are we meeting our customers' needs?

- Mission and Values: Who are we? What business are we in? What is our company trying to achieve?

- Vision and Objectives: Where are we going? What is our ideal future?

- Strategies and Action Plans: How will we reach our objectives?

- Infrastructure and Resources: What do we need to execute the plan?

- Culture: What environment do we need to support the implementation of the plan?

MARKET AND CUSTOMERS: WHAT'S GOING ON IN OUR MARKET? HOW ARE WE MEETING CUSTOMERS' NEEDS?

To grow your company, you have to understand what's going on in the market, how your company's products or services meet an important need in that market, and what is driving the growth of that need. The market and your customers are the context of your company.

Some entrepreneurs confuse market focus with marketing communications, branding, and positioning in the market. Market focus means developing a complete understanding of the milieu in which your company operates. It means never taking your eye off the market and constantly discovering the opportunities and threats it presents. By anticipating and being prepared for market shifts, you're not taken by surprise and forced to react. If you are market focused, you will discover, and sometimes even create, new markets where you can take the lead.

To develop this market focus, you need to understand your market, competitive trends, and the current and future needs of your ideal customers. Without this knowledge, planning will degenerate into an exercise of wishful thinking, and your plan will be based on internal guesses rather than informed by data and information about the environment in which your organization operates.

> "We weren't customer focused. We were producing products that were what our product development people or officers thought they should be, not what the market demanded. We really weren't in touch with our customers. Here's a typical symptom: We spent $500,000 or $600,000 developing a product, but there was no marketing plan in place when the product was ready for beta testing. Sales weren't ready to sell it, and the operations people couldn't find instructors who met development's requirements. We weren't sure we were solving any customers' real problem. Everybody was in their silos pointing fingers at other parts of the organization."

MISSION AND VALUES: WHO ARE WE? WHAT BUSINESS ARE WE IN? WHAT ARE WE TRYING TO ACCOMPLISH?

Many entrepreneurs have a difficult time deciding what they want their company to be, what business they are in, and what they want the company to accomplish. When entrepreneurs cannot articulate their mission, values, and vision, and have no rationale for responding to one market opportunity versus another, they confuse their employees and their customers. Your company will not be able to sustain growth if you are not able to describe who you are, what business you are in, and where you're going.

> "You have to focus on what you do best and decide what business you're really in. I see too many entrepreneurs get bored with what they're doing. They see something else out there and change their focus and mission and the business goes this way and that and they don't have an impact or achieve their goals. If you want to be successful, I think you need to set the course and stay with what you know how to do."

Many company leaders think the words *mission* and *vision* are interchangeable. In many organizations, they are merely corporate mottos or taglines with little or no significance.

> "Nearly all the planning we did in the past was financial based, around a spreadsheet. I mostly made up the vision and mission. They were more like rallying cries and good motivational statements than carefully planned and thought-out statements of what our future should be. They were more short-term. Now that we're doing real planning in a collaborative way that involves the whole company, we have real buy-in and great alignment around our mission, vision, and values."

The definitions of *mission* and *vision* we use in this book are different from those used by traditional corporate planners. But as we have worked with entrepreneurial companies, we have found that the following definitions are most useful:

Mission: A powerful and compelling statement of the broad purpose of the business; the legacy it intends to create.

Values: The principles that guide everyday interactions and define the way people work together to fulfill the mission.

Vision: A detailed picture of your company in the next 24 to 36 months, a period of time that most growing businesses can envision. Your objectives, strategies, and plans should all be tied to this vision and move your company toward achieving it.

Here is an example of one company's mission, values, and vision statements. The top team of a software company specializing in dynamic, personalized Web-based communications developed the following:

Mission Statement: To build a community of great leaders and innovators who improve people's lives through personalized technologies.

Core Values: Act with integrity and respect; demand personal excellence; deliver what you promise; lead and innovate; collaborate; and win.

Three-Year Vision: We have developed a culture that attracts, develops, and retains leaders and innovators. Our products dominate our chosen markets and we have entered significant new markets. Our financial growth and operating efficiency allow us to consistently build significant new products. We have the premier distribution system in our chosen markets. We have achieved "best-in-class" customer satisfaction. We build products on time, on budget, and have paperless internal processes that help us grow.

(See appendix E, "Examples of Mission, Values, and Vision Statements," for more examples of mission, values, and vision statements.)

Never underestimate the power of well-conceived mission, values, and vision statements that everyone understands. Together, these form the bedrock of your growth plan.

Even though the mission and vision may never be totally achievable, people want to know what you are trying to accomplish. And you want people to get excited about the mission and vision — so excited that they are willing to spend a portion of their lives helping you achieve them. Your mission statement should describe your organization's grand purpose, tell what you stand for, and how you're going to make a difference in the world. To create the mission statement, you need to define what business the company is really in, its core strengths, and its fundamental uniqueness. You must be able to describe what your company enables your customers to do and what it does better and differently than any other company. (See appendix F, "Helping Build Your Company's Profit Spiral™," for more information on creating mission statements.)

> "Our mission statement gave some people a gyroscope and told them which way to point. For others of us, it confirmed what we knew, but added subtleties we hadn't appreciated."

❁

> "Employees need a reason to give their enthusiastic support. Most will not mind if you make lots of money, especially if they share in the gain, but they need a mission or purpose that is grander than making you rich. Your customers, associates, suppliers, and investors want a purpose beyond increasing your personal wealth before they are willing to share the risk with you. You must realize that each of these must share your risk in order for you to

succeed. 'Becoming the first' or 'Becoming the best' — or even 'Doing what no one else has ever done' — are missions to get excited about. 'Helping people solve problems, or lead better, safer, healthier, more productive lives' calls upon the best of human values. The opportunity to meet a need better, quicker, or less expensively often provides the real purpose for an organization. Give your associates the opportunity to build and create a business where none has existed before."

Articulating your values is a critical step in fulfilling your mission. Values help you create the culture you want for your organization. They are the behavioral guidelines that you establish for the people who join and help you develop the company. Thus, mission and values are closely intertwined, and both need to be carefully worded as compelling statements that people really believe in. (See appendix C, "Creating a Core Values Statement for Growth," for an exercise you can use to create your core values statement and appendix E for examples of values statements.)

> "I saw our small company values slipping away as we grew larger and communication got more fragmented. I think the process of redefining our values has helped us get back to that place where people feel much closer to what's going on, where everyone feels they have real input on the direction of the company."

VISION AND OBJECTIVES: WHERE ARE WE GOING? WHAT IS OUR IDEAL FUTURE?

> "My vision grew from 20 years of working for asset-based carriers who set the rules. Their whole game was trying to get customers to conform to those rules. So the fun part of developing my vision was taking a blank sheet of paper saying, 'Let's change this, let's put the customer in the center and meet their needs by whatever means possible.' Then when I talked my CIO into coming on board, I said, 'From a technical standpoint, take a blank sheet of paper.' Same thing happened to the finance guy. We invited everybody in our company to come to the table with a blank sheet of paper, and we said, 'Let's try and reinvent this whole industry.' And we did it!"

It's important to clearly define the destination, or "vision," your company is trying to reach. Develop a highly detailed word picture of your organization's ideal future state within a two- to three-year time frame. Describe what happens when people are fulfilling the mission. The more specific and detailed the word picture, the better you and your people will be able to visualize the results you want, recognize the key priorities, and plan the best route to get where you're going. Set stretch goals and objectives for your organization, but make sure they are achievable, not just pie-in-the-sky wishing.

> "This is how I do it. I try to imagine that the business will be generating $1 billion in revenue in a few years, and then step back and ask, 'What will that look like?' First you have to stretch your imagination to think about what it will look like, in every part of the business, when you get there. Then you can work backwards and think about what changes you will need to make and what you will have to do in order to get there."

To develop this word picture, think about where you'd like the company to be in 10 years and then look at what the organization would need to do or what changes will be needed in the next two to three years to enable the company to move toward that goal. This creative exercise of looking far into the future frees your thinking from the constraints of your current business environment, opens up new possibilities to explore, and clarifies priorities and results to be achieved in the next few years. After you've created this word picture, create a set of objectives that outline what will need to be accomplished throughout the organization for this vision to be realized, and how you will measure progress and achievement of goals and objectives. Update these objectives each year so that the company is continuously focused two to three years in the future. (See appendix F for more information about creating your vision.)

> "Our vision is to have one technology-driven office in each country we're in, with a central office here in the U.S. and a very mobile, connected sales team. I want to create an environment that enables free thinking and empowers everyone's entrepreneurial spirit, one that is flexible, open, team-oriented, high-energy, and supports intellectual, emotional, and spiritual growth. I also want to create great wealth. I want to devote my time to travel and discovery for the enterprise and for sales."

> "I think you have to decide what you want to be, what you want to do. And you have to set the parameters for excellence in that. Then you want to focus your organization on achieving that kind of excellence, and you want to hire people who are focused on it, too. You must have a vision of where you want the company to be and what you want it to do. And you want to drive people toward that vision and mission so that everyone has a common goal and can

achieve success. You also need a strong set of values that apply to all the people within the corporation: one set of rules, one set of standards, everybody lives by them, everybody behaves accordingly and acts consistent with the values statement. And if people understand the vision, mission, and values, you can really move exponentially towards accomplishing any and all challenges and tasks — and you can be sure it will get done with consistency."

"My experience with vision is that you are only limited by your imagination. When you say you can't do something, that's what you can't do. Determine goals that take you where you want to go. Go way out there; make it very exciting. Even if you don't know how to get from here to there, you create excitement by saying, 'We're going to make this happen. How? I don't know how, but it's worth going for it; we'll figure it out as we go along.'"

STRATEGIES AND ACTION PLANS: HOW WILL WE REACH OUR OBJECTIVES?

Strategies and action plans are the way to turn the vision and objectives into reality. Begin by defining Strategic Growth Initiatives (SGIs), which are specific, broad actionable statements that link the mission and vision to reality by defining how the company will implement the vision. A good strategy will include three to seven key SGIs for the current year. This set of SGIs outlines how your company will satisfy customers' needs, distinguish itself from the competition, and effectively manage internal strengths and weaknesses. Examples of SGIs might be to grow 30 percent next year, to have 15 percent of your products be new products, or to sell to 100 new customers. Organize these one-year SGIs by quarters, set goals and targets for each SGI, determine action steps, and identify metrics for tracking progress toward these targets. These metrics will become the critical numbers of the business as you assess progress (or lack thereof) toward achieving your goals.

"I've learned that operating metrics are one of the things that separate successful companies from unsuccessful ones. For early stage or first-time entrepreneurs, there's a tendency not to recognize the importance of measuring — they'd rather be out selling and generating revenue. But you really do need to measure progress to determine if your company is on track."

"We looked at our total market size and saw it in the billions, yet last year we only did $8.5 million. I asked my management team, 'If we're in a billion-dollar market, and we claim we have the products and services to service that market, why are we so small?' There was an embarrassing silence and someone said, 'Because we limit ourselves.' Right then we set a goal to grow 20 percent or more a year, and since that moment we have grown 21 percent a year for five years, even though we were flat two years in a row before that. So now, the group says we want to be a $50-million company, at a minimum. That's the floor, not the ceiling. We looked at the obstacles we needed to overcome to get there, and mainly it's getting the right people — and we're now implementing the plan."

"We identify a critical number, which can change from year to year. This year we had two goals: increased profitability and increasing our data management unit's revenues. We educate our employees about the critical numbers and why we've chosen to focus on those numbers. Each year we do a massive rollout at the beginning of the year: 'Here's what the company must do and here's what you're going to get as a bonus if the company does that.' Then we report back on how we're doing. We give them monthly updates, both verbal and hard copy, and hold meetings to discuss changes we must make to meet the numbers. If the company achieves the numbers, we all get a bonus. If not, we get nothing. And that applies to everyone in the entire organization."

INFRASTRUCTURE AND RESOURCES: WHAT DO WE NEED TO EXECUTE THE PLAN?

Infrastructure includes the organizational structure that clearly defines the roles, responsibilities, and accountabilities, as well as the processes for getting the work done. People need to understand how the infrastructure contributes to and aligns with the mission, values, vision, and strategy. The infrastructure should make the execution of the plan easy, efficient, and well coordinated. (See chapter 8, "Establish Your Infrastructure for Growth," for more information about infrastructure.) When people have helped develop the plan, it is easier for them to understand and adapt to changes in the organizational structure or reallocations of resources because they know the changes are an outgrowth of the mission, vision, values, and strategy.

"A plan is a plan, but you must get down to specific tactics and identify who's responsible for what in order to implement the plan."

"A key challenge in a growing business is the coordination of 'Who's going to do what?' 'What part of the job is mine and what is yours?' and 'Whose responsibility is it?' As a company grows, establishing the right structure becomes a consuming task of leadership. Developing an organization chart is not enough. You must communicate the roles, responsibilities, and account- abilities of each member so they can devote their efforts fully and confidently to doing their best."

Implementation requires that you specify which functional areas are responsible for what tasks and activities, and how individuals, teams, and units will be held accountable for achieving the plan. In addition, you need to estimate the costs of what you plan to do, develop a budget, and then allocate the people, money, and other resources required to implement the plans.

CULTURE: WHAT ENVIRONMENT DO WE NEED TO SUPPORT THE IMPLEMENTATION OF THE PLAN?

Always remember the importance of culture in enabling your company to achieve its plan. No matter how well defined the rest of the plan is, it can't be implemented successfully if the culture doesn't attract the kinds of people you need to create, innovate — and accelerate — your growth. Make sure your strategic plans include an explicit section about building the culture and environment you need for growth. Be sure to define SGIs with goals and action steps that are aimed at developing and strengthening each of the 7 C's of Culture as outlined in chapter 3, "Develop an Innovative Culture for Growth."

"Culture was really important to me as the leader of the company. From the very beginning, I wanted to make sure that we set up the kind of culture that would focus people in the right ways. We had an outside consultant ask everyone in the company to fill out a survey about all the aspects of our envi- ronment and our organization. Additionally they took our values statement, which emphasizes results and being a hotbed of problem solving and new ideas, and asked each person to rate, on a scale of 1 to 10, how well we were fulfilling each value. The top team used the survey results to create initiatives that would help build the culture from our leadership perspective. We also set up a Culture Team to work with employees on other areas of improvement. Every quarter we reassess the values and the progress on the initiatives."

The Profit Spiral™, described below, is one model you can use to develop your company's plan. Many growth companies have used it successfully. (See appendixes E and F for tools you can use to develop various aspects of your plan, such as mission, vision, and values statements.)

A PLANNING MODEL: THE PROFIT SPIRAL™

BUILDING THE PROFIT SPIRAL™

INNOVATIVE CULTURE

Structure & Processes

Strategies & Plans

Vision & Objectives

Mission & Values

Market & Customer Focus

©2001, The Catlin Group, *Building The Profit Spiral*™ is a trademark of Katherine Catlin.

BACKGROUND

Organizations grow best in upward spirals: continuous, well-aligned loops reaching toward a common goal. This growth path is not the straight-line growth envisioned by many boards of directors and shareholders — although it may result in straight-line growth at the top and bottom line.

When we think of spirals, we usually think of downward spirals. Although it's difficult to build an upward spiral, when you do, you'll have a much healthier company with movement that is upward, flexible, profitable, market-sensitive, and ahead of the game. Upwardly spiraling growth is a controlled, sustainable, healthy growth, not a straight-line dash that quickly depletes resources.

Healthy businesses grow in a spiral that loops five critical business elements — market and customer focus, mission and values, vision and objectives, strategies and plans, and structure and processes — around a sixth element, a supporting core of culture. These elements build on and reinforce each other. We call this model the Profit Spiral™.

One important way in which the Profit Spiral differs from most planning models is the inclusion of culture. Culture provides the effective customer and market focus, communication, collaboration, creativity and proactive problem solving, constructive leaders and leadership, continuous learning, and change management (the 7 C's of Culture) that are essential to supporting the other elements of the Profit Spiral. Without these characteristics in the cultural environment, nothing works. The growth spiral collapses, and the organization's growth is stagnant, never achieving its potential.

VITAL SIGNS: ELEMENTS OF BUILDING THE PROFIT SPIRAL™

Market and Customer Focus — companywide knowledge of highest potential markets and customer groups.

What do our customers and target prospects value most? Why? Why will they want to buy from us? How are we constantly staying in close touch with them?

Mission and Values — a powerful and compelling sense of purpose and beliefs.

Who are we in business to serve? What do we enable our customers to do so they can win? What distinguishes us from everyone else? What do we stand for?

continues

-continued

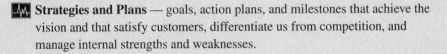 **Vision and Objectives** — a specific picture of the ideal future.

Where are we going? What will be new, different, and better two to three years from now in all aspects of business: products/services, market position, core competencies, operations, marketing and sales, infrastructure, people and teams, and financial growth?

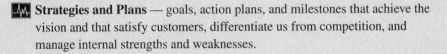 **Strategies and Plans** — goals, action plans, and milestones that achieve the vision and that satisfy customers, differentiate us from competition, and manage internal strengths and weaknesses.

How are we getting there? What are the annual and quarterly roadmaps for the overall company and for each functional department? What are the critical milestones and metrics?

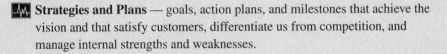 **Structure and Processes** — clearly defined roles, responsibilities, and accountabilities.

How are we managing the plan? How does the work flow efficiently? Who's doing what? How are people linked? How are they rewarded?

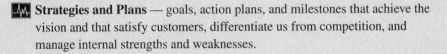 **Innovative Culture** — an environment empowering people to perform at their best.

Under what fundamental principles and values do we operate? How are we promoting and supporting customer focus, communication, collaboration, creativity, constructive leadership, continuous learning, and the management of change?

THE PLANNING PROCESS

CHARACTERISTICS OF AN EFFECTIVE PLANNING PROCESS

Your written plan will become the road map for your company's future. But, in order to create this road map, you need to establish a planning process that will ensure the best thinking and generate commitment to the plan.

"Your plan has got to be big enough to be exciting and small enough to be realistic. Plans are great, but they do change. Goals are great, but sometimes you underachieve them, sometimes you overachieve them. If you're over-achieving a goal, then it's no longer a motivating force, so you have to give it up. If you're way underachieving it, sometimes it isn't realistic, so it's no longer a viable goal."

An effective planning process is:

- **Comprehensive.** The process covers all the bases, raises all the issues of growth, and addresses all the fundamentals of your business.

- **Open and participatory.** People are involved both functionally and cross-functionally in giving ideas and feedback all through the process.

- **A compelling catalyst for change.** People see the need for change to support desired growth, so they see change as positive and want to help make it happen.

- **Immediately actionable.** The product of planning includes a vision for two to three years out, but also a one-year plan with quarterly segments that describe actions to be taken right away.

- **Supportive of an innovative culture.** By participating in the process itself, people learn to use specific techniques for creative thinking, planning, and teamwork that will foster innovation in all aspects of their work.

PHASES OF THE PLANNING CYCLE

Because growth continually changes your organization, you never outgrow your need to plan. The figure below describes a four-phase planning cycle that you can use at every stage of growth. It begins and ends with Discovery and has Communication at the center. The annual cycle of planning devotes approximately one month to Discovery, two to three months to Visioning and Planning, the rest of the year to Action and Results, and then repeats itself. Throughout the year, you'll need to engage in two-way communication with all parts of the organization about the plan, progress toward objectives, new discoveries, and modifications or additions to the plan.

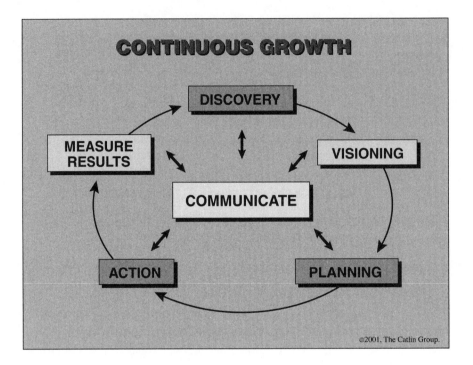

THE DISCOVERY PHASE

In the Discovery Phase, you explore your organization's strengths, weaknesses, opportunities, and threats (SWOT), as well as future possibilities for growth. Use interviews, surveys (including the *BAO SCAN: Create Your Plan for Growth* at the end of this chapter). Gather information and feedback from managers, employees, board members, and external sources, such as current, former, and prospective customers, vendors, suppliers, and market and industry analysts. Determine how these constituencies view the market, how they perceive your company versus competitors, challenges and hurdles they identify for your company, and ways they would solve problems or capitalize on opportunities. Be sure to listen carefully to those who challenge your assumptions and have perceptions that are different from yours.

Sometimes it's useful to have a consultant conduct the interviews, compile the data from the environmental scan and the interviews, and prepare a summary document. The document should include all the Discovery information and be shared with members of the top team in preparation for the Visioning and Planning phase. Each team member should analyze the document and identify key themes, critical messages, and top priorities for future action. They should also consider whether and how the company is aligned with future market needs.

"We start with the SWOT [Strengths, Weaknesses, Opportunities, Threats], and then we listen to each group's goals. Then we can see how our corporate goals line up with each group's goals, because they can be two different things — where each group wants to go and where we need to go as a company. Then we have to pick and choose."

Use the Discovery document to help you and your top team "pick and choose" and develop the outline and first draft of your written plan. While the top team should be responsible for leading the development of the final plan, the entire organization needs to be involved, as described in the following section.

VISIONING AND PLANNING

Visioning and Planning are best carried out through a series of off-site sessions where people get away from their daily responsibilities and have a chance to focus on planning the company's future.

"I wanted to make sure we were solidified in who we wanted to be. I also wanted the team to be able to come to consensus on the fundamentals for growth, including our market position, mission, and values. So we went off site for two days to define those key pieces of the company. Fortunately we had gone out and talked to customers, so we had some new ideas to think about when developing our plan."

Here's what occurs at these off-site meetings:

SESSION 1

The top team explores and prioritizes the insights gained in the Discovery phase. The team then creates (or reconfirms) the market and customer focus, the mission, and the values, and determines how it wants to grow the company over the next two to three years. (See appendix F for an exercise on creating a vision.) Cross-functional teams are formed to work over the next several weeks, developing proposed strategies and action plans.

SESSION 2

The cross-functional teams present the results of their work. The proposed strategies, Strategic Growth Initiatives (SGIs), goals, and action steps are critiqued (see appendix F for information about Creative Reaction Feedback), and solutions are recommended for any barriers or problems identified. Metrics for tracking progress are discussed. Departmental units and cross-functional teams are assigned responsibility for defining the action steps needed to implement strategies. The leadership team's responsibilities include managing the planning process and making decisions based on desired results.

SESSION 3

During the third off-site session, the leadership team presents the written document containing market focus, mission, values, vision, and Strategic Growth Initiatives (SGIs) to all managers. Be sure to schedule enough time for managers to respond to the presentation, suggest additional ideas, discuss implications, identify major challenges, and determine how they can gain everyone's commitment to successful implementation and achieving the target metrics. After agreeing on the plan, the entire group should then discuss the best way to roll out the plan at a companywide meeting.

THE ROLLOUT

Schedule a companywide meeting as soon as possible after the third off-site session, during which you and the top team present the vision, values, mission, and the new plan. Describe how the plan will help the company grow, how people will be expected to contribute to and support the plan, the SGIs, metrics, and bonuses or incentives for achieving or surpassing the plan. Use focus groups and/or surveys to gather people's reactions and ideas. Involving people in thinking and working on the plan is critical to gaining their understanding and commitment. Departmental managers should give their team members a chance to ask additional questions about the plan in team meetings after the companywide meeting.

DEPARTMENTAL PLANNING

Within a week of the companywide meeting, the VPs should lead their respective departments in the development of their departmental plans. At planning sessions, they should discuss how the company's new plan will impact what they're now doing in their departments and what will need to change. Some departments will have internal customers (other employees), and others will have external customers. Each department should undertake a Discovery phase, explore the needs of their customers, and then use that input in their Visioning and Planning phase to develop their own written market and customer focus, mission, vision, strategies, action plans, and metrics.

> "We use the company's mission and vision statements as we develop our departmental strategies to ensure that our plans are consistent across the

company. In fact, we have each department identify how their functional area will help achieve the company's mission. They use that as the basis for developing their own departmental missions."

"Each department is now taking the company mission and looking at what part of achieving it rests with their functional area. They take those pieces and use them as the basis for developing their own departmental missions. We also use the mission and vision statements as we develop our strategies, to ensure that our plans are consistent. We don't need to wait until the document is completed to implement some of the ideas that come up during the process. We found that many of the best concepts that came out of our discussions could be implemented immediately."

SGI TEAMS

It is extremely useful to convene cross-functional teams to work on the Strategic Growth Initiatives because the SGIs often have organization-wide impact and are almost always cross functional in nature. Teams might examine ways to stay close to markets and customers, systematize internal communications, define and launch new products, and manage key partnerships. These cross-functional teams also help mitigate the damaging effect of departmental silos, make the organization more efficient, and often develop creative solutions for high-priority challenges. Be sure that your people have the skills to work in teams and handle team-related conflicts. If they don't, get them into team-development training as soon as possible.

"During the planning process, we encourage people to seek input from all the other functions and departments with whom they interface. We establish a system of cross-functional teams and form teams focusing on markets and customers. This huge team system has been a much-needed major cultural change for the company. We've worked hard to make sure people had the skills to work on teams and handle issues such as, 'How do people operate on teams?' 'Who drives the team?' and 'What happens when the head of this team and the head of that team disagree and priorities need to be established?'"

FINALIZE ALL PLANS

When plans are being developed, it's useful for department heads and cross-functional team leaders to have at least one meeting where they can talk about new ideas; give each other feedback on proposed strategies, action steps, and accountabilities; and reach final agreement on the metrics. Once completed, all plans should be presented to the top team as well as all department heads and team leaders to develop a common understanding and agreement, and to identify interdependencies among all functional and cross-functional teams.

Finally, budgets for each department and cross-functional team need to be developed and processes established for managing the plans and budgets in the Action and Results phase.

ACTION AND RESULTS

This phase is all about execution of the plan. It's important to establish processes to keep the plan on track throughout the year. Make sure each individual understands what she or he needs to do to help achieve the plan. Make this an integral part of each individual's performance review and performance plan for the next year. Recognize and reward progress and hold people accountable for achieving the company's plan. Raise issues and solve problems, define new challenges and opportunities throughout the year, and make sure they are reflected in the next Discovery document that is developed.

> "We have two retreats annually. The winter retreat is where we hear from the staff, and the fall retreat is where management reports back. The process is based on a SWOT analysis. For years, it was always about systems and operations and who was doing what, but we've evolved beyond that. Now we focus on clients, that is, we talk about how we are thinking about a client's business, what we can do better, and how we are going to continue to diversify our client base. We establish strategies and set goals, and then we measure them every six months."

A critical part of ensuring that the desired results are achieved is to put in place a systematic process for tracking the plan's metrics. These metrics measure financial goals and other key indicators of success, such as customer satisfaction, employee satisfaction, product development, and other factors that support the achievement of the financial objectives.

Each metric definition should include the following elements:

- Standards for performance. What defines achievement or success and how will we know when we are there?

- A list of people responsible for tracking each metric and communicating it to others in the organization. This means alerting people when the company

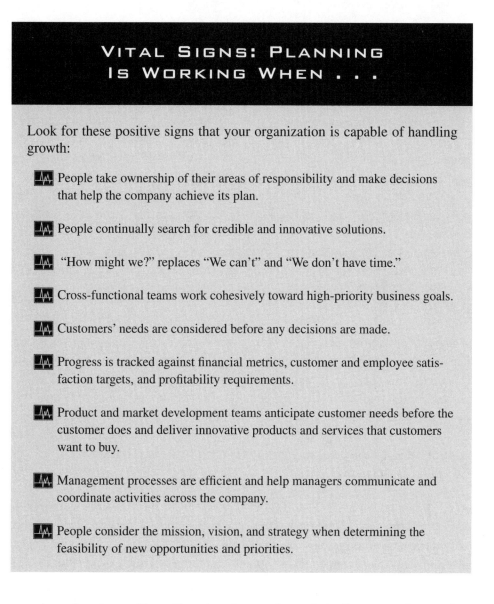

VITAL SIGNS: PLANNING IS WORKING WHEN . . .

Look for these positive signs that your organization is capable of handling growth:

- People take ownership of their areas of responsibility and make decisions that help the company achieve its plan.

- People continually search for credible and innovative solutions.

- "How might we?" replaces "We can't" and "We don't have time."

- Cross-functional teams work cohesively toward high-priority business goals.

- Customers' needs are considered before any decisions are made.

- Progress is tracked against financial metrics, customer and employee satisfaction targets, and profitability requirements.

- Product and market development teams anticipate customer needs before the customer does and deliver innovative products and services that customers want to buy.

- Management processes are efficient and help managers communicate and coordinate activities across the company.

- People consider the mission, vision, and strategy when determining the feasibility of new opportunities and priorities.

is performing really well against the metrics and sending out early warning signals when performance starts to weaken.

- Actions to take if performance falls below the desired level. Identify what actions will be taken when performance is off just a little and what actions may be necessary if performance falls through the floor.

"There's an adage that if you can't measure it, you can't manage it. I think the key is for you and your management people to identify the fundamental

> measures that determine the economics of your business, the three, four, or five variables that really determine your success. Then set measurable targets for those variables, measure them periodically, report progress, and hold people accountable for achieving the targets they agreed to."

Hold weekly, monthly, and quarterly meetings to review performance to plan, track progress, and make changes as needed. The plan must stay flexible because the market, the customer's needs, and the company itself are always changing. Continually introduce new information about the market and engage in Discovery to determine how this new input affects the existing plan. This will enable the company to stay proactive and nimble. Keeping the plan flexible is particularly important for very early-stage companies, where key market, technology, and financing requirements often deviate sharply from what was originally anticipated. Don't be afraid of changing your plan, based on new information. Just make sure that all parts of the plan are thought through and that the appropriate people are involved in decision making.

If the entire planning process is done right, the corporate plan for growth, the departmental and SGI cross-functional team plans will never be in danger of gathering dust on a shelf. Instead, they will become the focus of all work and will be constantly referenced in both formal and informal communication. People will bring plans to meetings, discuss issues within the context provided by the plan, and use them as a basis for decision making. Managers will use the company and departmental plans to delegate and empower people to come up with ideas that will help the company grow.

Note: A major event such as an IPO, a merger or acquisition, a major shift on Wall Street, the launch of a new product line, or a major strategic partnership or alliance should trigger a new round of planning, even if it doesn't coincide with your annual planning cycle. It is easy to underestimate the impact of such events, but they all will dramatically affect the vision, strategy, and operations of the company and require a new growth plan.

COMMUNICATION

All phases of this annual planning cycle depend on clear, consistent, and continuous two-way communication. Make sure the plan is a living document. Refer to it when communicating the company's direction and progress. Solicit new ideas, encourage people to share new insights, and update the plan as appropriate. Be sure to communicate progress against the plan. Remember that people won't follow the plan if you don't remind them that it's guiding the company's growth and if you don't report progress on a regular basis. Communication fosters accountability.

> "We did three off-site meetings, followed by an internal rollout of our plan to 240 people. We shared the vision, the values, the Strategic Growth Initiatives, and all of the specific action steps. The next step was rolling it out through departmental meetings. We also set up our Intranet to allow any employee to see exactly what cross-functional tasks people are accountable for and how we're doing against the goal. When we hire new people, they can see this; they recognize that we're holding ourselves accountable, and that's very empowering."

YOUR ROLE AS LEADER

> "It's important to identify what percentage of time is spent on being CEO versus COO. Make sure enough time is spent on the CEO role, addressing strategic issues and new business ideas."

The process of planning requires people to think strategically and stay focused on the future. People make better short-term decisions when they understand the company's long-term objectives. Planning is a healthy discipline that keeps companies strong and able to meet the many challenges of growth.

As leader of the planning effort, your roles are to:

- Assure that planning is an ongoing process and an essential component of your organization. Establish a planning process with regular meetings and milestones. Hold people accountable for fulfilling their roles in the process, such as participating in the off-sites, completing work assignments between off-sites, communicating the finished plans to their departments, and fulfilling the charters of their teams.

- Let people know you expect their very best thinking during the planning process and make sure to model this yourself in planning meetings. Stretch your own and other people's thinking.

- Keep people aligned with the plan, listen to suggestions and innovations, support continued discovery, and address people's issues.

- Keep discovering new ideas and continuously fine-tuning the plan as outside forces change your market.

● Track progress and make regular reports to all employees about what's been achieved, how well the company is performing versus plan, what still needs to be accomplished, and how it needs to be accomplished within the culture of the company.

BIG LESSONS

1. Successful companies develop plans for growth and measure progress against plan. Plans enable you to align the company around shared goals and stay focused on the prize.

2. The market and the needs of the customer should be the basis for planning and must be represented in your vision and mission.

3. Planning is not a one-time event, but a repetitive process. The demands of growth will change your company, so you need to revisit the plan regularly and make appropriate changes.

4. A plan should be a living document that constantly informs decision making at all levels.

5. The process of planning is as important as the plan itself; it facilitates communication, understanding, and buy-in from employees, board members, customers, and vendors and suppliers.

6. A healthy culture is necessary for growth and needs to be clearly defined in the written plan. It is the core that supports your organization as it grows and enables you to execute the plan.

BAO SCAN: CREATE YOUR PLAN FOR GROWTH

Use this *SCAN** to determine how well your company is developing its plan for growth. Take this *BAO SCAN* yourself, and then have your top team and other key people complete it as well. Compare your responses and perceptions with theirs. Work together to identify innovative ways to develop better plans and strengthen the planning process.

*This BAO SCAN is adapted from The Growth Potential Survey, © 2001, The Catlin Group.

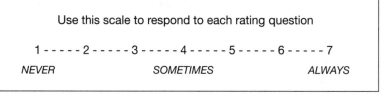

RATING SCALE

Use this scale to respond to each rating question

1 - - - - - 2 - - - - - 3 - - - - - 4 - - - - - 5 - - - - - 6 - - - - - 7
NEVER   *SOMETIMES*   *ALWAYS*

PART A. MARKET AND CUSTOMER FOCUS

Growth happens when companies stay in touch with those who keep them in business and when everyone in the company understands key markets and is keenly aware of customer values and needs.

1. We keep up with trends and needs in our highest-
potential markets.   Rating: _____

2. We know the perceived value of our products and
services in solving our customers' problems and
contributing to their success.   Rating: _____

3. Everyone in the organization understands and
considers the needs of the customer in daily operations.   Rating: _____

4. We build strong, long-term customer relationships
that impact the bottom line positively.   Rating: _____

PART B. MISSION, VISION, AND VALUES

Successful growth companies have a commitment to a clear, customer-driven statement of purpose (mission), a specific picture of the corporate future (vision), and agreement on what values and behaviors will be used to get them there (values).

1. Our mission guides employees in planning, decision
making, and prioritizing to meet business goals.   Rating: _____

2. We agree on the company's strategic targets two to
three years down the road.   Rating: _____

3. Our mission and vision drive our business strategy.   Rating: _____

4. Our corporate values are defined and used as operating principles for achieving our mission and vision.   Rating: _____

PART C. STRATEGIES AND PLANS

The ideal strategy provides a series of steps, clearly defined and articulated, that will enable the company to achieve its vision and goals.

1. Our strategy positions us to achieve sustainable competitive advantage. Rating: _____

2. People throughout the company understand our strategy and use it to focus their activities and priorities. Rating: _____

3. Our strategy is effective in winning and satisfying more customers. Rating: _____

4. Our strategy builds on our strengths and addresses our weaknesses. Rating: _____

PART D. STRUCTURE AND PROCESSES

The appropriate design of a company links people, processes, and systems to achieve corporate growth strategies.

1. Our work processes, systems, and infrastructure enable our people to do business effectively. Rating: _____

2. We define targets and measure each individual's performance against the company's strategies and bottom line. Rating: _____

3. People are held accountable for achieving unit and corporate objectives. Rating: _____

4. We recognize and reward people for achieving those objectives. Rating: _____

PART E. INNOVATIVE CULTURE

An outstanding corporate culture catalyzes enterprisewide commitment and high performance, and supports continued growth.

1. Our environment motivates people to take initiative and find innovative solutions to business problems. Rating: _____

2. We communicate — up, down, and across — to ensure that everyone has the information to make good decisions that are in accord with the company's goals and core values.   Rating: _____

3. People avoid stovepipes and silos; they collaborate effectively across functional areas and move the company toward its strategies and vision.   Rating: _____

4. Our Executive Team is cohesive and effective in leading everyone toward the achievement of company goals.   Rating: _____

SCORE SUMMARY AND INTERPRETATION

A Rating Score of **7** in any area indicates this is a prime area of strength that will facilitate and support the company's growth. Scores of **5** and **6** indicate that you have considerable strength in these areas, but you will want to consider making incremental improvements to increase the score. A score of **4** is a cause for worry. A rating of "Sometimes" indicates a lack of consistency that sends conflicting signals to employees and inhibits growth; thus significant improvements will be needed. Scores of **3 or below** are big red flags indicating areas or behaviors that hinder the company's growth and require your immediate attention.

RESULTS ANALYSIS

Look back over the *BAO SCAN: Create Your Plan for Growth:*

1. List three statements that you rated the highest. Choose those you feel are key strengths and contribute most to the success of the company.

A. _____

B. _____

C. _____

2. List three statements that received the lowest rating. Choose those you feel are the most critical weaknesses and should be targeted for improvement.

A. _____

B. _____

C. _____

3. Write three statements that define your priorities for change (for example, capitalize on the strengths or improve the weaknesses).

A. _____

B. _____

C. _____

4. List three things our company could do to implement those changes.

A. _____

B. _____

C. _____

ACTION PLAN

Recognize what you and your company are doing well and celebrate! Think about what you have done that enabled you to achieve these great results and how that can be applied to your weaknesses. But, do not overlook areas that need improvement or think they will improve on their own over time. Use these steps to develop your Action Plan for Improvement:

1. Ask your top team to complete the *BAO SCAN: Create Your Plan for Growth* and the Results Analysis. You may also want others in the company to complete the *SCAN* to get more comprehensive feedback.

2. Meet with your top team to:

- Compare and contrast your ratings on various statements with their ratings, as well as areas you have identified as strengths with those needing work.

- If applicable, discuss the reasons why their responses are different from yours.

- Agree on areas for improvement or change; be as specific as possible.

3. Prioritize those areas that must be addressed and will make the biggest difference. Develop them into Action Plans for Improvement.

4. Get consensus on the Action Plans and the resources and budgets needed to make the necessary changes.

   • For each Action Plan, specify the goal, desired outcomes, steps to take, team members responsible for implementation, resources required, key measures of success, and time frames for achieving the goal and tracking results.

   • Assign a cross-functional team to implement each Action Plan. Include members from different departments who will be affected by the changes. Members should have the necessary skills and insights to accomplish the plan. Identify a team leader and/or executive sponsor who will be held accountable for managing the team, tracking progress, and achieving the desired goal.

5. Communicate the Action Plans for Improvement to everyone in the company. Get involvement, input, and feedback.

6. Hold yourself and others accountable for achieving the new goals and milestones.

7. After a designated period of time (three to six months), evaluate progress, identify new or emerging problems or opportunities, set new goals, make new team assignments (if appropriate), and take action. In a year, retake the *BAO SCAN: Create Your Plan for Growth* and repeat Steps 1 through 6 as required. Remember: Continuous assessment, action, and improvement are essential to building an awesome organization that is strong enough to support continuous growth.

Top Team

CHAPTER 7

PRIME YOUR TOP TEAM FOR GROWTH

"If you depend on yourself to be the only leader, you will find it physically and emotionally impossible. Your top team or Executive Team must be a group of people you completely trust. You learn from them, and they learn from you. You work smoothly together as the leaders of the company. You can't be the only one concerned with the issues of growth and attracting and retaining great people; you've got to bring in people who are smarter than you are and who know how to do things you may not know how to do."

In prior chapters, we discussed three of the six elements of an awesome organization: culture, people, and planning. In this chapter, we explore the fourth element: the team of top executives who help you lead the company through growth. A cohesive Executive Team united by shared values and mutual respect enhances and extends your leadership, and enables the company to achieve its vision and plan for growth.

Your top team members must share your values and passion, and coordinate their activities to support the company's growth. They help you develop the company's goals and plans, protect and defend the values and culture, and attract and retain awesome people in each functional area.

A well-functioning Executive Team fills gaps in your experience and knowledge, and provides strengths in the areas where you are weak.

RED FLAGS: SIGNS OF DYSFUNCTIONAL LEADERSHIP FROM THE TOP TEAM

Do you see these signs in your company? These are signals that some or all members of your top Executive Team are not fulfilling their role as leaders of growth:

 Top team members are focused solely on running their own departments and have little consideration or appreciation of other departments, each other, or the whole company.

 People get inconsistent messages from different top team members about vital issues such as mission, vision, strategy, values, and priorities.

 It's difficult to achieve consensus among top team members, and they seem to be in constant competition with each other.

 Top team members complain they don't get enough time with you or you don't communicate enough with them.

 Your team members are still coming to you for decisions.

 Top team members "don't have time for meetings."

 There's a communications gap between your top team and middle managers.

 People believe that the leadership team is constantly changing direction — with no clue as to why.

 Big decisions are announced, but the rationale is not explained.

 You worry that one or more members of your team isn't right for the job.

Members of the top team need to have a clear understanding of the company's big picture and of how the functional units they manage interact and support each other to enable the company to fulfill its mission, vision, plan, and goals. As the most public examples of the culture, team members are role models for the company's values and accepted behaviors. As a positive model for all other teams, they learn from each other and help each other succeed.

"I've always been an entrepreneur, and one of the things I learned early on is that I couldn't get any traction in my business until I had a group of people working as entrepreneurs together. We have that now, and we also have a plan in place that we created together. It will guide our future growth while helping to preserve our unique culture, even as we add more and more employees here and around the world."

ASSEMBLING THE TOP TEAM

There are many ways to assemble a top team. Some entrepreneurs start with a team of colleagues who are expected to lead the company together and hope they will grow as their responsibilities grow. Others start a company by themselves and add team members one by one. They hope that the people they add will continue to grow in their jobs as the company's needs change. Other entrepreneurs dig deep to find the resources necessary to hire the very best people as soon as possible. Some even try to "overhire," hiring people who have more skills and experience than the company needs at its current stage of development. They hope that having these experienced people on board will accelerate the company's growth.

"In our early stage of growth, I left holes in the organization chart. I knew there would be additional roles that would need to be filled later, and I hired people with the clear expectation that eventually we would hire other people, above them, to fill those holes. I knew a top team was essential for growth, but I also knew that at different stages, the team would need to be different. The people I hired at the beginning might not be the ones I needed when we got bigger. This is my third company, and I've learned that it's important not to give away the vice president slots too freely, too early, and to be clear with people that those jobs will be filled down the road."

"I put a top team in place. As we grew and needed to add skills, we did it in a zigzag pattern. Over time, some people left. Others who weren't performing well enough were encouraged to leave. Each time I brought in someone better, and was able to ratchet up the capabilities of the team, slowly but surely. This probably isn't the ideal approach, and if I had it to do over again, I'd take a more thoughtful approach. I'd do more planning ahead to assure we have the right people in the right spots at the right time in the company's growth path."

Although there are different ways to assemble a team, it's unlikely that the people you hire in the beginning will have the skills to take your company all the way. The important point is that the company's needs will change as it goes through different stages of growth. Analyze what the organization needs in terms of leadership to support future growth and try to overhire whenever possible. Look for people who are experienced at the levels of success you hope to attain in the future, not just your current level. Hire executives who share your values and your commitment to growth, leaders who are capable of fulfilling the six critical top team leadership responsibilities discussed later in this chapter in the box, "Vital Signs: Top Team's Six Areas of Responsibility as Leaders of Growth."

What follows are guidelines for assembling your top team.

MAKE SURE THEY ARE AWESOME PEOPLE

The executives in your top team need to have all the characteristics of awesome people described in chapter 4, "Attract Awesome People for Growth," and chapter 5, "Retain Awesome People for Growth." Surround yourself with creative, passionate people who will be strong drivers of growth. Awesome people expect the CEO and the top team to provide the leadership needed to grow the company. They are unlikely to join a company with less than awesome leadership, and they certainly won't stay at a company that has a dysfunctional top team.

> "The critical ingredients for hiring the top team are talent and fit with the culture. We brought in a very talented person as our COO, but we ended up with a total mismatch with our culture. People tend to underrate the culture and environments in which top executives will have to work. It is absolutely critical to make a good match. This deserves much more attention than it gets."

> "We've gotten better over the years at hiring for values. It makes a big difference when we get that right. All it takes is one person who is not value aligned and the top team won't work. Determining values in an interview is hard. We get candidates to tell anecdotes about their life and business life. We learn how they dealt with failure and setbacks, how they dealt with projects as a team. If you find someone who finger points, you have a values issue; if you get someone who never had a failure, you have a values issue. Or, if someone claims credit for everything they've ever touched, you probably have a values issue."

BUILD THE TEAM FOR GROWTH

Regardless of your company's stage of growth, you need to hire executives who can grow at least two levels — even if you can't imagine what the organizational structure will look like in a year or two. Hire really strong, experienced people who are smarter than you are in their areas of expertise and to whom you can delegate significant responsibility for decision making in their functional areas. The right people will grow the company; the wrong people will sap energy and stunt growth.

> "We place a ton of importance on hiring people who match our corporate values and culture. We hire for trait and temperament. For a senior level person, you're going to spend over $100,000 in salary, benefits, and training, so you need to treat it as a key acquisition. To find out if they're a match for our corporate values, we ask questions about their last work environment, about what kind of work environments they've been successful in, and what's been wrong with their work environments in the past. We ask for examples of continuous improvement and of situations in which they've gone the extra mile to get the job done. We want examples of when they've taken risks and personal responsibility for mistakes or omissions. These are the ways we judge their commitment to excellence, their self-confidence, their teamwork, and whether they have the kind of insight and experience we need."

HIRE AND FIRE FOR VALUES

Hiring for values is important at all levels of the organization, as we discussed in chapter 4, but it is absolutely essential with the people you handpick for the Executive Team. Having a team that shares your values and practices them every day is one way to ensure that the culture you want will thrive. Just one Executive Team member who does not live by the values can have a devastating impact on your culture and organization, as the following stories illustrate.

> "I've made the mistake in the past of hiring someone whose skills were so impressive that I ignored a mismatch of values. That ended up being deadly. We had huge turnover in that guy's department because his values were so different from the ones we built in the company."

> "We use references a lot for checking values; one of the things I check on reference calls is how are these people in real life. My favorite question is 'We all have a bad day every now and then; how is this person on a bad day?'"

"One of our original management team members always delivered tangible results for the business. He had a lot of autonomy, but began to diverge too much from company strategy, our brand identity, and customer focus. His style and attitude changed from being a useful devil's advocate to being a destructive force. I was constantly fielding complaints about his negativity. In October I spelled out how he had to change, but by December it was clear he wasn't responding, so we negotiated a separation agreement in January. When I hired a replacement, I made sure the new VP was on the same page as me. Then I met with his four key direct reports to explain the change, why I did it, and why they weren't considered for the VP position. By February, the new VP was able to participate very successfully in our three-year visioning offsite."

The longer you tolerate top team members not living by the values, the more it will impact your culture and create morale problems, so make changes as soon as possible. On the other hand, take the time to compliment and reinforce members of the team who walk the talk and do live by the values. Point to them as great examples for everyone in the company to emulate.

SEEK DIVERSITY

Don't hire your clones. Seek people who have different skills, backgrounds, and thinking styles to enable the team to analyze issues from a variety of perspectives. This diversity of backgrounds and viewpoints leads to better planning and stronger decision making. Balance your Executive Team with introverts and extroverts, with creative people who have new ideas every day and those who excel at details and implementation, and with people who are analytical and those who follow their intuition. Include men and women, and seek team members who have had experiences in other countries and cultures. Create a top team that's representative of the full gamut of employees and customers you're likely to have, rather than include only people whose backgrounds and experiences match yours.

"On my top team, I want people with different thinking and communication styles within the context of everyone sharing the same core values. It makes a company stronger if you build in diversity. You want people who are relationship focused and can get key influencers to buy into a new idea; but you also want people who focus on execution inside the company, too. One is an inward focus and one is outward focus; having both makes us a stronger company."

"At my first company, we learned a lesson that the different kinds of thinking on the Executive Team was definitely an asset, so it is something I have focused on here. I'm trying to be careful not to hire people who are just like me."

UNDERSTAND THAT THE TEAM COMPOSITION WILL CHANGE

As the company grows, you'll notice gaps in certain functions. You'll need to hire people who have higher levels of expertise in finance, operations, product development, marketing, business development, sales, or human resources in order to take the company further up the growth curve.

With growth will come a need to divide functions that formerly could be led by one person. For instance, sales and marketing might operate as one department early on, but eventually you'll want to separate these functions and have strong experts leading each. Another change that accompanies growth is separating human resources from the finance function, where it normally resides in the early stages of the company when the main HR duties relate to administration, payroll, and benefits. But as the company grows and HR becomes a more strategic, organization-building function, it needs to be managed by a vice president who becomes part of the top team and a peer to the CFO.

"Top team stuff is tough. It's a complicated scenario because the characteristics you need in the top team are different as you go through growth. The person I would kill for right now is a big money CFO, somebody who knows about IPOs and about investment banks. The guy we've got in that slot right now is a buddy of mine. He's a brilliant controller and no dollar remains uncounted — anywhere — but he's not a Harvard MBA and doesn't hang around with venture capital guys. So the problem I face with the top team from one year to the next, sometimes one situation to the next, is that they often don't have the knowledge, experiences, and contacts I need. It's hard to justify getting rid of perfectly good people who are performing, but in some cases the people I need are different from the ones I have."

PROMOTE FROM WITHIN WHEN POSSIBLE; HIRE FROM OUTSIDE WHEN NECESSARY

Give current employees, including top team members, opportunities to grow and consider them for leadership positions that become available. Make sure outside recruiters consider internal as well as external candidates concurrently. Promoting from within maintains your culture, saves time, and sends signals that this is an organization that appreciates and recognizes employees who have the capacity to grow and develop. But sometimes you need new skills and experiences that are different from the ones anyone in the company has. In that situation, you'll need to bring someone new onto the team. But, understand that doing so will have a major impact on the top team because the dynamics of the group will change.

INTEGRATE NEW MEMBERS WITH CONTINUOUS TEAM BUILDING

A new person, even someone who shares your values and is a good match with the culture, will have different perspectives, won't know the history and lore of your company, and will probably have a different management style, and different contacts and experiences. Help integrate the new person and coach him or her as well as other members of the top team to appreciate and value those differences. When new team members present new ideas at meetings, don't allow them to be greeted with "We tried that idea; it didn't work," or "Around here, we don't do things that way." Instead, remind everyone that these team members bring knowledge and creativity to the organization that make it feasible to try new things — or do old things in new ways.

Get new top team members involved in the company's planning process as soon as possible. Help them get the big-picture perspective so they can see how their roles and responsibilities fit with other functional areas and with the company as a whole. It's often useful for new team members to interview existing team members as part of their orientation process. These interviews provide opportunities for two-way discussions in which current team members provide background and orientation as well as listen to the ideas and learn from the experiences of the new team member.

UNDERSTANDING THE TWO-HAT CHALLENGE

Even when an awesome top team is assembled, many CEOs and their executives don't understand that each member of the top team has to wear two hats; each has to be (1) an outstanding manager of his or her function and (2) a company leader who helps the CEO grow the company by building the components of the awesome organization. The latter duty involves taking on the six very specific responsibilities described in the following box, "Vital Signs: Top Team's Six Areas of Responsibility as Leaders of Growth."

It's not easy to wear these two hats because it's really like having two full-time jobs. To meet this challenge, each member of the top team must hire great people and build his or her own team in that functional area. Top team members must then delegate to those awesome people and let them manage so the executives have the time required to handle the responsibilities of company leadership. If every functional leader does a good job with the two-hat challenge, the company has a depth and breadth of leadership that a lone entrepreneur or CEO could never provide.

Most entrepreneurs hire Executive Team members for their functional expertise and hope they will fit well with other members of the top team and be able to master the two-hat challenge. But past success as a member of another company's management team does not guarantee that someone will fit well with your top team, operating within your company's particular culture. You can have a very strong group of individual leaders, but if they don't function well together as a team, this will create chaos in your company.

> "After starting and building two companies, I've learned a few things about managing growth. If you want to take off like a rocket, getting the funding for growth is the rocket fuel. But the only way to grow is to bring in a full team of really strong VPs who can be the rocket engines. Then your responsibility is to learn how to manage them. They need to be harnessed and directed so they work together. The hard part is that they're highly egotistical and independent (that's why you hired them), so they'll tell you they don't need to be harnessed and directed. But if you don't give that direction, they'll compete with each other and build their own power structures as separate entities within the company. That's the last thing you need for fast growth. The rocket engines must move the rocket in the same direction or the whole thing will explode."

You need to get the top team focusing their combined energy to produce liftoff for your company. During periods of high growth, team members tend to focus on fighting fires in their own areas, meeting short-term objectives, and providing leadership in the areas for which they have functional responsibility. They often find it difficult to take time to come together and play the role they must play as leaders of the company, address companywide issues, and set future direction.

VITAL SIGNS: TOP TEAM'S SIX AREAS OF RESPONSIBILITY AS LEADERS OF GROWTH

To be leaders of growth, all top team members must fulfill the following six key responsibilities. This aspect of their job description is seldom made explicit. These responsibilities should be reviewed during the recruiting and selection process. They should also be part of the executive development and performance review processes. Top team members must be great at leading their functional areas *and* at fulfilling these leadership responsibilities to provide the strong leadership needed for growth and innovation. Use the *BAO SCAN* at the end of this chapter to measure how well your team is handling these responsibilities.

Create the plan for growth. The Executive Team provides the big picture for everyone in the organization by creating a written plan for growth. Whether you use the Profit Spiral described in chapter 6, "Create Your Plan for Growth," or some other good planning process, it should clearly define market and customer focus, mission and values, vision and objectives, strategy and initiatives, structure and process, and culture. The top team uses this plan to focus and drive team and individual objectives throughout the company and to measure progress. Hold team members accountable for participating in the planning process as well as seeking information that will be useful during the Discovery phase. Expect them to take an active role in the discussions and decision making during the Visioning and Planning phase, not just be observers of the process; consensus and commitment are required. Discuss how they will communicate the company plan to their functional and cross-functional teams, and lead those teams in developing their own plans and budgets.

Communicate for alignment. The Executive Team must make sure everyone in the organization is in complete agreement with the company's mission, vision, structure, and culture, and understands what metrics will be used to measure their performance. Gaining clarity and alignment on these topics through systematic efforts to communicate consistent messages requires significant energy, time, and patience. Team members must be held accountable for soliciting input and feedback so people at all levels understand these critical areas, feel involved, and take ownership of the plan's successful implementation.

Build and protect the culture. The Executive Team must be constantly focused on developing and reinforcing the innovative culture required for growth. First, their behavior must mirror the desired culture and values at all times. Second, they are responsible for ensuring that the people on their functional teams adhere to the cultural values and for taking corrective action when individuals violate those values. Finally, top team members must be held responsible for strengthening all 7 C's of a great culture (see chapter 3, "Develop an Innovative Culture for Growth," for more information).

Attract and retain awesome people. As described in chapter 4 and chapter 5, hiring and then retaining awesome people are both vital objectives for the leadership team. Team members need to follow agreed-on processes for achieving these aims. They should recognize and reward employees who help the company achieve its goals. In addition, team members should be held accountable for any turnover of awesome people.

Manage team pitfalls as a role model for all teams. As part of the leadership team and as head of the team in his or her own functional area, each Executive Team member needs to know how to overcome pitfalls that are common to all teams. These include misunderstandings, not being on the same page, not listening respectfully to each other, allowing disagreements to linger without resolution, killing other's ideas, ignoring adversarial relationships, and power grabs. Team members also need to be skilled at processes such as balanced decision making, creative problem solving, giving direction and feedback, learning from successes and failures, holding each other accountable, and handling conflict resolution to manage their top team interactions as well as the interactions of their individual functional teams. The top team must be a role model of cohesive teamwork, effectively collaborating in a visible way that inspires other teams to follow its lead.

Learn from each other. An effective Executive Team has a diversity of expertise, experience, priorities, perspectives, and styles. The success of the top team in leading your company will be directly related to its ability to understand, value, and respect these differences. Team members should be held accountable for maintaining a supportive environment in which they give each other feedback, continually learn from each other, and help each other succeed.

Adapted from Building the Executive Team as Leaders of Growth™, a trademark of Katherine Catlin.
© 2001, The Catlin Group.

Team members have to learn to balance their tendency to say, "I can't afford the time for meetings," with the realization that "the company needs me to be involved in these meetings." One key to doing this is to make sure that meetings are effectively managed so that issues do get resolved in a timely fashion, enabling people to realize the power of good meetings.

You need to select and hire people who can play the dual role of company leader and functional leader, and then coach and mentor them so they excel at both jobs. Be very explicit and hold top team members accountable for the six responsibilities as company leaders, as well as for managing the operation of their functional areas.

> "One of the challenges of leading the top team is maintaining a balance between strategy and tactics — finding the time to sit down and think about the future of the company as opposed to solving the day-to-day, minute-by-minute tactical challenges. The planning process we used was a way to formalize getting our heads away from the tactics and into strategic issues. People participated in a collaborative and high-level way; people really showed up for it; there was no holding back, no lack of interest. Since then, we've changed the agenda of our weekly meetings to talk more about strategic issues and the tactical issues are handled in weekly written reports rather than in our meetings. These reports get distributed before the weekly executive meetings so everyone has read them and if there is a question, a comment, or an idea, they can bring it to the meeting."

> "The only way a top team can lead the company is through collaboration among peers. There is a natural tendency for managers to lead their people very well, but collaboration with peers is harder because you can't control your peers. But, it's more important for the long-term success of the company, so it comes down to the CEO doing a good job of encouraging informal networks and collaboration and driving accountability for things on a strategic, cross-functional basis."

One of the best ways to get a top team working in unison in support of their company leadership responsibilities is to guide them through the planning process described in chapter 6. Working together to develop a plan and define the future direction of the company is significant work. Designing, developing, and communicating the plan to the rest of the company — and then holding everyone accountable for achieving it — requires everyone on the top team to pull together as a unit and thereby helps align the whole company.

MASTERING COMMUNICATION, ROLE MODELING, AND CONTINUOUS INNOVATION

Executive Team members must excel as communicators and cultural role models who know how to foster innovation. You simply can't afford to have people on the team who aren't skilled communicators or who don't promote and model the collaboration, communication, creativity, and continuous learning that lead to innovation. The following three sections describe why these responsibilities are critical.

COMMUNICATE FOR ALIGNMENT

In an ideal organization, everyone is aligned; they understand and agree with the mission, vision, values, strategies, structure, and culture. There's clarity about how the organization works, how decisions get made, how success is measured and rewarded, and the consequences of failure. Clarity and alignment create the focus, consistency, accountability, and commitment required for successful growth. An aligned organization can move very fast, with great power. In contrast, a lack of alignment causes bad decision making, costly delays, departmental silos, and other major organizational difficulties that kill innovation and stall growth.

As CEO, you are ultimately responsible for achieving this alignment, but you can't do it alone. Your top team plays a critical role and amplifies your voice throughout the company. Getting alignment is perhaps the hardest job of the CEO and top team; it is something that cannot be taken for granted and requires constant attention.

> "I have a great top team; I hired them all personally and they're terrific people. We work well as a team, have a strong plan, and there is great consensus on decisions when we meet. I thought they were going out and communicating our decisions to other people, but when I walked around the organization, I discovered there were lots of people who weren't clued in. It made me realize that I wasn't holding the top team accountable for helping us achieve alignment. I guess I hadn't made it clear that I expected this — I thought it would just happen naturally. So, first I made it clear that I expected them to help with communications and alignment of the company. Then I began having them take a bigger role at company meetings in describing some of the things we were doing — to give them more experience and visibility as 'communicators.' Then we set up three major initiatives throughout the company related to our product strategy, our partnering strategy, and making sure our culture was great. By getting more people involved, we were able to do a better job of communicating our direction, and the top team began to understand how all these things helped align the company."

"I thought the vision was clear to everyone because I thought of little else and it was extremely clear to me. But I found the thinking behind the vision wasn't being shared, so people had a sort of one-dimensional view of the vision that didn't help them translate it into methodologies, systems, and plans that worked across all departments. I had to work with my top team to make sure they understood the vision, and that they knew how to communicate it to others at meetings, in memos, in speeches, in performance reviews, and so on."

"I think the Executive Team has to be messengers of the vision, interpreters of the vision, and supporters of the vision. If the Executive Team goes out and just mouths the party line, that's going to have zero credibility with the rest of the people. They have to understand and buy into the vision so well that they can defend it, translate it, and show staff how it applies to everyday situations."

Members of your Executive Team must be good communicators to create the needed alignment. This is especially true during times of change and rapid growth. It is very easy to get off track, and when things are moving at warp speed, communication often slips. At such times, people forget to copy other people on e-mails and memos, they mention something to one person and forget to tell another person who needs to know, they only hit the high spots when they write and talk — leaving out important details — or try to cover strategic information in five minutes of a meeting. All these small, inadvertent communication mistakes result in confusion and distraction — at the very time you need people to be the most focused and completely aligned. Good communication at all times is a primary responsibility of the entire team of leaders of a high-growth company.

"The pace of high growth means that at any given time there are a lot of things going on, so communication is the biggest challenge. You need constant communication and constant alignment. You have to make sure you have enough forms of communication and recognize that people have different kinds of communication styles. You need to get those styles to work together so communication doesn't become miscommunication. For example, some people are voice mail people and some are e-mail people. Voice mailers tend to be more communicative, and it drives them nuts when other people don't respond quickly to their voice mail. E-mail people, on the other hand, tend to be more reflective, and they want to get something polished before they send it, so getting those styles to collaborate takes an awareness of this difference and constant focus on it."

"We have 'Ask Anything' meetings where my team and I do a forum for employees; it's usually a brown-bag lunch. Anyone can sign up, and we usually get a good turnout. We do a 10-minute presentation on a specific topic and then have a Q&A session where people can ask questions about anything. We have quarterly all-hands meetings and we use 'Ask Anything' for the theme of those, too. We have a culture where whoever asks the toughest question is recognized. Our communication style is very open in terms of what's going on. One of our core values is deliver what you promise. We encourage people to talk about what's wrong and what's broken; and to have integrity in how they talk to customers and each other about what we're doing as a company."

Leaders who filter information and only tell employees what they think they need to know are walking on a slippery slope. Employees who feel they are only getting part of the story tend to fill information vacuums with assumptions about the truth — often erroneous — and false rumors abound. Or, people do not accept responsibility for achieving certain results because they feel they don't have all the information. All of this wastes valuable energy. It's much better for you and your top team to describe the problem and its cause. Then, explain what you propose to do about it and how your decision will impact employees, you and the top team, customers, vendors, and shareholders. Next, ask for their help and ideas about how best to implement the solution.

Executive Team members must be skilled in two-way communication, presenting as well as soliciting information. They need to be good listeners, encourage people to contribute ideas and feedback, and then use those ideas and feedback. They also need to remove bureaucratic roadblocks that might impede effective teamwork. (See appendix D, "Model for Creative Problem Solving," for an example of a model that fosters idea generation.)

RECOGNIZE THAT THE TOP TEAM MUST MODEL THE VALUES

"My experience has taught me that the impact of the CEO and the senior team in modeling awesome behavior is probably 10 times greater than what many people realize. Everybody recognizes it's important, but I think the magnitude is enormous when you factor in the exponential ripple effects."

People throughout the company watch to see how you and the top team act. They pick up cues about what is really important to the organization and what behavior you support or will not tolerate. They observe how supportive you are of people who come up with new ideas, take risks, and then stumble. They also watch to see what you do about people who don't achieve the expected results. Both as functional team leaders and as members of the leadership team, top team members can inspire people to achieve — or discourage them from even trying.

A great top team works together to achieve critical goals and solve problems. In all of their interactions with each other, they must visibly exhibit the kinds of cross-functional collaboration and creative problem solving you want to foster throughout the company. Each team member should be responsible for chairing at least one cross-functional team involving people from their own area as well as others from across the organization. When employees experience their departmental leader working smoothly and supportively with people from other parts of the company, demonstrating mutual respect and trust, they get a powerful message about the importance of collaborating to achieve the company's goals.

> "If you told me I could be a fly on the wall to observe something that would tell me whether this was an awesome company or not, my answer would be easy: 'Let me observe a meeting where a cross-functional team is tackling a tough issue.' The senior Executive Team is a good litmus test, and a standing cross-functional team is one, too. But I think an even better test would be to watch a cross-functional team of people from many levels of the company dig into a difficult challenge — for example, an unhappy customer in which six different people had contributed in some way to the problem. Or the task of cutting overall costs 30 percent on a product or service. I guarantee you I would see good or bad behavior come out right away that would tell me a lot about that company and its ability to be awesome or not."

ENCOURAGE CONTINUOUS INNOVATION

Continuous innovation is essential to growth. The top team must develop and continually drive a process that enables the organization to turn new, fragile ideas into exciting new processes, products, and services. Individually and together, the top team must seek out these ideas from many sources, break down barriers that hamper innovation, foster great teamwork and coordination, create effective reward systems for innovation and creativity, and gain commitment to innovation from all involved. They must lead cross-functional teams that focus on innovation and continuous improvement.

A good innovation process includes the following:

- Listening to the market, learning, and constantly searching for break-through ideas

- Developing new products and services, so you have a steady stream of exciting new offerings for customers and/or partners

- Creating and managing innovations so fresh new ideas are protected and nourished instead of killed

- Making time for reviews and postmortems, so you are constantly learning from experience — both good and bad

You and your top team members need to be sure your people know that the company's pursuit of innovation and continuous improvement is not limited to products and services, but also covers new processes and new and better ways of operating. Make problem solving, initiating improvement, and searching for innovations an explicit part of everyone's job. Then, define how success will be measured, how people will be rewarded, and provide training to develop their skills in problem solving and solution development. Help them turn their ideas into reality, and establish regular forums and channels of communication to uncover issues and opportunities and to develop ideas and solutions. The top team must always ask these three key questions:

- "Are we doing the right (or best) things?

- "Are we doing them in the right (or best) way?"

- "Can we be more efficient and do them in less time and with less money?"

When people raise issues and identify patterns of problems, your top team needs to create improvement teams and ask people to evaluate problems or find ways to increase the effectiveness of product development, market development, sales, operations, information systems, cultural processes, and so on. Innovation teams can also focus on specific opportunities for the future, anticipate changes and new requirements for growth, and reinvent the company's strategies, systems, or processes. All improvement and innovation teams should be cross functional, operate with input from both internal and external sources beyond the team, and be held accountable by the top team for delivering defined proposals and/or results.

"The key to our innovation is creativity, giving ourselves the freedom to think. Our Executive Team has regular brainstorming meetings to play 'what if.' We're constantly looking for new products and new ways to provide extraordinary service. This makes innovation a way of life for us. We stress it. We think about it. We keep it at a conscious level, constantly."

"To encourage cross-functional idea sharing, we have weekly meetings led by our top team that include all the managers from the next level (about 20 people). Each week an idea is formally presented and then we go to a flip chart. We write down all the pluses of the proposed idea on one side of the paper; on the other side, which we call the delta side, we write ideas for improving the proposal. We also use this process to critique projects that have just been completed; we use the same treatment for ideas about what we would do differently the next time. This simple process keeps us focused on both innovation and continuous improvement."

For more information about how the top team supports innovation, see the following box, "Vital Signs: How the Top Team Supports Continuous Innovation."

A top team that supports and encourages innovation will enable the company to continuously reinvent itself and develop new products, services, and processes to meet emerging customer needs. If your top team can anticipate the inevitable market, technology, and economic changes and manage them with innovative planning and problem solving, the company will be able to move to the next stage of growth and development. If not, it will hit the wall and stall or begin the downward spiral.

"We had one executive on our top team who consistently killed ideas, especially from people who were 'not as smart' as he was. Now, a lot of the ideas deserve to be killed — they would never make any money. But what about that one great idea that could lead to a whole wave of new growth? It is so fragile in its early form that it could die unless nurtured. This guy was excellent at many aspects of his job, but I had to get rid of him before his idea killing killed the whole company."

"Get your Executive Team to help you develop an innovation process, a process for evaluating new ideas and for deciding what's going to work and what's not going to work. Entrepreneurs are often accused of coming up with a new idea, making a unilateral decision, and telling everyone it's a done deal. You don't want to be that kind of a leader; that doesn't work with people at the top team level — or with anyone else in the organization for that matter. So develop a process for evaluating new ideas and use it."

VITAL SIGNS: HOW THE TOP TEAM SUPPORTS CONTINUOUS INNOVATION

The top team's goal is to provide all of the following so maximum innovation can thrive:

Vision. For any new opportunity, challenge, initiative, or problem, define how the ideal end result will support the company's vision.

Involvement. Solicit input and ideas for each initiative and form teams to generate creative ideas and achieve results that are critical to the company.

Information. Provide and/or encourage a steady flow of useful information, especially from the market and the customer.

Communication. Be a good two-way communicator — a succinct presenter of information and an active listener.

Empowerment. Give others the responsibility and the resources to implement plans and achieve desired results.

Creativity. Foster "out-of-the-box" thinking, make "what if" brainstorming a regular part of every meeting, and seek new and better ways to make and deliver current as well as new products and services. (See appendix D for an exercise that boosts idea generation and solution development.)

Risk taking. Encourage and reward those who take calculated risks, and take time to review lessons learned from successes as well as failures.

Customer focus. Know your target customer's business. Use feedback and ideas from external customers, especially about their competitive and strategic issues, to make informed decisions and focus efforts on delivering high value to customers.

MANAGING YOUR TOP TEAM

Your role with the top team is to be their coach and the leader who drives consensus. As the leader, you have the right and responsibility to identify critical problems, find solutions, and make the final decision. But if you've hired the right people, you will want to ask for their insights and perspectives, and take those into account before making decisions. You and the top team members need to listen respectfully to each other's explanation and definition of the problem, and then discuss the pros and cons of alternative ways of solving the problem.

Sometimes the decision will be obvious to all. Other times it will be difficult to get agreement on the definition of the problem, let alone the solution. But at some point you will need to make a decision based on the best information available, what's best for the customer, and what's best for the company. Hopefully you can achieve consensus. But even if you do not, it is imperative that all team members understand that they must support, communicate, and implement the final decision — even if they argued for and preferred another one.

Don't underestimate the importance and difficulty of your role as coach and leader. If you hire great people who are masters of their functional areas and who came highly recommended as terrific team players, your natural assumption will be that they will fit right in with your existing top team and that everything will go smoothly. Often, that is not the case. Even a team of great athletes who come together for an all-star game can have problems if they don't have effective coaching.

Being an effective coach for your top team involves mastering four skills that will build great teamwork among this group. As the team benefits from your strong guidance and develops into a powerful team, they learn how to improve their leadership of the functional and cross-functional teams they head. Great teamwork at the top filters throughout the organization as people observe the top team working together in harmony and shared commitment.

1. KEEP THE TEAM ALIGNED

Clearly, if the top team isn't aligned, the rest of the organization won't be either. So your #1 objective is to keep the top team aligned around the company's vision, mission, values, strategies, structure, and culture. Once they have agreed and committed to all parts of the plan, thousands of daily decisions can be delegated throughout the organization. Using the planning process described in chapter 6 is a critical way to foster alignment.

Frequent communication and meetings are essential to providing opportunities to uncover and hammer out any differences of opinion early on, before they have a chance to fester and cause alignment problems.

"If the top team isn't aligned, it makes everything take twice as long. You work through a process, make progress, and then watch someone run around to the front of the train and act like they're driving it. That just slows everything down. If someone isn't aligned, you need to work with him on his shortcomings, and if he's coachable and willing to change and able to learn, then he'll have an opportunity to grow with the organization. If not, then you work with the person on an opportunity outside the company and offer a severance package."

"If the top team doesn't 'get it,' there is little hope that the rest of the company will, so it is even more critical that the top team be in alignment on culture, values, and the direction of the company. It is so difficult to determine this in an interview, which is why I believe companies should always look inside first to fill management positions. As a company grows, it becomes too big for any one person to control it and make the tough decisions. If the top team doesn't work well together and have the same basis for making hard decisions, then you waste a lot of time arguing and questioning every decision."

"Whenever a decision is made, it's important that team members feel they've had a chance to present their viewpoint, as well as understand your thought process and how you came to the decision you made. We work together well as a team, and usually arrive at decisions through consensus. There are only two or three times a year where I'll say, 'No, we're not doing that. We're going to do it this way.' And I always tell them why and how I reached my decision. Then we concentrate on how to implement the decision."

The toughest part of keeping people aligned is conflict resolution, and conflicts are bound to occur if you have done what we advised earlier in this chapter: selected a team of diverse thinkers. If you don't have skills or experience in conflict resolution, you may be uncomfortable taking on this role. You'll either need to develop your capacity to resolve conflicts or rely on a trained facilitator who knows how to bring people to agreement.

2. MANAGE THE TEAM AS A GROUP, NOT AS INDIVIDUALS

In the company's early days, you probably used a "hub-and-spoke" style of leadership with you at the hub. The top team was small, and you communicated and made decisions with each member individually rather than as a group. But as the company becomes more complex and the Executive Team grows, this style of communication becomes increasingly dangerous. If you continue to work with the team members as individuals, the members will never come together as a truly cohesive unit, and they will compete with each other for your time and recognition.

Unfortunately, the hub-and-spoke style of leadership is a hard habit to break. It's very easy to continue communicating this way, and it may seem more efficient to have one-on-one meetings rather than calling everyone together for a team meeting. But leading in this way contributes to the formation of silos. When one department doesn't know what the other is doing, this leads to suspicion and mistrust.

To avoid these problems, you need to switch from one-on-one meetings to team meetings. Your job is now to coach the team, create an environment that leverages each person's skills and knowledge, and make sure team members communicate with each other directly, not just through you.

3. USE CONSTRUCTIVE FEEDBACK TO ENCOURAGE TEAMWORK

All team members must learn to be comfortable with discussing their ideas in an open forum where everyone can assess the ideas, talk about them, and think constructively about how to make it better. Learning how to engage in healthy, nonantagonistic debate on company issues requires team members to accept constructive criticism of their ideas and to provide others with feedback that is not personally destructive. Good leaders allow all ideas to be heard, explored, and critiqued. Cutting off dissent or acting as though disagreement doesn't exist discourages people from pursuing potentially breakthrough ideas.

> "We had a meeting this week where we kept going back and forth on an issue, and the team was split about what to do. I thought I knew the answer because I had sold the job, but I said, 'Let's walk through this.' We walked through it, and in the end I came to understand that the customer was no longer seeing it the way I'd originally sold the account. Our original model wasn't good anymore because our assumptions were wrong. The people who were in contact with the customer knew this, and it all became clear when

we took the time to walk through the problem and be honest with each other. By admitting I was wrong, I signaled to my team that they could admit they were wrong, too."

4. LEARN TO HOLD PRODUCTIVE MEETINGS

Everyone says they hate meetings, but what they really mean is that they hate unproductive meetings that waste time because there's no agenda and/or nothing gets resolved. Successful growth companies have teams that are skilled at managing meetings, problem solving, and making good use of people's time.

To be effective, you and your top team need to have a schedule of meetings that cover specific topics. For instance, you might want to have weekly operational meetings, monthly strategic meetings, and quarterly meetings to evaluate progress on the plan and hear reports from cross-functional teams.

You should require attendance, set agendas, accomplish the work in the time allocated, and hold everyone accountable for making the meeting a productive one. Send out prework for people to read ahead of time so they come prepared to discuss the issues on the agenda. Announce the purpose of the meeting, identify the chair, and assign roles so that someone takes notes and tracks time. List issues that are important, but that are off the agenda, on a page marked "parking lot" for later discussion. The chair needs to manage the discussion, make sure everyone who has something to contribute has a chance to talk about the issue on the agenda, call time out when discussions get too polarized, and pull people back to the main issue when the discussion is going off track.

> "At the end of our meetings, we ask people to rate three things on a scale of 1 to 5: How well did we accomplish the results we expected for this meeting, how satisfied are you with how the team worked as a group, and how satisfied are you with your participation and contribution as an individual. We also ask how we can make future meetings more effective. Making this a routine part of meeting keeps us focused on making sure we spend our time together effectively, and it's made a real positive difference. People around here now see meetings as a way to get things done rather than as a waste of time."

It's important to separate operational issues from strategic ones. Successful growth companies have separate meetings in which they focus on the vision, goals, and strategies. Day-to-day tactical matters are deliberately kept out of these sessions. A final key to productive meetings is to ask participants to evaluate the effectiveness of each meeting, and then make changes as necessary.

IDENTIFYING THE PITFALLS OF MANAGING THE TOP TEAM

Thus far, we've provided guidance about what you need to do to manage your top team. Now we'll review some common pitfalls entrepreneurs experience in leading their top teams:

ALLOWING TEAM MEMBERS TO IGNORE THEIR ROLE AS COMPANY LEADERS AND FOCUS ON THEIR FUNCTIONAL AREAS

As growth occurs, pressures build that tempt top team members to concentrate solely on their functional responsibilities. They need to add new people to their departments to keep up with customer demands, and there's a premium on getting the work done and getting it done quickly. Given these pressures to perform, the top team may be tempted to put off planning or skip a monthly strategy session because everyone is just too busy. But if you allow this to happen, soon the left hand won't know what the right hand is doing. Communication will falter, cross-functional teamwork will stop, and silos will start to form. Even in the most well-intentioned groups, distrust can creep in and walls can start to form between departments if the top team doesn't meet and talk at regular intervals. You, the leader, must make sure this does not happen. Hold your team members accountable for their six leadership responsibilities at all times.

DISMISSING TEAM CONFLICTS BECAUSE "EVERY TEAM HAS PROBLEMS"

Don't use the fact that few teams function in perfect harmony as an excuse for tolerating ongoing conflicts in your top team. Knowing how to manage conflicts, turf wars, and conflicting or hidden agendas can significantly improve the group's ability to work together as a team. This, in turn, can have an impact on teamwork throughout the organization, because the top team is a role model for all other teams. Remember that healthy dissent is good. Help team members learn how to raise issues, address and resolve conflicts as a team, and create win-win situations. Don't dismiss conflicts and problems; learn to manage them.

"When we did our planning, there were some rough spots that needed to be addressed — some personal conflicts on the Executive Team. We had one person we finally had to dismiss because he didn't match the culture of the rest of the team. Each unresolvable conflict was pretty minor, but in total these began to get in the way of progress. What was interesting was how painfully obvious it was to the consultants working with us on strategic planning that this one person was a misfit. I was certainly aware of it, but it was so obvious to them that it solidified my thinking that this really wasn't working and I had to get rid of him."

❀

"In the early days, the culture mirrored a trait I had. I grew up in Kentucky and was taught that if you don't have something good to say about someone, don't say anything at all. This was the way our culture worked for the most part too, so when people had conflicts, they didn't confront each other and try to resolve them. Instead, sides seemed to be drawn up and we'd have conflicts that affected day-to-day work but weren't out in the open. Changing our culture and insisting that people always talk to people they are disagreeing with before going to other people has made a big difference, and the company now runs much smoother. We still have conflicts, but we manage them."

NOT UNDERSTANDING WHAT CONSTITUTES REAL CROSS-FUNCTIONAL TEAMWORK

Real cross-functional interaction and feedback are actually rare in growing organizations. Your company may have an atmosphere of camaraderie in which people enjoy working together but still not have true cross-functional teamwork. Just because people get along and work well together doesn't mean they're sharing ideas and moving the company forward together. To achieve this goal, you need to establish a network of cross-functional teams that work on important issues and are held accountable, as teams, for results.

Be sure that people on these teams are truly listening to each other and giving each other feedback about ideas. This requires a healthy, innovative culture. The model for good cross-functional behavior must come from the leaders of these teams — the members of your top team. Hold them accountable for making this critical form of teamwork happen so that innovation and continuous improvement can thrive.

ALLOWING TEAM MEMBERS TO PUT THEIR DECISION-MAKING RESPONSIBILITIES BACK IN YOUR LAP

If team members are constantly asking to spend more time with you, it often means they want you to make decisions instead of making them themselves. But, if you have to make all the decisions, you'll become the bottleneck to growth! If this "upward delegation" is happening, you may need to look at your own behavior. Have you made it clear that the company is entering a new stage of growth and that you and they need to change from one-on-one meetings to top team meetings? Are you blindsiding team members by pulling back decisions after telling them they have authority to make them? Are you supporting their decisions or second-guessing them? Have you clarified at what level you are delegating (see the box "Vital Signs: Six Levels of Delegation," in chapter 5, "Retain Awesome People for Growth"), or are you abdicating your decision-making responsibility?

> "Don't make decisions for your top team. If they come to you and you make a decision for them, they'll come the next time; if they come to you and you give them some coaching, guidance, and feedback, then the next time they'll make the decision themselves. It's important to have people who thrive on autonomy and responsibility but who are also able to work collaboratively."

Entrepreneurs often find it difficult to move from individual to team management, and some are tempted to play one team member off against another. They may give an assignment to one member of the team, and the same assignment to another member and wait to see who comes up with the best idea. They forget that internal competition wastes time and energy that's needed to compete in the market, and that this kind of behavior will stunt the company's growth. You need to stop relating to team members as individuals and begin relating to them as members of your team. Make it clear to them why you are changing, clarify your expectation that team members operate as a unified group, and give them the processes and tools to do so. Review the vision and the plan they helped create and work together to develop strategies that they will all have a role in implementing. Establish a compensation and incentive structure that rewards them for the accomplishment of team goals and company growth rather than rewards them solely on the achievement of individual or departmental goals.

YOUR ROLE AS LEADER

Leading the top team is one of your most critical roles. In addition to hiring and integrating these highly talented executives, your role as top team leader includes eight responsibilities:

1. **Clarify each team member's two-hat challenge to provide company leadership as well as functional leadership.** Team members must understand they have to provide leadership to the company as well as lead their functional areas. Make sure each one understands explicitly that you will evaluate her or his performance in both roles because both "hats" are critical to the company's success.

   > "If I say to the top team, 'You are responsible for this cross-functional issue,' then we get people taking much more strategic leadership roles. If I don't tell them that, they fall into a more departmental or functional role. So it's crucial for the CEO to make people think about strategic ownership of the business."

2. **Communicate expectations about performance and values.** As leaders of the culture, top team members must be held accountable for both talking and walking the values of the company. You must be willing to let members of the top team go who violate the values or fail to meet performance expectations on a timely basis. Anything less will erode the culture needed for high growth.

3. **Establish a process that keeps the team focused on the vision, strategies, and actions to achieve growth, and on developing their staff to run their departments.** If you don't put an explicit process in place that requires the team to meet regularly to develop and refine the plan for growth, review progress, and make adjustments as needed, it simply won't get done. It's very easy to stay focused on day-to-day operations and near-term objectives rather than focus on the future. But the role of the top team is to help you plot the company's future. Hold them responsible for developing their directors and managers. Teach them to delegate appropriately.

   > "I was working late and called one of my top team members. His wife answered and told me I was crazy — it was after midnight and I should get some sleep. I was upset at first, then realized I was in total overload. I talked with my mentor and he said, 'Make a list of all the things

you need to do. And recognize that if that list doesn't change, you're going to die, because you can't keep working like this. Put a check mark next to the things that only you can do. Put an X next to those things that someone else can do if you take the time to teach him or her to do it. Then circle those things that no one knows how to do and you need to hire a new person to do. Go through that list every six months.' This sure helped me figure out how to transfer responsibilities to my top team, and I had them use the same process to figure out what they could delegate to their directors and managers and who else they needed to hire."

4. **Break down silos and functional barriers that impede innovation.** It's your job as top team leader to insist on collaboration between and among functional areas. Make sure the top team creates cross-functional teams to tackle issues with companywide implications or to solve problems that impact multiple areas of the organization. In addition, require top team members to provide written and oral reports on their departments' activities. Give team members opportunities to ask questions of each other and get clarification around various decisions and projects. Search for areas of synergy between departments. Encourage feedback from everyone on the team and all areas of the company. Help your top team members strengthen their functions, learn to delegate, and free up their time to work with you on strategic issues.

> "I set up a rule for cross-functional projects. If members of the different departments weren't there, we didn't have the meeting. We had a marketing and product meeting every week; if the marketing people weren't there, we would cancel the meeting. I required their presence and participation — no excuses. It soon became clear that this was not something they could ignore. So they began to come, and we got better at working and thinking together."

5. **Nurture new strategic ideas and initiatives that no one else owns.** Provide your top team with new ideas and information from external sources that you have discovered in your role as outside spokesperson and thought leader for the company. Encourage and support new ideas until they are ready to be transferred to a team member's area of responsibility or need to be dropped because they no longer fit the company's strategy.

6. **Instill an experimental, learning attitude and facilitate strategic skill development.** Make sure the top team is skilled in brainstorming, scenario development, experimenting, and group problem solving. Know how to lead effective decision-making sessions. Never stop learning, and encourage other team members to continually build their knowledge and skills.

7. **Establish two-way feedback mechanisms.** Insist on having a formal process for getting feedback on your performance and the team's performance. Help other members of the top team understand the value of such feedback for themselves and for their direct reports. Seek to improve your own performance. Build in processes for the top team, employees, the board, and external advisors to provide feedback on the team's strengths and areas for improvement. Create an environment that supports innovation and growth, a culture where people are encouraged to do "out of the box" thinking, provide feedback and critique each other's ideas, and develop new ways to accelerate your company's growth.

8. **Build effective teamwork and synergy.** Be aware of friction among top team members and move quickly to help them resolve conflicts. If someone is out of step with the company's values, promptly resolve the problem to preserve the team's harmony and trust. Show team members that you value them as individuals and as team members. Make sure they understand that strength comes from having a team that blends diverse experiences and viewpoints. Have them take the *BAO SCAN* at the end of this chapter. Discuss differences in scores, strengths, and weaknesses, and develop an action plan.

These responsibilities must be on your radar screen at all times. If you are not an active coach for the top team and are not constantly working to make that group stronger and better, the culture will deteriorate, business performance will falter, and growth will stall.

BIG LESSONS

1. Require top team members to be as effective in their role as company leaders as they are in leading their functional areas.

2. Recognize that improving the top team is one of your highest priorities. Add and integrate strong new members when necessary, help existing members improve their leadership skills, and constantly work to improve the group's collaboration skills.

3. Guide top team members to become great communicators, active listeners, and superb role models for the culture you're trying to build. They must also be comfortable managing continuous innovation and change.

continues

-continued

4. Be certain the top team is in alignment with the company's vision, mission, values, and strategies, and that team members keep their staffs aligned as well.

5. Understand the destructive potential of a top team member who is not in sync with the company values and take immediate steps to remedy such situations.

6. Anticipate, watch out for, and quickly eliminate functional silos. A company that operates with silos lacks the coordination and power to be agile, flexible, and innovative in achieving growth.

BAO SCAN: PRIME YOUR TEAM FOR GROWTH

Use this *SCAN** to determine how well you are priming your team for growth. Take this *BAO SCAN* yourself, and then have your top team and other key people complete it as well. Compare your responses and perceptions with theirs. Work together to identify innovative ways to strengthen the top team's ability to handle their six key areas of responsibility as leaders of the company's growth.

RATING SCALE

Use this scale to respond to each rating question

1 - - - - - 2 - - - - - 3 - - - - - 4 - - - - - 5 - - - - - 6 - - - - - 7
NEVER   *SOMETIMES*   *ALWAYS*

PART A. LEADING THE PLANNING FOR GROWTH

Effective Executive Teams paint the big picture and create a plan that builds all the requirements for growth. They then use the plan to focus and drive every individual objective throughout the company.

1. The Executive Team articulates a clear statement of the company's purpose and sets specific strategic targets that are understood throughout the company.   Rating: _____

*This BAO SCAN is adapted from Building the Executive Team as Leaders of Growth™.
© 2001, The Catlin Group.

2. The Executive Team's culture of innovation, open communication, and cross-functional collaboration supports the growth of the company. Rating: _____

3. The Executive Team's strategic plan, with annual objectives, helps achieve sustainable growth. Rating: _____

4. The Executive Team allocates resources in ways that support the company's strategic plan. Rating: _____

5. The organizational structure, processes, and incentives defined by the Executive Team hold people accountable for implementing the plan. Rating: _____

6. The Executive Team tracks the plan's milestones and metrics and continuously determines how the strategy needs to evolve. Rating: _____

7. The Executive Team uses external input about market opportunities and customer needs when making decisions. Rating: _____

8. The Executive Team is proactive about making fundamental changes that will lead to the next level of growth. Rating: _____

PART B. LEADING FOR ALIGNMENT

Effective Executive Teams create clarity and alignment throughout the organization through frequent, consistent, and systematic communication and involvement of staff.

1. Executive Team members are "on the same page" with each other on the strategic plan for growth and the cultural values of the company. Rating: _____

2. The Executive Team communicates the strategic plan for growth and cultural values, and uses them to focus and drive every work group and staff member. Rating: _____

3. Executive Team members coordinate cross-functional input and feedback in getting the work done. Rating: _____

4. The Executive Team seeks the ideas and involvement of staff in raising issues, solving problems, and making decisions. Rating: _____

5. Decisions and changes made at Executive Team meetings are communicated throughout the organization.   Rating: _____

PART C. LEADING THE CULTURE

Effective Executive Teams define and spread the innovative culture required for growth. They work together in ways that mirror and support the culture.

1. Executive Team members mirror, support, and contribute to the desired culture by their individual actions.   Rating: _____

2. Executive Team members work together as a unit in ways that model and reinforce the culture.   Rating: _____

3. The Executive Team keeps the staff linked closely to markets and customers.   Rating: _____

4. Executive Team members hold each other and their staff accountable for living the cultural values.   Rating: _____

5. Executive Team members develop innovative strategies, ideas, and solutions to problems with one another.   Rating: _____

6. The Executive Team promotes open communication and cross-functional collaboration throughout the company.   Rating: _____

PART D. ATTRACTING AND RETAINING AWESOME PEOPLE

Effective Executive Teams are accountable for using processes to hire, motivate, and keep awesome people who will drive the company's growth.

1. Executive Team members use agreed-on criteria for hiring to ensure "fit" with values and culture, along with competency and relevant experience for the job.   Rating: _____

2. Executive Team members are effective in recruiting, interviewing, and selecting awesome people who are "smarter" than they.   Rating: _____

3. The Executive Team orients and integrates new hires so they understand and feel motivated to achieve the company's vision and goals.   Rating: _____

4. The Executive Team challenges, motivates, and develops awesome people so they want to stay with the company.   Rating: _____

PART E. MANAGING TEAM PITFALLS

Effective Executive Teams work hard to avoid the pitfalls common to all teams as well as the pitfalls that are unique to their team.

1. Executive Team members step out of their roles as leaders and advocates of functions to consider the needs of the company as a whole.   Rating: _____

2. The Executive Team spends its time on important strategic issues that affect the growth of the company.   Rating: _____

3. The Executive Team manages its discussions, meetings, and agendas to address the company's top priorities.   Rating: _____

4. The Executive Team evaluates itself as a team and identifies and addresses problems in the way it works together.   Rating: _____

PART F. LEARNING FROM EACH OTHER

Effective Executive Teams leverage their differences and learn from each other.

1. The Executive Team uses and learns from the different perspectives and skills of its members to increase its own effectiveness.   Rating: _____

2. Executive Team members ask for and give feedback to one another on business activities as well as cultural behaviors.   Rating: _____

3. Executive Team members listen and respond to one another and respect each other's unique perspectives.   Rating: _____

4. Executive Team member interactions are characterized by mutual respect, trust, and commitment to one another's success.   Rating: _____

PART G. SUMMARY QUESTIONS

1. Overall, the Executive Team is cohesive and effective in carrying out its leadership role.   Rating: _____

2. Individual members effectively manage their functional units.   Rating: _____

3. Individual members understand how to work effectively with each other as members of the Executive Team.   Rating: _____

4. The CEO is effective in leading and managing this team.   Rating: _____

SCORE SUMMARY AND INTERPRETATION

A Rating Score of **7** in any area indicates this is a prime area of strength that will facilitate and support the company's growth. Scores of **5** and **6** indicate considerable strength in these areas, but you will want to consider making incremental improvements to increase the score. A score of **4** is a cause for worry. A rating of "Sometimes" indicates a lack of consistency that sends conflicting signals to employees and inhibits growth; thus significant improvements will be needed. Scores of **3 or below** are big red flags indicating areas or behaviors that hinder the company's growth and require your immediate attention.

RESULTS ANALYSIS

Look back over the *BAO SCAN: Prime Your Team for Growth:*

1. List three statements that you rated the highest. Choose those you feel are key strengths and contribute most to the success of the company.

A. _____

B. _____

C. _____

2. List three statements that received the lowest rating. Choose those you feel are the most critical weaknesses and should be targeted for improvement.

A. _____

B. _____

C. _____

3. Write three statements that define your priorities for change (for example, capitalize more on the strengths or improve the weaknesses).

A. _____

B. _____

C. _____

4. List three things our company could do to implement these changes.

A. _____

B. _____

C. _____

ACTION PLAN

Recognize what you and your company are doing well and celebrate! Think about what you have done that enabled you to achieve these great results and how that can be applied to your weaknesses. But, do not overlook areas that need improvement or think they will improve on their own over time. Use these steps to develop your Action Plan for Improvement:

1. Ask your top team to complete the *BAO SCAN: Prime Your Team for Growth* and the Results Analysis. You may also want others in the company to complete the *SCAN* in order to get more comprehensive feedback.

2. Meet with your top team to:

- Compare and contrast your ratings on various statements with their ratings, as well as areas you have identified as strengths with those needing work.

- If applicable, discuss the reasons why their responses are different from yours.

- Agree on areas for improvement or change; be as specific as possible.

3. Prioritize those areas that must be addressed and that will make the biggest difference. Develop them into Action Plans for Improvement.

4. Get consensus on the Action Plans and the resources and budgets needed to make the necessary changes.

- For each Action Plan, specify the goal, desired outcomes, steps to take, team members responsible for implementation, resources required, key measures of success, and time frames for achieving the goal and tracking results.

- Assign a cross-functional team to implement each Action Plan. Include members from different departments who will be affected by the changes. Members should have the necessary skills and insights to accomplish the plan. Identify a team leader and/or executive sponsor who will be held accountable for managing the team, tracking progress, and achieving the desired goal.

5. Communicate the Action Plans for Improvement to everyone in the company. Get involvement, input, and feedback.

6. Hold yourself and others accountable for achieving the new goals and milestones.

7. After a designated period of time (three to six months), evaluate progress, identify new or emerging problems or opportunities, set new goals, make new team assignments (if appropriate), and take action. In a year, retake the *BAO SCAN: Prime Your Team for Growth* and repeat Steps 1 through 6 as required. Remember: Continuous assessment, action, and improvement are essential to building an awesome organization that is strong enough to support continuous growth.

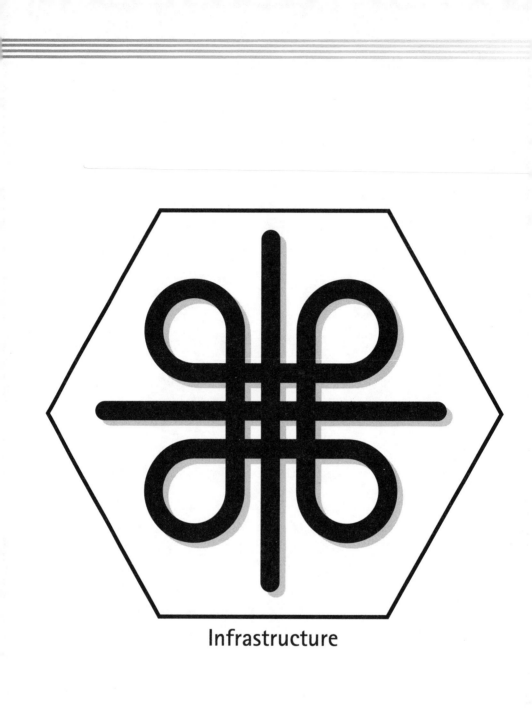

Infrastructure

CHAPTER 8

ESTABLISH YOUR INFRASTRUCTURE FOR GROWTH

"I had a meeting with my top team and described how I hated processes and procedures and didn't want to have anything to do with them. Then my new VP said, 'I've been here for two weeks, and I've spent all my time trying to figure out how we do things around here. I finally sketched out what appeared to be a couple of procedures and asked some of the staff to review what I had written and give me feedback. All of them came back within a day and thanked me, said it was about time we had some systems and procedures — it would make it much easier to explain to new people how things get done.' That's when it hit me that we were growing too fast to keep winging it. My VP convinced me we needed to develop some policies and procedures so people don't have to keep making them up each time. This has cut some of the cycle time and helped us be more consistent about how we do things."

Infrastructure, the fifth element of an awesome organization, helps a company develop tremendous forward momentum by organizing and streamlining the work so people can produce the best possible results with minimal time and effort. Many entrepreneurs don't understand how having a good infrastructure supports productivity and growth. They claim to hate organization charts, processes, and procedures, or say they don't have time to develop them. But what really stops many of them from instituting standardized processes is a fear that this will signal the onset of a big company bureaucracy. In other cases, entrepreneurs do see the need for a better compensation system, a budgeting system, or a more rigorous orientation process but don't recognize how these individual components fit together in the larger system of highly interconnected pieces that we call the infrastructure for growth.

Successful leaders know the value of a clear organizational structure that describes how the company functions and a standardized set of processes that define how things get done. A strong infrastructure enables people to determine who is responsible for what (which creates accountability and responsibility), what needs to be done (which facilitates execution on plans and strategies), and how they are expected to do the work (which reinforces the culture and values). As you read this chapter, you'll recognize issues discussed in the chapters on culture, attracting and retaining people, and planning. All of these processes and procedures are interrelated. They cannot stand alone, but need to be mutually reinforcing if you're going to achieve your larger organizational goal of building an awesome organization.

> "Last year we grew over 50 percent to surpass the $50-million level. It seemed like all of a sudden every middle manager in our company of 250 people was screaming that we needed more systematic processes for hiring, budgeting, planning, innovating, communicating, and prioritizing. They also wanted much more autonomy from the senior executives to run with their piece of the company to make it grow. In fact, they ranked the lack of infrastructure as the number-one potential inhibitor of our success. I thought they would be more worried about products, technology, and marketing. I wasn't surprised that employees wanted more structure and processes, but the suddenness and vehemence of the reaction was quite striking and was probably exacerbated by our fast growth."

A company cannot survive rapid growth if it does not have a good infrastructure. Chaos, lack of focus, duplication of effort, and confusion are indicators that you don't have good systems in place. All of these problems drain people's energy and create negative attitudes. In contrast, a strong infrastructure institutionalizes the mission, vision, values, and culture in the organization, and makes them come alive. Work becomes easier and more streamlined, and people don't waste energy and time trying to figure out how to get things done. This greater efficiency and coordination enables your company to move faster and be more agile and flexible.

RED FLAGS: SIGNALS THAT THE INFRASTRUCTURE NEEDS WORK

The following Red Flags are signals that your organization's infrastructure is not functioning well:

- You change the organizational structure over and over again.

- People don't understand why you're changing the structure, and you don't have a good rationale to give them.

- You don't seem to get better results — even after you change the structure.

- You can't answer when someone asks how the new structure supports the strategy.

- 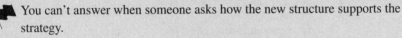 Delays are routine; critical milestones are missed, and timetables have to be revised.

- 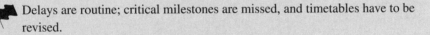 There is no consistency in how work gets done; everybody does things differently.

- People are frustrated because they feel as if they're constantly reinventing the wheel.

- The left hand doesn't know what the right hand is doing.

- It's harder to get work done than it used to be and everything takes longer.

- 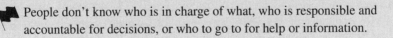 People say, "I thought *they* were the ones responsible for that."

- People don't know who is in charge of what, who is responsible and accountable for decisions, or who to go to for help or information.

In addition, a good infrastructure helps define the differences between your company and some other company. For example, when hiring someone, you can point to specific policies for training, compensation, and other infrastructure elements that make your company more attractive than another company that is competing for the same awesome person.

VITAL SIGNS: THE RIGHT ORGANIZATIONAL STRUCTURE FOR YOUR COMPANY

No single organizational structure is right for every company. The structure should grow out of your strategy for growth, and this will change over time. Therefore, you'll need to redraw your organization chart as you grow. Regardless of whether you organize by functions or by business units, or want centralized or decentralized control, the organizational structure you adapt should always:

 Fit the growth strategy, making it easy to implement.

 Be connected cross-functionally by a network of teams that spreads throughout the organization like a spider's web.

 Be as flat and simple as possible.

 Enable decision making to occur at levels where people are closest to customers.

 Facilitate communication up, down, and across the company.

 Enable the formation of small work units to get work done and produce breakthrough innovation.

 Keep the customer at the center of the organization. Be sure that everyone stays focused on customer needs and expectations.

"I had to learn that an organization can be designed. It's a dynamic system. You have to think about how it feels to be a person working within that organization. What works? What doesn't work, and so forth. Building a great place to work and focusing on the organizational details as an end in itself has become my second passion in life — which certainly wasn't the case when I first got started. We'd probably have been more successful, quicker, if I'd focused on it sooner."

THREE CRITICAL SETS OF PROCESSES

You need to put in place three sets of processes to build the awesome organization: (1) processes for managing and leading people, (2) processes for planning and alignment, and (3) processes for management and control. Because this book is focused on organization building, we will only be describing the processes and procedures required to build an organization. In addition, you will need a set of well-defined processes for product development, acquiring and retaining customers, marketing and brand development, order processing, and shipping — and more — to get the work done. If your organizational infrastructure processes are working well, they will support these other critical processes and help the work flow more smoothly. That's why it's important to have teams working on all the infrastructure processes to continually refine and improve them, just as you have teams working on other top priority issues, such as new products, customer service, and sales channels.

Our intent in describing these three sets of processes is to provide a high-level checklist you can use to gauge whether your infrastructure includes all the interrelated processes necessary to support growth. As you read this chapter, you will find that we've already discussed many of the individual elements of the infrastructure in other chapters, but this checklist shows how everything links together to form a cohesive, efficient organization that will support rapid growth. For more information about how to build each infrastructure element, visit www.entreworld.org, a Web site for entrepreneurs developed by the Kauffman Center for Entrepreneurial Leadership.

> "Most entrepreneurs are running from something, and they are trying to prove something. Often they are running from bureaucracy and hope to prove that it doesn't have to be that way in their venture. But there is a big difference between process and bureaucracy. Processes and systems are critical to building a sustainable business of any size. It is a balancing act. You want people who have the core understanding of the business to have the freedom to be flexible, but you don't want people constantly changing the way they do every part of their job. Process is all about repetition and fine-tuning, so people can really learn the best and most efficient ways to do their tasks."

VITAL SIGNS: PROCESSES THAT WORK

In order to build the proper infrastructure, you need to ensure that:

- The processes are written down and people understand them and acknowledge their value in streamlining the organization's work.

- Employees throughout the organization know and use the same processes and are able to describe them to new people.

- People know who in the organization is responsible for which processes.

- The people who are responsible for a process provide training and support so employees know how to use the process and know where to turn when they need information or help.

"If you don't have policies, procedures, and standards, then every decision has to be escalated — to you or the top team. Good policies and standards allow the organization to run on autopilot, so you can focus your time and energy on the strategic, rather than operational, decisions. The more you do that, the faster you can grow. Having salary grids for Human Resources, a forecasting process that works, a legal contract process that minimizes risk — those are the kinds of things that make an organization more efficient and better able to work."

Understanding the relationship among and between the three sets of processes described here is key. Your infrastructure needs to be viewed as a whole system, not as individual parts. For example, if you improve your recruiting processes and attract more awesome people, that's great. But, your hard work on recruitment might not matter if those new awesome people get off to a terrible start because you put them through the same inadequate orientation process you've used in the past. Recognize that you'll need an across-the-board approach to improve all parts of the infrastructure so that the elements strongly support each other.

MANAGING AND LEADING PEOPLE

"Certainly I am not involved in every hiring loop, but I do stay involved in the hiring. For instance, I meet with groups of prospective employees who have been through initial interviews and have been identified as people we want to hire. I get 20 people in a room, and we talk about our values and our vision. This works really well, and it says a lot about our culture when the CEO takes time to meet with a group of candidates. It also sends a message to our managers about how important I think good hiring is."

"We have a buddy program for new employees that works really well. We also send people gifts to their homes before they start working here, and that makes an impression on the whole family."

"Cross-functional teams are important because they bring perspectives that any one person from a single area can't bring alone. When a team makes a decision together, there is more likelihood that it will work because all have a stake in the decision and want it to work. This doesn't mean that you need a team for every decision, but you do for the important ones. Teams enable you to get more input, make better decisions, and get buy-in across the company."

PROCESS FOR ATTRACTING, RECRUITING, SELECTING, AND HIRING AWESOME PEOPLE

As we discussed in chapter 4, "Attract Awesome People for Growth," your company's future depends on finding self-motivated, awesome people who can provide the innovative ideas, passion, and commitment that drive growth. To achieve this goal, you need to avoid an ad hoc hiring process that really is no process at all. Develop a well-defined hiring process, and then make sure everyone follows it. Develop job profiles and use objective criteria to identify the best technical and cultural fit for jobs. Train all managers to follow the same processes, use behavioral interviewing, and check references. Involve the right people in the hiring process, carefully screen for the right individuals, and hire selectively to fit your standards.

PROCESS FOR ORIENTATION AND INTEGRATION

Your goal in developing an orientation and integration process is to get new hires up to speed so they can be productive and immersed in the culture as quickly as possible. This requires that you have a formalized process to introduce people to the company's mission, vision, values, goals, and strategies, as well as their own jobs. You also need a process that enables them to learn about their jobs by interviewing others and by participating in boot camps or workshops to learn and practice the skills that will help them succeed in the company.

Process for performance management, review, and development

All employees want to know what's expected of them, the criteria for success and failure, how their performance will be measured and rewarded, requirements for promotion, and what kind of investment the company is willing to make in their personal and professional development. Managers need to be taught to follow a defined performance management process, to work with employees to develop a set of mutual expectations and goals with high standards of performance, and to show employees how their individual goals and the company's strategies and values are mutually reinforcing. The process should also require managers to provide regular feedback and coaching, review performance according to specified criteria, and develop plans for the personal and professional development of their people.

In many organizations, employee evaluations have been transformed from the dreaded once-a-year event to vital tools for the development of awesome people. Some companies have moved to quarterly performance reviews, and many use the best practices method of "360° reviews," in which managers ask employees to assess their own performance, and ask peers, staff, and other managers to provide input as well. Because performance on cross-functional teams is an integral part of an individual's job, you also need to get feedback from the leader(s) of any cross-functional teams the employee has worked on. Use all this information to assess an employee's performance, and then sit down with her or him and discuss the roles and responsibilities of the position, how the employee performed and what's expected of her or him in the next quarter (or year), and identify what the employee needs (education and training, people, budget, or other resources) in order to perform at or above expectation.

Process for continuous learning

Your organization needs defined processes for mentoring, coaching, and training that develop the skills essential to support growth. The following skills must become your company's core competencies if you want to grow: staying close to market/customers; learning how to learn; and encouraging creativity, innovation, and problem solving. In addition to learning these skills, people need to know it's their responsibility to gather new information, develop new goals, plan, experiment with new ideas, learn from each other, and learn from successes and failures. Your continuous learning process should include regular forums and channels where people can share their experiences and knowledge with other employees.

In addition, you need to make a conscious effort to develop your managers and offer courses or send them to programs that will develop their management skills.

They need to learn to manage people, resources, and change. They need to be able to plan, budget, and delegate appropriately. They need to learn how to guide and coach their people to perform at the highest levels, and what to do about those who are not meeting expectations. They need to know how to be great team players as well as team leaders.

PROCESS FOR DEVELOPING EFFECTIVE TEAMS

Another core competency of growth companies is teamwork. Your company needs a process for developing a network of close-knit, high-performance teams that operate throughout the organization. Identify company priorities for teams to tackle, focus teams on creating a win for the company, and set guidelines for team effectiveness that are used throughout the organization. Everyone should participate in one or more teams beyond their functional area. This will facilitate the implementation of plans, better decision making, conflict resolution, and camaraderie throughout the organization.

PROCESS FOR COMPENSATION, REWARDS, AND RECOGNITION

Compensation was discussed in chapter 5, "Retain Awesome People for Growth." The guiding principle in developing a compensation system is to make sure that it rewards employees for the performance and behavior you want in your organization — reward people for acting in ways that are consistent with the company's values and compensate them for achieving results that support company goals. Compensation should be based on the achievement of company, team, and individual results. Start with a salary base at or slightly below the industry average, benefits and a variable based on performance, and then add bonuses and other incentives, as appropriate. In addition, develop nonmonetary mechanisms to recognize and reinforce the desired values, behaviors, and performance.

PROCESS FOR SUCCESSION PLANNING

Entrepreneurs often overlook the need to plan for the promotion or departure of a key executive. Having a succession plan can make the difference between floundering for weeks or months versus promoting or bringing in a new person without missing a beat. The process for developing your succession plan starts with listing all your key people and the options for replacing each person if he or she were to be promoted or leave the organization.

Your first task is to list internal candidates who could fill each position immediately — or who might be able to fill it if they were coached, mentored, or received more education or training. (Be sure to review the performance development plans for these people to make sure they are receiving the coaching and mentoring needed for their development.) Then, list any external candidates you've met whom you'd like to interview if an opening occurred for a specific position. Finally, identify recruiters who could help you find candidates with the skills and values you will need. Review the succession plan as needed, but at least once a quarter, and add new internal or external candidates to the list who might be able to take over key positions.

PROCESS FOR TERMINATION

You must have well-defined processes for dealing with people who aren't performing well or whose behavior does not match the values of the company. Managers need training on how to handle various kinds of performance problems, and they need support when they have to deal with one. The performance review process described in chapter 5 provides a mechanism to identify and address performance problems. Do not ignore performance problems in hopes that they will go away or that performance will improve. Address the problem with the employee and develop a performance improvement plan. The process should include documentation of attempts to discuss, coach, and turn around poor performance or values conflicts, and any improvements in performance.

If performance does not improve after feedback and coaching are provided, you need a process that describes how to formalize and develop a termination plan. Remember to analyze all terminations to uncover root causes and determine whether the problems are due to poor hiring decisions, failure to give adequate performance feedback, or some other reason that needs to be addressed and improved on in the future.

PLANNING AND ALIGNMENT

"You want to design a participative organization. Communication needs to be top down from you and your managers, and cascade throughout the organization — but it also has to be bottom up. There are tons of people in your organization who have ideas about how things could be or should be operating. You need to capture all of that creativity, all those ideas, and engage people so they understand what the issues are at the corporate level. Then, have them develop the plans and activities and momentum within the department and in the cross-functional teams."

"Since we implemented daily team huddles and weekly one-on-one meetings between employees and managers, the company has been in a great rhythm where communication is flowing, issues arise, get captured, and get resolved. It's amazing how many types of communications are needed to keep everyone current. Sometimes I hear a comment that we have 'too many meetings,' and then a comment like 'I don't know about that.' It's so easy for things to fall between the cracks if we are not vigilant about keeping everyone updated. The one-to-one meetings provide a time for employees to talk with managers, be accountable for their actions last week, and review their plan for this week. I'm amazed when I ask friends who work in other companies how often they meet with their manager and they say once or twice a month. How do they stay on track? How can they be expected to stay on track?"

PROCESS FOR PLANNING

As we noted in chapter 6, "Create Your Plan for Growth," everyone needs to have a clear understanding of the company's mission, vision, and core values, as well as its market position and opportunity. This needs to drive all functional and cross-functional planning, including planning for sales, marketing, product development, operations, hiring, and people development. The company needs to establish an annual cycle for planning and needs to schedule annual, quarterly, monthly, and weekly meetings during which the top team develops, tracks, evaluates, and refines the company's written plan. The planning process should require input from all constituencies as the plan is developed and tracked. In addition, it should include well-defined mechanisms for communicating the plan throughout the organization and getting feedback from all areas.

Each department and cross-functional team needs a defined process for developing its own plan and needs to make sure that its plan is aligned with and supports the overall company plan. In addition, you need to develop good departmental and cross-functional communications processes so everyone on the team can participate in problem solving and is informed about progress toward goals.

PROCESS FOR MARKET AND CUSTOMER INFORMATION

You must have processes that enable everyone in the organization to understand who the customer/potential customer is and what he or she needs or values the most. Make use of market intelligence data to track competitive trends in your target customer's industry. Encourage your employees to identify customers' problems and provide solutions even before customers articulate their needs. Develop a process for compiling and disseminating customer and market information, and provide ways for everyone in the organization to review, analyze, and learn from competitive trends data. Always review your decisions and plans from the perspective of current and future customers, and make adjustments as needed.

Staying close to the customer and having effective information-gathering processes help your company build strong customer relationships, stay focused on innovation, deliver products and services that satisfy existing customers, and attract new customers.

PROCESS FOR COMMUNICATION

In order to make good decisions and do their best work, employees need clear and accurate information. Develop a companywide communications plan to ensure that information moves quickly up, down, and across the organization. Make members of the top team responsible for implementing and overseeing this plan. Use regular meetings, special meetings, e-mails, voice mails, memos, and written or electronic newsletters to provide open and honest information about business realities, issues, changes, successes, and new goals. All these will help keep your employees aligned with the plan and focused on the company's goals.

PROCESS FOR CONTINUOUS INNOVATION AND IMPROVEMENT

Everyone in the company must understand that their job includes making incremental improvements as well as searching for breakthrough innovations. Put processes in place to get people focused on exploring new ideas and solutions, improving what they are now doing, simplifying the handoff of ideas from one group to another, measuring and keeping score, and learning from experience. Assign "innovation teams" to focus on specific opportunities for the future, anticipate changes and new requirements for growth, and recommend ways to reinvent the company's strategies or operations. Charter "improvement teams" to evaluate and find ways to improve the efficiency and effectiveness of current processes, products, or market activities. These cross-functional teams will need to operate with input from both internal and external sources and should be held accountable for delivering defined proposals and/or results.

PROCESS FOR MEASUREMENT

Determine performance standards and track key performance indicators that signal how your company is performing. At a minimum, you need to measure and track financial health, customer satisfaction, and employee satisfaction against a set of standards that you develop for your company or that are industry standards. In addition to establishing metrics in these three areas, decide what other variables you should track that have a major impact on your company's health and growth rate.

Develop some standards against which to measure performance on these variables, and then regularly track performance using these indicators. Highly successful companies measure everything they can, develop benchmarks, note variances, and check into the reasons for those variances.

For example, review cash flow projections and check into why the expenses over a two-month period were way over or under projection. Did customers pay late? Did products get shipped sooner or later than planned? Did customers return a product because it was defective? Did your vendor spend half as long and charge half as much as you'd planned because he or she is behind schedule developing that new software you needed six months ago? These different explanations for the variance indicate different problems in the organization that someone needs to investigate because they will have consequences for the rest of the organization.

Here's another example. When you see that the numbers of telephone transactions completed per minute is decreasing, you ask, why. Are the transactions more complicated, hence taking longer — if so, why? Is the staff taking longer to chat with customers, hence requiring training in more efficient telephone conversations? Or, do you need more staff to handle an increasing workload?

And, don't forget that measuring performance against a baseline gives you an opportunity to spot and reward high performance. For example, you need to know the ratio of sales calls required to land a contract or numbers of months, on average, it requires to develop a lead into a paying customer. If you don't know this, you won't be able to develop staffing plans, know how many salespersons you need to hire, or how to make reasonable cash flow projections. So when you see that your salespeople are able to land a contract in half the time, or convert a lead to a contract in four months rather than six, that's cause to celebrate — and to have them share what they've learned so that everyone else can use that learning to decrease the sales cycle time. If you don't measure, you won't know how well you are doing, how fast you'll run out of cash, or when employees are turning in exceptional performances.

If you need some help with financial benchmarking, check out the financial benchmarking tool at the Kauffman Center for Entrepreneurial Leadership. (See Kauffman Business EKG at www.businessekg.com.) It will provide a comprehensive assessment of your company's financial "vital signs." You will discover insights about your company's financial health and how you compare to the "best of the class" in your industry. The assessment requires only a few minutes and will give you ideas and strategies for improving your company's long-term financial health.

Regardless of what tools you use, identify key ratios and numbers that you can track against a baseline or benchmark. Like signals on your car's dashboard, they will help you know whether your organization's engine is running smoothly and taking you where you want to go. If a red light comes on, if performance is over or under the standard, pay attention, check into the reason for the deviation, and make adjustments as needed.

In addition to companywide metrics, each department and project team should have its own metrics and accountability for measuring performance against a standard. For example, customer service might measure the number of complaints, by day or week or season, and the time it takes to resolve each complaint. Finance might measure the number of days it requires to collect receivables — or process payables. Manufacturing might want to measure the time it takes to process an order and send a product to the customer. Choose your performance standards carefully and make sure everyone understands which numbers are being tracked and why they are critical. Then, hold your top team and employees accountable for achieving or exceeding the standards and provide incentives and rewards for doing so.

PROCESS FOR POLICY DEVELOPMENT AND IMPLEMENTATION

From one perspective, policies are the "rights" and "responsibilities" of employees who are productive and committed. They need to be worded positively and be based on the premise that each individual has the ability and desire to perform well and succeed in his or her job. If you have used the processes we described in chapters 4 and 5, you will need fewer policies than if you have hired bodies for slots and have a lot of employees who don't match the values or culture, and/or are not performing.

Most employees want to do a good job when they come to work. You only need to give them a few parameters, make sure you don't create roadblocks, and let them do their work. Policies should provide a few critical guidelines that are proactive, positive, designed to support the culture, and help people run the business efficiently and effectively.

Think carefully about how to write your employee handbook and policy manual. Describe the behavior you want, rather than the rules that govern that behavior. Start with the mission and values and indicate how each policy will help people contribute to them. Make sure the handbook is clearly written, useful, and easily accessible; develop it into a tool that employees enjoy using.

MANAGEMENT AND CONTROL

"Tracking and knowing how to measure the financial and operating results in your business is as essential as knowing how to keep score in an athletic event. We have more statistics on every aspect of individual and team performance in baseball and basketball than the inventors of the games ever imagined, but we often overlook the importance of similar measurements in our business."

PROCESS FOR BUDGETING AND TRACKING

Having completed the strategic plan and identified your financial targets regarding sales, revenue, and profitability, you should then quantify the targets and develop the budget. Examples of targets include head count, unit sales, square feet, or average training expenditure per employee. Budgets are estimates of the resources needed to accomplish specific goals such as launching a product, conducting R&D, achieving a certain level of sales, or providing information technology to all employees. They are also estimates of revenue expected, based on an investment of money and employees' time. Think carefully about the return you want on that investment. Make sure that everyone understands that budgets specify the resources allocated to enable individuals, departments, and the company to achieve the plan. Base them on a set of assumptions about the future and the company's ability to control the future. Hold your managers accountable for estimating costs and revenues. Good budgeting systems are critical to the health and development of a growing company. They provide the financial road map to achieving the strategic plan.

Use the budget as a tool to track performance. Budget reports will enable you to monitor results and follow up on variances such as revenue above or below plan, or cost overruns. Use these budget reports to ask the important "who, what, when, how, and why" questions, seek answers, find solutions, and make midcourse corrections as needed.

PROCESS FOR FINANCIAL MANAGEMENT AND CAPITAL ACQUISITION

The financial management process is typically focused on generating revenue, controlling expenditures, and managing cash flow. But growth companies need more money than they are usually able to generate internally, so processes for raising money need to be developed as well. Budgets will enable you to control expenditures and project revenues, but a high-growth company will generally need more money than the company itself can generate or the founders can provide — unless you are willing to invest considerable personal wealth. Debt financing can help smooth out your cash flow, but understand that banks do not provide the capital you need to grow. That's not their role, and unsecured debt is too risky for them. So you need to find growth capital from other sources. Develop processes to search for strategic partners, angel investors, perhaps even venture capitalists who can add knowledge as well as financial capital to your company. Then, when you find them, conduct your own due diligence to identify, then screen potential investors.

Bankers, lawyers, and accountants are all likely to know angel investors and local venture capitalists. Talk with your banker about your plans for the company and what kind of capital you need for growth, and then ask her or him to provide suggestions. Do the same with your lawyer and accountant. They will often be able to point you to formal or informal "bands of angels," individuals who invest in companies alone, or in groups. Local incubator directors may also be a good source of names, as well as directors of entrepreneurship centers at nearby universities. Ask other growth entrepreneurs how they are financing their growth, and learn from their positive and negative experiences. Think about companies who are vendors or customers of yours who might have a strategic interest in the success of your company. Outline your pitch on why and how their success is dependent on your success, then talk with them about providing financing or investing in your company. Go to www.entreworld.org for more ideas about financing your growth.

You'll need to provide a different "face" to your company depending on which of these funding sources you approach. Banks will want to know that you are a safe bet and have enough assets or collateral to pay back any loans they might provide. Angel investors will be as interested in you, the leader of the company, and may check to see whether you are coachable. Venture capitalists will try to decide if your company can provide a 10-fold return on their investment, and whether you can manage that kind of growth or need to be replaced. Strategic partners will check you out as a business partner and possibly as a potential acquisition. Recognize that all these sources of financing will ask different questions and will be measuring their return on investment from different perspectives. Develop a process that enables you to respond to each of them promptly with accurate information. Choose carefully. Your decision about how to finance your company may well determine your growth rate and possibly your personal future with the company.

PROCESS FOR INFORMATION TECHNOLOGY (IT) AND SUPPORT

Your information technology strategy should be tied to your growth strategy. Make sure you have the hardware, software, telecommunications, and networking support needed to underpin your anticipated growth. Get the best computer and communications systems you can afford and train people to use them to greatest advantage.

Involve key managers in the design of the financial systems and other management information systems. Find out what information they need and what are the keys to their success now, and in the future. Get their input in the design of the reports you want them to review and use for decision making, and then figure out how to get the data they need from internal or external sources. Expect them to do the same with managers working for them so that critical information flows to all levels.

PROCESS FOR FACILITIES MANAGEMENT

Your facilities must also support the strategic plan. It's very important to provide working facilities that will enable people to be productive and succeed. Provide them with the tools, equipment, and physical environment that reflect the desired culture and make it possible for them to do their best work. Light and airy surroundings with clean and comfortable workspaces and plenty of meeting areas for teams will improve productivity and support the success of your business. Develop processes for determining whether you have enough space for your people, whether the facilities are clean, safe, and comfortable, and whether other on-site amenities — for example, more parking, child care on the premises, a dining room, an exercise room — would enable you to retain awesome people and facilitate peak performance.

YOUR ROLE AS LEADER

Do not allow your fear of bureaucracy to blind you to the need to develop a solid infrastructure to support growth. Your responsibilities regarding your company's infrastructure are as follows:

- Develop an organizational structure that supports the strategy of your company's growth plan.

- Review the structure to see if it needs to be altered when you enter a new stage of growth or when your growth strategy changes.

- Make sure your top team members develop processes that will build the organization and enable people to work more efficiently and effectively.

- Hold top team members accountable for continually improving the infrastructure.

BIG LESSONS

1. Infrastructure is not synonymous with bureaucracy.

2. Develop an organizational structure that is appropriate for your company. Recognize that it will change as your company grows and develops.

3. Understand that sound policies and procedures simplify work and allow employees to work more efficiently and effectively, which enables the company to move faster.

4. Standardize processes across the company. Everyone in the company should be operating under the same set of policies and procedures.

5. A good infrastructure is essential for growth.

6. Your organizational structure must change as your strategy changes and as your company grows.

BAO SCAN: ESTABLISH YOUR INFRASTRUCTURE TO SUPPORT GROWTH

Use this *SCAN* to determine how well you are building the infrastructure to support growth. Take this *BAO SCAN* yourself, and then have your top team and other key people complete it as well. Compare your responses and perceptions with theirs. Work together to identify innovative ways to design and develop the organizational structure and processes for growth.

RATING SCALE

Use this scale to respond to each rating question

1 - - - - - 2 - - - - - 3 - - - - - 4 - - - - - 5 - - - - - 6 - - - - - 7

NEVER   *SOMETIMES*   *ALWAYS*

PART A. OUR ORGANIZATIONAL STRUCTURE

1. Fits the growth strategy.   Rating: _____

2. Is connected cross-functionally by a network of teams.   Rating: _____

3. Is as flat and simple as feasible.   Rating: _____

4. Encourages communication to flow up, down, and across.   Rating: _____

5. Has small work units for maximum innovation and efficiency.   Rating: _____

6. Is customer-centric with everyone at all levels focused on identifying and meeting customer needs and wants.   Rating: _____

PART B. OUR PROCESSES FOR MANAGING AND LEADING PEOPLE

1. Our processes for attracting, recruiting, selecting, and hiring awesome people:

a. Enable us to find self-motivated people who fit with the company's vision, values, and culture.   Rating: _____

b. Enable us to hire self-motivated people who fit with the company's vision, values, and culture.   Rating: _____

2. Our processes for orientation and integration help new employees:

a. Understand the mission, values, vision, goals, culture, and leadership.   Rating: _____

b. Get involved and engaged as active participants soon after joining the company.   Rating: _____

3. Our performance management, review, and development processes:

a. Clarify expectations and enables us to set mutual goals.   Rating: _____

b. Encourage coaching and performance feedback.   Rating: _____

c. Support delegation.   Rating: _____

d. Help employees create personal development plans.   Rating: _____

4. Our processes for continuous learning:

    a. Enable employees to learn from successes and failures. Rating: _____

    b. Help employees develop personally and acquire job skills.   Rating: _____

5. Our processes for developing effective teams:

    a. Help employees be effective team members.   Rating: _____

    b. Develop a network of close-knit, high-performance teams.   Rating: _____

6. Our processes for succession planning:

    a. Enable us to identify potential candidates for each key position.   Rating: _____

    b. Enable us to respond quickly when a key position becomes open.   Rating: _____

7. Our processes for compensation, rewards, and recognition:

    a. Reward people who are exceptional performers and live by the values.   Rating: _____

    b. Reinforce the behavior we want in our employees.   Rating: _____

8. Our processes for termination:

    a. Enable us to identify substandard performers, coach them, and then terminate the ones who aren't improving.   Rating: _____

    b. Enable us to identify employees who don't fit the values, coach them, and then terminate the ones who don't change.   Rating: _____

PART C. OUR PROCESSES FOR PLANNING AND ALIGNMENT

1. Our processes for planning:

    a. Require the top team to develop plans with involvement from everyone.   Rating: _____

    b. Require the top team to measure, track performance, and update progress on a regular basis.   Rating: _____

2. Our market and customer information processes:

    a. Effectively collect appropriate data about customers and markets.   Rating: _____

    b. Effectively analyze this data.   Rating: _____

    c. Effectively distribute market data throughout the company.   Rating: _____

    d. Encourage everyone in the company to focus on the customer and market needs.   Rating: _____

3. Our communication processes:

    a. Help align people with the company's mission, vision, values, and strategies.   Rating: _____

    b. Include written, oral, and electronic forms of communication.   Rating: _____

    c. Enable us quickly and easily to send and receive information on a regular basis.   Rating: _____

4. Our processes for continuous innovation and improvement:

    a. Encourage employees to focus on continual improvement and search for more efficient and effective ways to do their jobs.   Rating: _____

    b. Help all employees understand the importance of innovation to the future of our company.   Rating: _____

    c. Encourage and reward innovation within our company.   Rating: _____

5. Our measurement processes:

    a. Identify and describe why certain key performance indicators are important to our company's success.   Rating: _____

    b. Have identified metrics and standards against which to measure our performance.   Rating: _____

    c. Track performance and report progress on a regular basis.   Rating: _____

6. Our processes for developing and implementing policies:

    a. Define positive rules for an effective workplace.   Rating: _____

    b. Result in easy-to-use employee handbooks or
       Web-based documents.   Rating: _____

PART D. OUR PROCESSES FOR MANAGEMENT AND CONTROL

1. Our budgeting and tracking processes:

    a. Are developed to support the company's plans and
       strategies.   Rating: _____

    b. Provide the financial road map to guide the company.   Rating: _____

2. Our financial management processes:

    a. Enable us to track current, deferred, and anticipated
       revenue.   Rating: _____

    b. Enable us to track and control expenditures on a
       timely basis.   Rating: _____

    c. Enable us to manage cash flow.   Rating: _____

    d. Provide the information we need to present to
       various sources of financing for the company.   Rating: _____

3. Our information technology and support processes:

    a. Provide appropriate computing and communications
       tools and training needed for employees to perform
       at top levels.   Rating: _____

    b. Encourage our IT staff to be proactive in tracking
       changes in the IT/Telecomm fields.   Rating: _____

    c. Encourage our IT staff to anticipate our computing
       and communications needs.   Rating: _____

4. Our facilities management processes:

    a. Provide a pleasant and efficient physical environment
       in which to work.   Rating: _____

    b. Help our employees be productive and successful.   Rating: _____

SCORE SUMMARY AND INTERPRETATION

A Rating Score of **7** in any area indicates this is a prime area of strength that will facilitate and support the company's growth. Scores of **5** and **6** indicate considerable strength in these areas, but you will want to consider making incremental improvements to increase the score. A score of **4** is a cause for worry. A rating of "Sometimes" indicates a lack of consistency that sends conflicting signals to employees and inhibits growth; thus significant improvements will be needed. Scores of **3 or below** are big red flags indicating areas or behaviors that hinder the company's growth and require your immediate attention.

RESULTS ANALYSIS

Look back over the *BAO SCAN: Establish Your Infrastructure to Support Growth:*

1. List three statements that you rated the highest. Choose those you feel are key strengths and contribute most to the success of the company.

A. _____

B. _____

C. _____

2. List three statements that received the lowest rating. Choose those you feel are the most critical weaknesses and should be targeted for improvement.

A. _____

B. _____

C. _____

3. Write three statements that define your priorities for change (for example, capitalize more on the strengths or improve the weaknesses).

A. _____

B. _____

C. _____

4. List three things our company could do to implement these changes.

A. _____

B. _____

C. _____

ACTION PLAN

Recognize what you and your company are doing well and celebrate! Think about what you have done that enabled you to achieve these great results and how that can be applied to your weaknesses. But, do not overlook areas that need improvement or think they will improve on their own over time. Use these steps to develop your Action Plan for Improvement:

1. Ask your top team to complete the *BAO SCAN: Establish Your Infrastructure to Support Growth* and the Results Analysis. You may also want others in the company to complete the *SCAN* in order to get more comprehensive feedback.

2. Meet with your top team to:

   • Compare and contrast your ratings on various statements with their ratings, as well as areas you have identified as strengths with those needing work.

   • If applicable, discuss the reasons why their responses are different from yours.

   • Agree on areas for improvement or change; be as specific as possible.

3. Prioritize those areas that must be addressed and will make the biggest difference. Develop them into Action Plans for Improvement.

4. Get consensus on the Action Plans and the resources and budgets needed to make the necessary changes.

   • For each Action Plan, specify the goal, desired outcomes, steps to take, team members responsible for implementation, resources required, key measures of success, and time frames for achieving the goal and tracking results.

   • Assign a cross-functional team to implement each Action Plan. Include members from different departments who will be affected by the changes. Members should have the necessary skills and insights to accomplish the plan. Identify a team leader and/or executive sponsor who will be held accountable for managing the team, tracking progress, and achieving the desired goal.

5. Communicate the Action Plans for Improvement to everyone in the company. Get involvement, input, and feedback.

6. Hold yourself and others accountable for achieving the new goals and milestones.

7. After a designated period of time (three to six months), evaluate progress, identify new or emerging problems or opportunities, set new goals, make new team assignments (if appropriate), and take action. In a year, retake the *BAO SCAN: Establish Your Infrastructure to Support Growth* and repeat Steps 1 through 6 as required. Remember: Continuous assessment, action, and improvement are essential to building an awesome organization that is strong enough to support continuous growth.

Leader

CHAPTER **9**

BECOME THE AWESOME LEADER OF GROWTH

"If there's any one lesson I've learned, it's that it really is the leader who makes or breaks the company."

Because you are the leader, you are the driving force behind your organization. Every day you have to make choices about where to focus, what to do, whom to see, and what to delegate. You have to decide how to use your most precious resource: your time. Few first-time entrepreneurs or CEOs are clear about their roles and responsibilities. They aren't sure what they should do themselves, when to delegate, and how to make the trade-off between spending time on building the organization versus working on projects that will generate revenue. This chapter makes those roles and responsibilities clear. It also helps you understand that what you do as leader will affect the people who join you, your culture, the company's ability to develop and execute viable plans, the relationship between you and your top team, and the infrastructure you build to support growth. The six components of an awesome organization are inextricably intertwined. What you do in one area will affect all the others.

RED FLAGS: SIGNS THAT YOU HAVEN'T CLEARLY DEFINED YOUR ROLES AND RESPONSIBILITIES

Many CEOs and entrepreneurs have a difficult time knowing when to shift from working in the trenches to managing the business. If the following statements are true for you, then you may need to make that transition. Here's a list of hints that you may need to further define your roles and responsibilities as CEO:

 You aren't sure what you should do yourself and what to delegate to top team members.

You get ad hoc feedback about your decisions and comments about your performance, but you can't tell whether people think you're handling your CEO role effectively.

You want to move out of day-to-day operations and focus more on strategy and long-range issues, but you're not sure how to let go or where to focus.

 You're not sure whom to hold accountable when deadlines are missed, people aren't behaving according to the company's values, or performance is below expectation.

There's more and more to do, and you can never get caught up. The harder you work, the more work there is. You don't know how to get out of the 24/7 syndrome.

You wonder if you're the right person for this job.

We've noticed that media profiles of successful CEOs tend to focus on their leadership style. Though it certainly helps to have an effective style, you need more than that to do a good job as CEO of a growing company. You need to master a set of roles and responsibilities to lead your organization through growth. And you have to focus on more than making the numbers. In the next two sections, we look at what comprises "leadership style" and the roles and responsibilities of the leader of a growth company. If you focus on hiring the right people, supporting innovation, executing your plans, developing an infrastructure that supports growth, and creating a strong culture that attracts and enables awesome people to perform at high levels, then you will build shareholder value and make your numbers as well.

WHAT PEOPLE EXPECT OF THEIR LEADER

To achieve their dreams, leaders must have followers. The Kauffman Center for Entrepreneurial Leadership asked employees (identified by their CEOs as awesome) to describe what they look for in a leader and how they expect the leader to behave. These employees — the kind of people any company would want to attract and retain — identified 10 qualities in the leaders they are willing to follow. They are listed in the following box, "Vital Signs: What Awesome People Look for in a Leader."

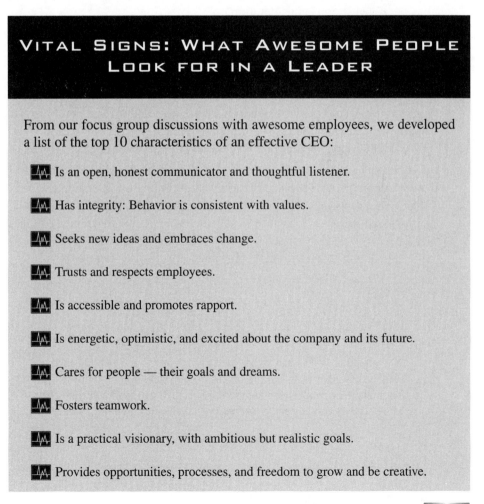

VITAL SIGNS: WHAT AWESOME PEOPLE LOOK FOR IN A LEADER

From our focus group discussions with awesome employees, we developed a list of the top 10 characteristics of an effective CEO:

- Is an open, honest communicator and thoughtful listener.
- Has integrity: Behavior is consistent with values.
- Seeks new ideas and embraces change.
- Trusts and respects employees.
- Is accessible and promotes rapport.
- Is energetic, optimistic, and excited about the company and its future.
- Cares for people — their goals and dreams.
- Fosters teamwork.
- Is a practical visionary, with ambitious but realistic goals.
- Provides opportunities, processes, and freedom to grow and be creative.

LEADERSHIP STYLE: EXPECTATIONS

Though the list of expectations regarding leadership style may be daunting, the good news is that we now know, with certainty, what awesome people are looking for and expect of their CEO. As you read the following descriptions, think about how well you are meeting the leadership style expectations of the awesome people in your organization.

- **Is an open, honest communicator and thoughtful listener.** Awesome people want to know what's happening and want you to listen to their suggestions for making the company an even better organization. They want you and your top team to share information — the good and the bad — to listen to their ideas and suggestions, and to value their input. They don't expect you to adopt every recommendation they make, but they want to feel that they are heard, that their ideas are valued, and that their suggestions are given serious consideration.

- **Has integrity: Behavior is consistent with values.** Awesome people will not follow leaders who are dishonest or whose actions are inconsistent with their words. Once you define your company's values, you and your top team must live those values and set the standard for the whole company. People watch what you do, listen to what you say, and measure that against what they understand the values of the company to be. If you say you want to be a leading-edge technology firm but your plan is to manufacture "me-too" components, if you tell a vendor the check is in the mail when it's not, if you cut corners on a project and joke about pulling a fast one on the customer, your employees will question your values and integrity — and the best ones will leave.

> "My advice to my fellow entrepreneurs: Never, ever cave on your values."

> "I've found that if I, the leader, don't hold myself accountable to the same standards the rest of the organization is held to, then people will not believe or support the standards. The slightest deviation from the values can be used as evidence that they really don't matter that much."

- **Seeks new ideas and embraces change.** Awesome people get frustrated when they don't feel they are being allowed to perform at their full potential. For them, "full potential" means more than just doing their jobs. It means being given increasing amounts of responsibility, being sought out for advice and feedback, and having opportunities to learn and to help the organization change and grow. They are not drawn to leaders who simply want to maintain the status quo. They want to follow leaders who are trying to grow their companies into market leaders and achieve something no other company has done before.

- **Trusts and respects employees.** Awesome people don't want to be micromanaged. They want you to set targets and then delegate projects to them. They want you to trust them to succeed, to take calculated risks and help them not to fail. They expect you to know what they're doing and to acknowledge their accomplishments. If they need to check signals now and then or discuss an unexpected variable that will affect the project, they want to know that you will make time for them, but they don't want you constantly looking over their shoulders.

- **Is accessible and promotes rapport.** Awesome people become frustrated when they cannot get access to the leader. They need to know that they can ask you questions and that you welcome their ideas. There are many ways you can make yourself more accessible to employees. One is by walking around. Another is by having "open hours" at a specific time each week and encouraging employees to drop by your office and talk about anything they want to talk about. Or, you could schedule lunch meetings on a regular basis with a cross-section of employees during which you talk about the company's vision, values, plans, and goals, and get a sense of what's working and not working from their perspective. You might also want to attend some meetings of cross-functional teams. And, you will always want to take a major and visible role at all company meetings. Make a conscious effort to be accessible to your employees and create mechanisms so you can hear what they want to tell you about themselves, their projects, and the company.

> "I hired a salesperson from a competitor and soon after he joined, I sat down and talked with him for an hour. When we were finished, he said that in the eight months he'd been with our competitor, he had never spoken with the CEO, let alone had an in-depth conversation about the direction of the company."

- **Is energetic, optimistic, and excited about the company and its future.**
  Awesome people want you to be clear about the company's direction and
  confident about its future. They expect to see you leading the company,
  actively participating in the planning, communicating on a regular basis,
  being upbeat about opportunities, and energizing the whole organization.

- **Cares for people — their goals and dreams.** Successful entrepreneurs
  and CEOs care for their people. Ewing Marion Kauffman felt that his
  success was directly related to his people skills. He genuinely cared for his
  employees and figured out that the best way to attract people was to show
  them how they could achieve their personal goals by working at Marion
  Laboratories. His advice to entrepreneurs was to "show people how they can
  reach their goals by helping you reach yours." Effective leaders understand
  how to connect with their employees and develop win-win relationships.

- **Fosters teamwork.** Awesome people want to work with other awesome
  people who are interesting and engaged in creating the company's future.
  They like being part of teams, attacking big challenges, hitting milestones,
  accomplishing goals, and moving the company along its growth path. Their
  leader needs to believe in the power of teams, understand how they work,
  reward team behavior and accomplishments, and foster strong teamwork at
  the top, within departments, and cross-functionally.

- **Is a practical visionary, with ambitious but realistic goals.** Awesome
  people want to be engaged in a mighty purpose and leave a legacy. Some
  want to leave a personal mark; others prefer to work in groups to achieve
  goals they could not achieve alone. When they find a leader whose vision is
  compatible with theirs, they will work with passion and enthusiasm. They
  can handle a temporary setback or a disappointing result if you can explain
  why it happened, what you intend to do differently, and what the new goals
  are. But if they begin to think the goals you establish are unattainable, or
  that your vision has no basis in reality, they will become disillusioned and
  perhaps even cynical.

- **Provides opportunities, processes, and freedom to grow and be creative.**
  An effective leader encourages people to try new ideas, take initiative,
  solve problems, learn new skills, and reflect on what they've learned from
  various experiences. Good leaders encourage and reward people who take
  calculated risks.

  > "I am the opposite of a micromanager. I'm very collaborative by nature.
  > I spend a lot of time encouraging people who have great ideas. I like
  > to reward and recognize people with great ideas at every level. I think

I'm good at setting goals and clarifying expectations about what we want to accomplish, then checking in on progress. I also advocate moving the boulders, not the pebbles."

LEADERSHIP ROLES AND RESPONSIBILITIES: THE OTHER SET OF EXPECTATIONS

In the last section, we described certain qualities that can be used to describe your leadership style — accessible, honest, upbeat, open to new ideas and change, respectful, caring for people, and so on. Now we want to focus on what you need to *do* as leader, that is, your roles and responsibilities.

RED FLAGS: SIGNS YOU ARE NOT FULFILLING YOUR LEADERSHIP ROLES AND RESPONSIBILITIES

When you are the leader, your team expects you to assume certain roles and responsibilities. If any of the following statements is true, you need to expand your understanding of the role of the leader:

 People are asking: "What are we doing?" "Why are we doing it?" "Where is this company going anyway?"

 The company is constantly revising goals because it never hits its targets.

People grumble that they don't get enough information about the company or get information too late for it to be used in decision making.

You find yourself thinking, "But I already told them that. Didn't they get it?"

 You see people working together in ways that do not fit your culture or values.

 You can see the culture changing as the company grows and more people are added, but you aren't sure what to do about it.

People complain that it's too difficult to get things done.

continues

-continued

 People come to meetings, listen to you and nod their heads, but don't challenge you or build on your ideas.

 You wonder whether some people, particularly top team members, are capable of handling their jobs.

You're thinking about reorganizing parts of the company and hope that doing so will improve performance.

You know the company needs to change and reinvent itself, but you're not sure how to manage the changes without sending the company into a tailspin.

For years we have talked and worked with CEOs as they led their companies through growth and transformation from one stage to the next. Based on their experiences, we've identified eight critical roles and responsibilities of the leader of a growth company, all of which require constant attention. None can be ignored for long without causing problems for the organization.

As you read the following explanations, understand that these are roles and responsibilities your awesome people expect you to perform. If you do not meet their expectations, your company will not reach its potential, and your people will begin to lose confidence in you and in the company.

RESPONSIBILITY #1: SET DIRECTION

"In my mind, there's a big distinction between management and leadership, and the CEO must clearly be the leader. Leadership is about setting goals and standards. It's about having a vision of where you want to be — even if you aren't there now, and it's not obvious how to get there. You want everybody thinking of solutions to problems, but they can only do that if they know where you're heading and what it is you want to get done. That's the role of the leader, the CEO."

Some entrepreneurs mistakenly believe that everyone expects them to have all the answers, and so they do all the planning and make all the decisions themselves. This won't work. No one person — not even you — has all the answers. Your awesome people expect and want to have a role in planning, and they want you to ask their opinion and welcome their ideas before you make any decisions. So your responsibility is to define an effective planning process, initiate the process, and provide leadership throughout the process so it moves forward and results in a plan that everyone understands and is aligned around. Make sure the plan includes goals, timetables, milestones, and ways to measure how well the company is accomplishing its plan, and how well individuals and teams are contributing to the achievement of the plan.

In addition to setting direction, you need to gather external information about trends and new developments so you can make forecasts about the future. Make sure everyone considers markets and customers first when making decisions. Constantly evaluate whether and how your company can capitalize on emerging trends and use that information to determine which new areas to pursue. In order to set the company's direction, you need to be outwardly focused and serve as a conduit to bring this outside information into the company. Then you need to help the company adapt to external developments that will affect where your company is headed.

As you strive to lead the company in ways that are innovative and make it more competitive, take time to step back and evaluate whether you're accomplishing the vision, mission, goals, and culture you want to achieve or whether you need to make midcourse corrections in strategy and tactics.

RESPONSIBILITY #2: ACT AS CHIEF COMMUNICATOR

Having set the direction for the company, you must keep the mission, vision, values, and strategies top of mind for everyone at all times. This will help employees become aligned and stay involved and committed to the organization. There are many ways to do this: Remind them of the mission, vision, values, and targets when you lead company meetings and strategic planning sessions; make sure you take time to describe the mission, vision, values, and plan when you meet with new employees during their orientation; have weekly lunches or breakfasts with a random group of employees from all levels of the company and talk about your vision for the company and how you need them to help achieve that mission; be responsive to employees who send you e-mails or leave voice mails; and write a regular column for the company Intranet or newsletter.

If you don't play the role of chief communicator, don't assume that someone else will do it for you. Your management team will not step in to fill the void. In fact, if they observe that communication isn't important to you, they'll assume that they don't need to bother with it either. You are the role model for communicating information about how the company is doing, where it is going, and how everyone is expected to contribute to its growth.

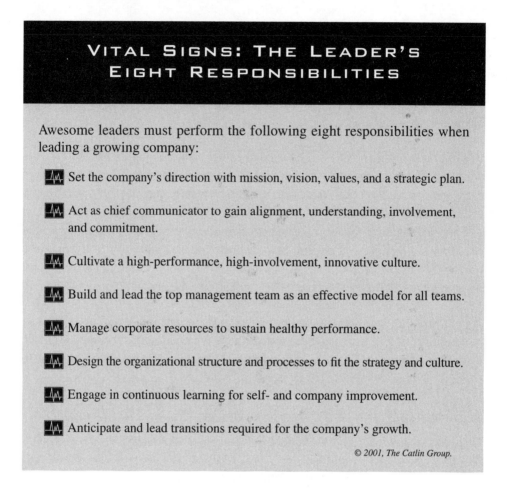

VITAL SIGNS: THE LEADER'S EIGHT RESPONSIBILITIES

Awesome leaders must perform the following eight responsibilities when leading a growing company:

- Set the company's direction with mission, vision, values, and a strategic plan.

- Act as chief communicator to gain alignment, understanding, involvement, and commitment.

- Cultivate a high-performance, high-involvement, innovative culture.

- Build and lead the top management team as an effective model for all teams.

- Manage corporate resources to sustain healthy performance.

- Design the organizational structure and processes to fit the strategy and culture.

- Engage in continuous learning for self- and company improvement.

- Anticipate and lead transitions required for the company's growth.

© 2001, The Catlin Group.

If you see signs that people are not getting the information they need, it's your responsibility to solve the problem. Face-to-face communication with everyone may have been possible when you started your company, but it becomes less feasible as the company grows, so you must rely on your top team to help deliver the messages, in a variety of ways, throughout the organization. Build in feedback mechanisms to check whether people throughout the organization are receiving the right messages at the right times and that they fully understand those messages.

> "I spend a lot of time calling people in the 18 branches of our company. I communicate with them about what we're doing, talk with them about their professional development, discuss proposed new products and services, and share success stories from office to office. I tell everybody I am most successful and effective when I am on the phone with our employees, promoting the company spirit. Our conversation is two-way, so I get feedback from them about how we can improve the services the corporate office provides."

Remember that different people prefer to receive information in different ways — some prefer it written, others verbal, and others want to watch your body language when you say the words — so use several different media to communicate and deliver messages: memos, newsletters, e-mail messages, video conferencing, company meetings, staff meetings, one-on-one conversations, lunches or breakfasts with small groups, and so forth. In addition, people comprehend information differently, so you should adapt your communication style accordingly. For instance, some people want metaphors and stories, others want just the facts, and still others need to be told how specific information applies to their job or circumstances.

> "We have company meetings once a quarter for an afternoon and talk about what's good and what's not so good. We pass out the income statements and talk about what we're making or losing each quarter and what corrections we might make. If we have a major course adjustment between those meetings, we pull everybody together right then and share the news — both the good news and the bad news. Since some people are reluctant to ask questions in front of a hundred other people, we always include a social activity at the end of these meetings so they can ask me questions in a more informal setting. We also make sure there is ample opportunity at the department and team level to get their feedback."

> "Every day I'm in the office, I spend a half hour walking around and talking to people. I deliberately take a different route each day. If people want to ask me a question but are intimidated to walk down to the corner office and do so, this gives them a chance to get their question in. I sort of take the company's temperature and they take mine! I learn a lot doing this. If there's an area of concern, I can ask the right question and pick up a lot of information."

Good communication pays off at several levels. Because effective decision making requires that you gather people's ideas and input before decisions are made, asking questions and being open to suggestions will enable you to have better information for decision making. Once you've made decisions, you need to communicate them, along with your rationale, and ask for ideas about how best to implement them. Finally, you need to monitor the implementation, ask questions, get feedback, and then determine whether to make midcourse corrections.

> "It's essential to be talking and listening to all levels of the organization about what our people are doing and saying, asking if we've made it easy or hard for them to get their work done, asking how we can make it more efficient, and what things we could do differently to be more successful. It's important to gather that kind of information regularly."

Make communication a conscious part of your job. Don't get frustrated by the need to repeat the same messages over and over again, in different media and different formats, to different people. Sometimes people filter out messages they hear once and wait to hear them a second or third time before they pay attention. Others pay more attention to messages delivered verbally than in writing — and vice versa. Communications about the mission, vision, values, and culture need to be repeated over and over so new people joining the company get the message, and longer-term employees are reassured that you are still using the same touchstones to guide the growth of the company.

> "The top person has to spend a ton of time communicating as the organization grows. People need to have messages repeated over and over again for them to really get it. And only talking about culture, values, and strategy at the annual meeting won't cut it. If you don't believe repetition and consistency of messages are important, why do you think they show the same TV commercials over and over again?"

The final aspect of your role as chief communicator is spokesperson on behalf of the company. One way to get customers, prospects, and other key external audiences to pay attention to your company is for you to be perceived as a thought leader within your industry. Think carefully about how to position the company with outside constituencies. To secure the information your company needs to compete, you must be in a position to hear about emerging trends and innovative developments before they become front-page news. This information is critical to your planning processes and to determining which companies will be collaborators and which will be competitors. Having gathered such information, you then need to make sure you share it inside the company as part of your role as chief communicator.

RESPONSIBILITY #3: CULTIVATE THE CORPORATE CULTURE

As we've said several times in this book, your company's culture is a reflection of you, the leader. Your actions and the behavior you encourage (and discourage) in others directly affect the culture.

"I believe life is better if you treat people with respect and you always tell the truth. I believe business is easier when you try to maintain a set of values and build a culture that focuses on how people treat each other. I wish I could say that all my life I've lived this way, but I can't. I've learned the hard way. Treating people with respect, so that they always feel respected, is tough. Telling the truth is hard, too. It isn't good enough just to not lie, you have to avoid misleading people — intentionally or unintentionally."

Entrepreneurs often underestimate the power of their position as leader. Everyone in the company is watching you and consciously or unconsciously will begin to imitate what you do and say. They listen to how you communicate the vision and values, watch how you behave toward others, and are influenced more by what you do than what you say. If you say you want feedback on your ideas but get upset when someone criticizes them, people will remember that. If you talk about the need to respect each other but publicly and routinely criticize individuals on your top team, you'll find that they will begin to act like you when dealing with members of their functional and cross-functional teams. Bottom line: Be very conscious of what you do and say and make sure you are always reinforcing the values and culture.

"I wish people didn't pay so much attention to every single thing I say and do, but they do. This makes me very conscious of my actions. It just goes with the CEO territory."

"I learned long ago that you don't stay honest for the IRS. You stay honest for the people in your company, because they are watching you, all the time. They watch what you do and imitate you."

As we discussed in chapter 3, "Develop an Innovative Culture for Growth," and chapter 8, "Establish Your Infrastructure for Growth," you can develop processes that help spread the values and culture you want. Be chief of culture and take the lead in making sure such processes are developed and are working smoothly.

"I learned I could set up systematic ways to create the culture I wanted based on our values of integrity, entrepreneurial spirit, innovation, teamwork, results-orientation, rewarding people for contributing to results, open communications, and customer focus. We set up systems and ways of doing things such as regular company meetings, feedback surveys, posting values on the wall, establishing performance reviews and compensation strategies that reflect the values. We also offer positive reinforcement and rewards for people and teams that exhibit the desired values and behaviors."

As your organization grows and your hire more people, always try to hire those who are a good fit with your values and culture. Unfortunately, there may be times that you discover people working together in ways that don't fit your culture and values. As you hire people who may have worked in other organizational cultures, they bring the values and norms of that culture with them and may behave in ways that are incompatible with your culture. It's critical that you clearly define the culture you want. Write it down, live it, talk about it, and make sure these new employees understand what you expect and what you will not tolerate, so they can adapt as quickly as possible to your culture.

"I'm a big believer in culture. If you get people who have the right attitudes and they understand their task well, you can make them awesome employees by teaching them what they don't understand. The converse is not usually true. People with the wrong values but great skills can't be made to fit in with your culture, and they can do a lot of damage."

"Every other month, all new employees have breakfast with me. I tell them about our values and try to do it on a very personal level, which is really part of our culture. It's less about what we do and more about how we do things. I tell them that I hate things like office politics and backstabbing and that I love things like honesty and mutual respect. It's a very personal talk."

Listen to what people say about the company, especially their complaints. Something is wrong with your culture if they say it's hard to get things done, that they don't know what's going on, or that they are only told what to do but not why. As you check around, you'll probably find that one (or more) of your management team is failing to model the values. You must take corrective action immediately. Meet with these individuals and make it clear that they must change their behavior — or they will have to leave. You can't afford to let anyone violate the values of your culture, no matter how well that person performs his or her job. Allowing people to continue when they don't match the values sends a message to the whole organization that will damage the culture, and your own credibility. (See "Deal with Misfits, Malcontents, and Nonperformers," in chapter 5, "Retain Awesome People for Growth.")

RESPONSIBILITY #4: LEAD THE EXECUTIVE TEAM

One of your most important and most difficult responsibilities is developing and leading a top team that can take the company to the next level of growth. You will have to manage big egos, add the right people to the team as the company grows, integrate these new people into the team quickly, and help every member of the team become a great team player and a great leader.

> "Job one of getting the top team aligned is to hire the right people because without that, it's not going to work. Job two is to make sure you spend enough time working as a team. Start by developing long-term goals so everyone on the team is working from the same sheet of paper. Job three is constant communication. Job four is encouraging them to work in small teams on tough strategic issues and not bring everything to me."

As we discussed in chapter 7, "Prime Your Top Team for Growth," your goal is to build a team with the strengths the company needs. For that to happen, you have to change from chief decision maker to coach. This means learning to delegate accountability to team members in both their functional and company leadership roles and providing guidance to help them succeed. Set and enforce ground rules for how the team and how individuals work together. Sometimes this requires having tough conversations with team members who are not fulfilling their roles as leaders or not modeling the company values. Do not delay; be sure you define the problem clearly, specify the improvements you expect, and outline the consequences if they don't change their behavior to be consistent with the company's values.

> "I had one sales VP who had one excuse after another for not making the numbers. The product was late; the price was too high, and so on. While some of that was legitimate, when you peeled all that away it turned out that his attitude was the problem. His attitude ended up dragging down the rest of the team. Deciding to let him go was easy. The execution was hard because he'd been with us four and a half years. I've gone through this a few times now, so I make those decisions faster now, but probably not fast enough. When it's all done, I usually regret I didn't do it sooner."

Look for signs that silos are developing within the company because they will stifle growth and innovation. Remind the team that part of their performance evaluation will be based on their being team players, which you define as working together effectively, solving problems, supporting each other, communicating well, giving each other feedback, and doing whatever it takes to avoid erecting and operating in silos.

> "We set up quarterly meetings where each VP gives feedback, both positive and negative, to the other VPs, in a group setting. Then we all discuss what we can do better — both individually and as a team. At first, people thought this was weird, but now we've come to realize how valuable it is."

> "Once a year we have a team meeting. Each VP gets three wishes. We each have to write down what we wish the other VPs would do or do differently. This forces us to identify solutions as well as problems, and to identify the 'big rocks' problems, rather than complain about the small ones. This exercise has helped us prioritize and move ahead."

RESPONSIBILITY #5: MANAGE CORPORATE RESOURCES

As CEO, it's up to you to secure and manage the financial resources required to sustain growth and stay focused on maintaining a healthy financial picture that balances short-term and long-term needs. This includes the difficult and time-consuming tasks of deciding how to finance your company's growth and then obtaining the necessary capital.

Raising funds and meeting the quarterly numbers are too often the only measurements used to rate a CEO's performance. But don't underestimate the importance of the company's other major resources: employees, investors, customers, and partners. Thinking about how to get the most from these resources is also your responsibility. Any or all of them could provide access to additional customers and strategic alliances, help you develop new products and services, be a source of financing for growth, help you reach your plan, or offer an exit strategy if you decide to sell the company. It's up to you to keep a constant eye on all of these groups, using systematic measures that help you gauge how well these key resources are being managed.

> "You have to understand the key arteries of the business; you have to get the financing, manage your cash flow, your people, have a plan, and be persistent. Leaders have to put all of those things together."

Make sure the organization closely tracks customer satisfaction and reacts appropriately and promptly to any early warning signs of dissatisfaction. Seek and use information about customers' current and future needs. Serve as an ambassador for the customer's perspective within the company and remind people that the customer is at the heart of the company's mission and vision.

For employees, act as the chief of hiring, ensuring that hiring practices focus on finding people with the best talents, the right values, and the capacity to grow with the company. In addition, make sure managers are doing everything possible to retain awesome people. Put mechanisms in place to track employee satisfaction as part of your role as chief of culture.

> "I rank my activities related to hiring as one of the top two functions of a CEO. If you don't hire well, your job is never-ending. I don't think many CEOs dedicate enough time to hiring because they don't recognize the long-reaching effects or costs — in terms of time and money — of a bad hire. With a bad hire, you've got the potential of bad morale within the company and damaging your relationships with customers. Then you have to build the case, fire the person, and start all over again to hire someone else — and all that costs time and money. So it's critical to do the job right the first time."

Finally, develop, manage, and leverage external relationships and partnerships to accomplish corporate objectives. As the company grows, you will eventually delegate part of this responsibility to people you hire to take on the business development function. However, you will always need to stay involved because alliances and partnerships are critical to the company's future.

As you manage corporate resources, make sure you avoid some common mistakes. Don't set goals and targets and then not hold people accountable for achieving them. Enforcing accountability is difficult, but if you see that progress is not being made, don't revise the goals; confront the person who is not performing as expected. A good manager establishes checkpoints, and then requests periodic reports or briefings. If you don't feel there's enough forward momentum when you do these periodic check-ins, say so, and hold people responsible for figuring out what to do to get the project back on track. Help people understand the consequences for failing to achieve goals, especially if they did not forewarn you. The worst message you can send the organization is to let underperformers off the hook. And make sure everyone understands that in an awesome organization, there are "No Surprises — Good or Bad."

Managing all of these resources requires the development of a set of metrics or measures that allow you to gauge how well the company's resources are being managed and a standard against which to measure them. You'll need to develop metrics and standards appropriate for your company, but here are a few ideas:

- Units shipped or hours billed per day versus plan
- Cash flow projections per week or quarter

- Aging receivables by month

- Average size of new customer accounts versus size of current accounts

- Numbers and types of customer complaints versus goal

- Ratio of new accounts to old

- Unwanted employee turnover by quarter

Everyone needs to understand the metrics and why they are important. People need to know how you define success and what it looks like when they are successful. Reward people who meet the standards you set. Provide feedback and training to those who fall short and help them improve their performance. If that fails, move them out of the organization.

RESPONSIBILITY #6: DESIGN STRUCTURE AND PROCESSES TO FIT THE STRATEGY AND CULTURE

As discussed in chapter 8, some entrepreneurs mistakenly believe that structure and processes will destroy creativity and flexibility. Successful entrepreneurs understand that a company must have a well-established infrastructure in order to grow. People need structure and processes to help them understand what to do and how to do it. Ask your team to help you develop a creative structure and processes that are appropriate for your unique strategy and culture. Be willing to modify them when it's time to reinvent the organization, but always recognize that a strong infrastructure is necessary to sustain growth.

> "I believe that business success is based on competency, communication, and consistency. We try to hire competent people. The top team and I work hard to communicate, and we've also worked hard to develop processes so we can be consistent. I believe that processes are critical to building a sustainable business of any size."

As CEO, you know who has the authority and responsibility to make which kinds of decisions throughout the organization. In addition, you also need to be paying attention to all the handoffs of responsibility between departments. Because you're the only one who has this all-encompassing view of the company's many interconnected pieces, you need to be the one to drive the structural change and reinvention needed to transform your company and move it to the next level of growth.

Structural change can create fear and uncertainty in a company. When change is imminent or even rumored, people worry about job security, as well as their titles and rank within the organization. But, as long as the structural change is explained in terms of its fit with the vision, strategy, and culture, and the rationale for change is clearly communicated, most people will accept and adapt to it. Make sure that any changes you make enable the company to continue to operate cross-functionally and stay customer-centric and nimble.

RESPONSIBILITY #7: ENGAGE IN CONTINUOUS LEARNING

As your company grows, it changes and becomes more complex. It requires a multi-faceted leader. You need to constantly strive to better understand your roles and responsibilities and improve your performance. Successful leaders keep learning — all the time.

Schedule periodic evaluations of your own performance with your top team, employees, and board members or advisors. You need feedback on whether you're meeting their expectations and fulfilling the role of CEO and leader. Use their feedback to make positive changes. Seek to continually improve your skills in leadership, particularly in leading your top team, doing strategic thinking and planning, communication, innovation, and monitoring changes in the industry or the world that will affect your business.

> "I have a really good board member who gave me some great advice. He said, 'There are some things where you're a 9 and some things where you're a 4 or 5. You can work on making the 9's into 10's or you can work to make the 4's into 7's and 8's.' It was a very simple way of determining what things I should focus on to make a real difference."

Realize that you need to ask for feedback on how to be more effective. People won't volunteer their opinions about your performance unless you ask them — in a way that's not intimidating. You're not likely to get useful feedback by asking people, "How am I doing?" Instead, use objective surveys, instruments, or outside consultants, and make sure the questions focus on your performance and your effectiveness in growing the business. The *BAO SCAN* at the end of this chapter can be an effective, nonthreatening way to let people share their perceptions of how well you're fulfilling your roles and responsibilities.

People are naturally hesitant about giving feedback on their leader's performance. However, acknowledging that there are things you're not good at or where you've made a mistake is a very powerful statement about you, as leader. If you make it clear that you really want to hear their opinions and improve your leadership skills, people will respect you and will share ideas about how you can do a better job.

"We have a pretty simple process at our company. Everyone has a list of five goals that he or she and their manager have agreed should be their focus that quarter. I have a list of five goals, too. Then once a quarter the manager and the people who report to him or her review the goals and rate how well they are doing, on a scale of 1–5 (5 being tops). I rate my top team, and I ask them to rate me, too. The first time a new person goes through this process, they often give me high marks. Then I sit down with them and say, 'I see you've rated me pretty high here — but I figure that rating includes a "suck up" factor. Here's how other people on our top team have rated me.' — and then I show them my 2's and 3's. At first they can't believe it, that someone rated me low and didn't get fired. But then they appreciate the fact that they work in a company where we're honest, trying to improve, and are expected to provide honest feedback so we can all learn and get better."

When you acknowledge that you've made mistakes or identify areas where you need to improve, you signal your commitment to feedback and learning. You model the behavior you want everyone in the company to adopt. Although you may feel vulnerable — especially the first time you ask for feedback — you will find that people respect and admire you for wanting to learn, that they will provide constructive feedback, and that they will be more committed to a leader who is trying to become better, than to a leader who acts like a know-it-all.

"The year of our 10th anniversary, I realized I hadn't had a performance review in 10 years. I give our Executive Team feedback all the time, but as CEO you're never sure whether people are being completely candid when they comment on your performance. I figured I was probably doing 80 percent of the job just fine, but I wanted to find out what that other 20 percent was. I decided to ask our Executive Team to critique my performance and to get their perspective on what my priorities should be as we moved into our second decade. I used an outside consultant to design a survey and interview process that solicited their input on my key areas of responsibility. During this process, we identified five key strengths that I can trust and count on in any situation that might arise. This was very reassuring. And learning what things team members wanted me to do — or stop doing — to help them achieve their goals was very useful. So it was a very powerful experience for us as we prepared for our second decade."

"Getting feedback from my team on my performance was a great learning process. When I read their evaluations of me, 95 percent of the stuff was absolutely accurate, whether I liked it or not. People also used the review process as an opportunity to raise business issues that they wanted to be sure were being worked on. I was already addressing many of these, so it gave me confidence that I was working on the right things. As part of this process, I fed back to the group what I had learned and what I was going to do about it. I made a commitment to report back to them in one quarter on what I'd done to address their issues. As a second part of this evaluation process, I told them they were going to have to do the same thing, to get a 360° review from their peers, from me, and from the people who report to them. People are doing that now, they are receiving really valuable information, and they are learning and growing as never before."

Don't be the emperor with no clothes. Try to see yourself as others see you. Other people can often identify problems you are having before you know what's happening. If you discover that people are talking behind your back, frustrated because decisions aren't being made, or second-guessing your decisions, these are signs you need to get feedback on your performance.

In addition to getting feedback from people associated with your company, get feedback from other CEOs. Join the Young Entrepreneurs' Organization or a CEO forum where you can discuss your challenges and gain insights from peers who are trying to manage growth and are facing the same problems you are. Because entrepreneurs learn best from people who have experienced the same challenges and have overcome the same pitfalls, a CEO peer group can be invaluable. Some entrepreneurs choose to work with an executive coach to get another perspective on what they are doing — or not doing. If you decide to work with a coach, look for a skilled professional who has experience working with CEOs of fast-growing companies.

"Participating in a peer group can really help you run your business. I've learned a lot by using my group as a sounding board for ideas and by participating in discussions about topics that impact us all. You get 10 reasonably intelligent people in a room who know what you're going through on a day-to-day basis; you think through thorny issues and learn how they were able to blast through what seem like insurmountable problems to you. This allows you to move your business forward. It's made a big difference in my company's growth. We're putting together a restart for the business, and several key parts of the business model came out of discussions with my CEO group."

If you feel like you're in over your head, don't know where you need to make improvements, or wonder if someone else could do the job better, feedback and coaching will help. It is indeed lonely at the top, but getting feedback from your Executive Team and employees, advisors, other CEOs in a peer group, and members of your board will help you identify your strengths and weaknesses and develop ideas for new goals and actions. Use the *BAO SCAN* at the end of this chapter.

Ask others to take it and compare your responses to theirs. Review the results, decide where you need to change, learn new skills, and improve your performance as CEO. Then develop an action plan — and do it.

RESPONSIBILITY #8: ANTICIPATE AND LEAD TRANSITIONS

As your company grows, your roles and responsibilities as leader will change. Our first book in this series, *Leading at the Speed of Growth: Journey from Entrepreneur to CEO,* identified three stages of growth beyond start-up — initial growth, rapid growth, and continuous growth — and described the different roles and responsibilities you need to play in each one. It's your job to anticipate and lead the company through these major transitions, to get it from one stage to another. (See appendix B, "Stages of Growth and the Leader's Roles," for more information on the stages of growth and the leader's roles at each stage.)

As your company moves through the stages of growth, it is up to you to provide the leadership, rationale, and impetus for growth and change. Internal growth will strain your current infrastructure. New customer demands, new competitors, shifts in technology, mergers or acquisitions, an IPO, new product or new market initiatives, major new strategic partnerships or alliances — all these will require that you reinvent and transform the company. You need to anticipate and make the necessary changes to move smoothly from one stage of growth to another — and that's difficult enough. But the really hard task is to engage your Executive Team in leading and planning so that they will be able to help you move the company through the turbulence as quickly as possible and keep the organization focused and moving ahead.

Inevitably there will be resistance to change. People will say, "We're doing fine. We've had the best year ever. Why do we need to change?" They will give lip service to the need for planning but claim they have no time to spend on it. Unlike you, they won't have been externally focused, spotted the new trends, or talked with other thought leaders. They won't have the big-picture focus that your position at the top provides you.

Don't give in to those who say, "Let's not rock the boat," or "We're too busy fighting fires to spend time on planning." It's your responsibility to lead the planning process that redefines the market focus, vision, strategy, and structure, and reinvents the company. This is not an easy role to play, but it won't happen if you don't lead it. It cannot be delegated to someone else. You have to help people get comfortable with the idea that the company needs to transform in order to meet changing market conditions. Otherwise, your company will stagnate and decline.

"We've gone through reinvention several times and if we hadn't, we wouldn't be here today. We've done a couple of acquisitions and made some fairly significant course adjustments. One of the issues when you do those things is communicating effectively from the top to the bottom. You have to take the time to explain why we're doing things because it may not always be obvious to others. For instance, you need to explain why we are buying a company because of its technology rather than developing that technology ourselves. People need answers to questions like that. The most critical element is explaining your thought process, your rationale for the reinvention and solution. This helps build your people's confidence in what you're doing."

As the company moves from one growth stage to another, you may wonder if some people are still capable of handling their jobs. Don't make the mistake of ignoring or dismissing these doubts. It is critical that you address these worries head-on and make the hard decisions that have to be made when your company outgrows an individual's ability to contribute. If you don't address the issue of people not pulling their weight, it will damage the culture you've worked so hard to establish, not to mention the business results you seek.

ALL RESPONSIBILITIES ARE IMPORTANT

All of these responsibilities are equally important to leading a high-growth organization. You can't decide to focus on some of them and ignore the rest. This may seem like an overwhelming job description, but you should count on your Executive Team to assist you. Seek advice and guidance from mentors, peers, and board members. Some roles and responsibilities may come naturally to you, but you'll struggle with others. Continually reevaluate your performance and effectiveness, and work on what you need to know and do to lead an awesome organization.

BIG LESSONS

1. Understand that *what* you do and *how* you do it are both important.

2. Recognize that having a great leadership style won't make you a great leader. You have to understand and perform the eight roles and responsibilities of the leader of a growth company.

3. Constantly seek feedback from many sources about how you're performing as a leader.

continues

-continued

4. Watch for the red flags that indicate you need feedback and coaching. Try to see yourself as others see you and then develop an action plan to make the necessary changes.

5. Don't focus just on making the numbers. Understand that building an awesome organization requires far more than short-term trade-offs to meet quarterly financial targets. Make sure you hire great people, manage your top team well, develop plans, build an infrastructure, and lead the company through its growth transitions.

BAO SCAN: BECOME THE AWESOME LEADER OF GROWTH

Use this *SCAN** to rate your performance as the company's leader. How effectively are you exemplifying the leadership style your awesome people expect? How well are you performing the eight critical roles and responsibilities of the leader of a growth company? Also give this *SCAN* to your top team and ask them to rate your effectiveness as well. Compare your responses and perceptions with theirs. Then, identify which aspects of style, and which roles and responsibilities you are performing well and where you need to make improvements.

RATING SCALE

Use this scale to respond to each rating question

1 - - - - - 2 - - - - - 3 - - - - - 4 - - - - - 5 - - - - - 6 - - - - - 7
NEVER   *SOMETIMES*   *ALWAYS*

PART A: USES AN EFFECTIVE LEADERSHIP STYLE

1. Is a good listener and open/honest communicator.

2. Has integrity; never compromises values; and behavior is consistent with values.

*This BAO SCAN is adapted from The CEO Performance Evaluator, © 2001, The Catlin Group.

3. Actively seeks new ideas and is comfortable with change.

4. Trusts and respects employees — and shows it.

5. Is accessible and promotes rapport.

6. Is energetic, optimistic, and excited about the company and its future.

7. Genuinely cares for other people, and helps them reach their goals and dreams.

8. Fosters teamwork.

9. Is a practical visionary, with ambitious but realistic goals.

10. Provides opportunities, freedom, and mechanisms for employees to grow and be creative.

A. Our leader, the CEO, exemplifies these qualities of leadership style that awesome people expect.   Rating: _____

B. Which statements best describe where the CEO is strongest?   Statement #s _____

C. Which statements best describe where the CEO needs to improve his/her leadership style?   Statement #s _____

PART B: SETS DIRECTION

1. Sets the company's direction with mission, vision, values, and a strategic plan.

2. Is clear about values and demonstrates them in actions.

3. Establishes the company's mission (purpose), vision (future direction), and plan (actions), and shares them with all employees.

4. Leads the planning process with the management team to define both short-term and long-term objectives, with strategies and metrics for achieving them.

5. Ensures a focus on markets and customer satisfaction in all decision making.

6. Drives the company into new areas where it will be innovative and competitive.

A. Our leader, the CEO, is fulfilling these roles and responsibilities to set the company's direction.   Rating: _____

B. Which statements best describe the roles and responsibilities the CEO is performing well?   Statement #s _____

C. Which statements best describe where the CEO
needs to make improvements?   Statement #s _____

PART C: COMMUNICATES FOR ALIGNMENT

1. Acts as chief communicator to gain alignment, understanding, involvement, and commitment.

2. Uses a variety of communication methods to keep important goals, facts, challenges, and future direction in front of people.

3. Proactively solicits and really listens to ideas, input, and feedback from people.

4. Establishes structured mechanisms for effective and continuous two-way communication among all people in the company so that everyone has the information needed to fully contribute to the mission and vision.

5. Recognizes that people communicate differently and adapts communication style accordingly.

A. Our leader, the CEO, is fulfilling the roles and
responsibilities of communicating for alignment.   Rating: _____

B. Which statements best describe the roles and
responsibilities that the CEO is performing well?   Statement #s _____

C. Which statements best describe where the CEO
needs to make improvements?   Statement #s _____

PART D: MODELS THE CULTURE

1. Acts as a role model for the core values, recognizing that behaviors and actions are a powerful and visible manifestation of the culture.

2. Offers positive reinforcement when people exhibit the desired values and behaviors, and is willing to get rid of those who don't.

3. Instills an "entrepreneurial spirit" to tap creativity in everyone, along with clear accountability for results and effective processes to resolve inevitable conflicts.

4. Provides for development of skills, recognizes and rewards performance of individuals and teams, and celebrates successes.

5. Establishes an environment that supports and empowers people, has high standards of performance, and provides many opportunities to check on the "health" of the company.

A. Our leader, the CEO, is fulfilling the roles and responsibilities for modeling the culture.   Rating: _____

B. Which statements best describe the roles and responsibilities that the CEO is performing well?   Statement #s _____

C. Which statements best describe where the CEO needs to make improvements?   Statement #s _____

PART E: LEADS THE TOP TEAM

1. Builds a strong, multitalented management team with complementary strengths.

2. Explicitly clarifies team members' accountability as leaders of the company to develop and implement the corporate vision and plan for growth, communicate for alignment, and maintain a culture that attracts, retains, and empowers awesome people.

3. Facilitates effective, creative teamwork and balanced decision making within the top team as a model for all teams.

4. Ensures that all members act as team players in supporting, leveraging, and giving feedback to each other.

5. Promotes cross-functional connections between departments and assigns team members as sponsors of cross-functional teams to address critical priorities in the company's plan.

A. The CEO fulfills the roles and responsibilities of leading the top team.   Rating: _____

B. Which statements best describe the roles and responsibilities that the CEO is performing well?   Statement #s _____

C. Which statements best describe where the CEO needs to make improvements?   Statement #s _____

PART F: MANAGES CORPORATE RESOURCES EFFECTIVELY

1. Maintains a healthy financial picture that balances short-term and long-term needs.

2. Uses appropriate measurements and accountability processes to ensure financial performance, customer satisfaction, and employee satisfaction.

3. Ensures that all hiring practices focus on finding the "right" people with the best talents, the best fit with the values and culture, and the capacity to grow as the company grows.

4. Develops, manages, and leverages strategic relationships and partnerships to accomplish corporate objectives.

A. The CEO is fulfilling the roles and responsibilities of managing corporate resources effectively.   Rating: _____

B. Which statements best describe the roles and responsibilities that the CEO is performing well?   Statement #s _____

C. Which statements best describe where the CEO needs to make improvements?   Statement #s _____

PART G: OVERSEES THE DEVELOPMENT OF THE ORGANIZATION'S INFRASTRUCTURE (STRUCTURE AND PROCESSES)

1. Keeps the organization as simple, flat, and as close to the customer as possible.

2. Ensures that all role definitions and expectations are clear and that every person has specific accountability for achieving established goals and making balanced decisions with appropriate input.

3. Facilitates cross-functional communication and coordination across all departments, among all employees, and with customers and markets.

4. Recognizes that the organizational structure will perpetually evolve and change as the company grows. Is prepared to reorganize periodically so the organization can move to the next stage of growth and development.

5. Builds and continuously improves the company's infrastructure, processes, and cross-functional teams so the work gets done with increasing efficiency and effectiveness.

A. The CEO fulfills these roles and responsibilities for overseeing the development of the organization's structure and processes.   Rating: _____

B. Which statements best describe the roles and responsibilities that the CEO is performing well?   Statement #s _____

C. Which statements best describe where the CEO needs to make improvements?   Statement #s _____

PART H: CONTINUOUSLY AND ACTIVELY LEARNS

1. Searches for and identifies new ways to improve the company.

2. Proactively asks for feedback on own performance and effectiveness; uses feedback to make positive changes in role and style.

3. Establishes relationships with mentors, advisors, and other entrepreneurial leaders.

4. Continues to develop leadership and strategic business skills.

A. The CEO fulfills the roles and responsibilities of a continuous and active learner.   Rating: _____

B. Which statements best describe the roles and responsibilities that the CEO is performing well?   Statement #s _____

C. Which statements best describe where the CEO needs to make improvements?   Statement #s _____

PART I: LEADS THE COMPANY THROUGH THE CHANGES REQUIRED FOR GROWTH

1. Is proactive in providing the leadership, rationale, and impetus for growth and change; watches for signals and leads the company through transitions to new stages of growth.

2. Leads the reinvention planning process that fundamentally transforms the company. Redefines market focus, mission, vision, strategy, structure, and culture as necessary.

3. Gathers input and ideas from everyone in the company. Engages them so they become owners of the change.

A. The CEO fulfills the roles and responsibilities for leading the company through the changes required for growth.   Rating: _____

B. Which statements best describe the roles and responsibilities that the CEO is performing well?   Statement #s _____

C. Which statements best describe where the CEO needs to make improvements?   Statement #s _____

PART J: QUESTIONS FOR OTHERS TO ANSWER

1. What is most rewarding or valuable about the way your CEO works with you? How is he or she most helpful to you?

_____

_____

_____

2. What is difficult or frustrating about what your CEO does? What gets in the way of working with him or her?

_____

_____

_____

3. What does your CEO do, as the leader, that enables you to achieve your goals?

_____

_____

_____

4. What does your CEO do, as the leader, that inhibits you from achieving your goals?

_____

_____

_____

5. What could he or she do to help improve the functioning and performance of the top team?

_____

_____

_____

6. If your CEO had two extra hours each week to devote to a leadership/ management activity, how would you recommend that time be spent?

_____

_____

_____

SCORE SUMMARY AND INTERPRETATION

A Rating Score of **7** in any area indicates this is a prime area of strength that will facilitate and support the company's growth. Scores of **5** and **6** indicate considerable strength in these areas, but you will want to consider making incremental improvements to increase the score. A score of **4** is a cause for worry. A rating of "Sometimes" indicates a lack of consistency that sends conflicting signals to employees and inhibits growth; thus significant improvements will be needed. Scores of **3 or below** are big red flags indicating areas or behaviors that hinder the company's growth and require your immediate attention.

RESULTS ANALYSIS

Look back over the *BAO SCAN: Become the Awesome Leader of Growth:*

1. List three statements that you rated the highest. Choose those you feel are key strengths and contribute most to the success of the company.

A. _____

B. _____

C. _____

2. List three statements that received the lowest rating. Choose those you feel are the most critical weaknesses and should be targeted for improvement.

A. _____

B. _____

C. _____

3. Write three statements that define your priorities for change (for example, capitalize on the strengths or improve the weaknesses).

A. _____

B. _____

C. _____

4. List three things our company could do to implement these changes.

A. _____

B. _____

C. _____

ACTION PLAN

Recognize what you and your company are doing well and celebrate! Think about what you have done that enabled you to achieve these great results and how that can be applied to your weaknesses. But, do not overlook areas that need improvement or think they will improve on their own over time. Use these steps to develop your Action Plan for Improvement:

1. Ask your top team to complete the *BAO SCAN: Become the Awesome Leader of Growth* and the Results Analysis. You may also want others in the company to complete the *SCAN* to get more comprehensive feedback.

2. Meet with your top team to:

• Compare and contrast your ratings on various statements with their ratings, as well as areas you have identified as strengths with those needing work.

- If applicable, discuss the reasons why their responses are different from yours.

- Agree on areas for improvement or change; be as specific as possible.

3. Prioritize those areas that must be addressed and will make the biggest difference. Develop them into Action Plans for Improvement.

4. Identify the resources and budgets needed to make the necessary changes.

- For each Action Plan, specify the goal, desired outcomes, steps to take, resources required, key measures of success, and time frames for achieving the goal and tracking results.

5. Communicate the Action Plans for Improvement to your top team. Get involvement, input, and feedback.

6. Hold yourself accountable for achieving the new goals and milestones.

7. After a designated period of time (three to six months), evaluate progress, identify new or emerging problems or opportunities, set new goals, and take action. In a year, retake the *BAO SCAN: Become the Awesome Leader of Growth* and repeat Steps 1 through 6 as required. Remember: Continuous assessment, action, and improvement are essential to building an awesome organization that is strong enough to support continuous growth.

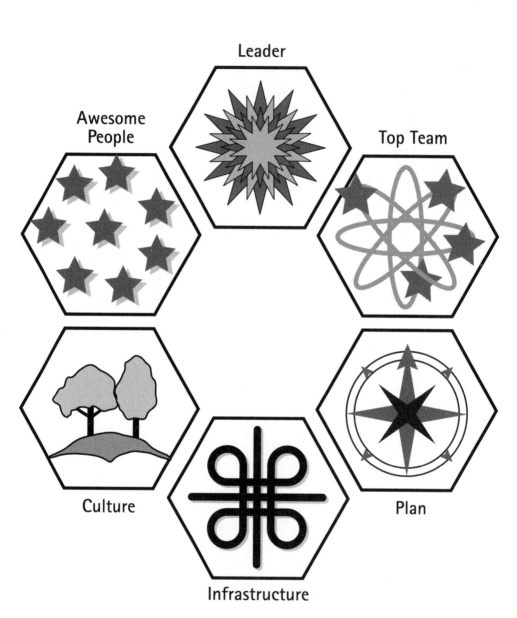

Six Essential Components that Drive Entrepreneurial Growth

CHAPTER 10

IN THE END, IT'S UP TO YOU

Now that you know what makes an organization awesome, we hope you're excited and energized by the many ways you can foster innovation and drive growth in your company. This book contains the knowledge and the tools that you and your top team need to build a great company:

- Savvy advice from your fellow entrepreneurs and CEOs

- Vital Signs of a strong organization against which you can compare your company

- Red Flags that warn your company is headed for danger

- Sections describing "Your Role as Leader" that define your responsibilities for building each component of an outstanding organization

- Assessment tools that you can use to identify areas of strength and weakness and determine whether you, your top team, and/or your employees have similar or different perceptions of the company's strengths or weaknesses

Although all these tools are valuable, we believe the *Overview Quiz* and the seven *BAO SCANs* are most valuable for two reasons. First, using these instruments regularly with your top team and others will help you determine where you need to focus time and resources to strengthen your organization. Second, the assessment process itself will actually help build the innovative culture you want for your company. Broad-based assessments provide opportunities for your people to think about what they are doing and how to do it better. It signals that you want them to contribute new ideas and will consider making changes, if change is warranted. The assessment process gets your people more vested in the company and its success. Regular use of these assessment tools will signal your intent to build a creative, open culture that is dedicated to continuous learning. This, in turn, will encourage your people to develop innovations and pursue new opportunities that will accelerate your company's growth.

We assume that, by now, you have taken the *Overview Quiz* and one or more *BAO SCANs* and developed an Action Plan — or you might have taken several *BAO SCANs* and developed several Action Plans. Don't be concerned if you have several lists of actions you need to take. Work with your top team and (1) identify actions that appear on two or more Action Plans, (2) identify the actions that, if taken, will impact three or more of the six components, and (3) select the two or three actions that will make the biggest difference and focus on them. Remember the 80/20 rule: Identify the 20 percent of the issues or problems that, if resolved, will make 80 percent of the difference. In other words, focus your energy on those changes or improvements that will have the greatest impact on the development of your organization and will enhance its ability to grow.

Once you and your top team have determined your top-level Action Plan, communicate it to the entire company. If people feel that you have identified the problems and have a strategy and timetable for making improvements, they will be encouraged and will support your efforts.

Because your organization is a system, problems in one area will often create problems in other areas. Fortunately, improvements in one area will often have a positive impact on other areas as well. So as you begin to make the 20 percent of the changes that will have the greatest impact on the organization, you should start seeing improvements in culture, retention of people, the way the top team works together, and the plans that get developed. It won't happen overnight because correcting problems, changing the culture, or developing new processes takes time.

Building an awesome organization is a long-term endeavor that you will need to focus on throughout the life of your company. When you hit roadblocks, refer to the stories and lessons your CEO peers have learned. Review the "Vital Signs" and "Your Role as Leader" sections for guidance on how to regain forward momentum. Chart progress, identify improvements, communicate results, and celebrate victories!

Great leaders acknowledge they don't know everything and are able to engage people from all parts of the company to solve problems, generate ideas, and build the organization. Be a great leader — be open to feedback and the new insights you'll get from repeated use of this book and the assessments. The Kauffman Center Series on Managing Growth is being written to help you learn what you need to know to be a great leader. *Leading at the Speed of Growth: Journey from Entrepreneur to CEO,* the first book in the series, outlines your roles and responsibilities at different stages of your company's growth. It provides a valuable road map for you and your team to achieve extraordinary success. Read this and other books in the series, join a forum for entrepreneurs, use www.entreworld.org, find mentors — keep learning.

It's not easy to build the right kind of culture, manage the top team, recruit and retain great people, develop a growth plan, and lay in a solid infrastructure. But if you do it right, you'll be a great leader. And in the process, your organization will reap tremendous rewards in the form of enhanced innovation, greater agility, and faster, more profitable growth. Your company will become a magnet for awesome people. Your company will be an awesome organization.

APPENDIX A

GLOSSARY OF GROWTH AND ORGANIZATION-BUILDING TERMS

ACCOUNTABILITY—Assignment of ultimate responsibility for achieving specific goals as defined in a plan. Holding someone accountable means clearly defining expected results, milestones, and measures of success. Establishing accountability requires: (1) getting agreement with the individual on the expectations; (2) clearly delineating the rewards for achieving the expectations and the consequences of failure; (3) periodically reviewing performance against expectations; and (4) taking appropriate action based on results.

ACTION PLAN—A written plan for implementing a strategy, solving a problem, or turning a creative idea into a reality. Action plans include a stated goal, steps to take, team members responsible for implementation, resources required, key measures of success, and time frames for steps and for tracking results. Action plans should also include feedback mechanisms for indicating when milestones have been reached or actions completed.

ALIGNMENT—Having everyone in the company understand, accept, and commit to common goals, values, and plans as well as processes for achieving them. Alignment is achieved with frequent, consistent, and systematic communication and involvement of people throughout the organization.

AWESOME—Amazing, extraordinary, superior, incredible, successful beyond your wildest dreams.

BALANCED DECISION MAKING—A technique of (1) soliciting input from everyone affected by the decision that needs to be made; (2) making the decision considering that input; and (3) communicating to all constituents how and why the decision was made.

BAO SCAN—Assessment tool that serves as a checkup on your company's strength and capabilities for building each of the six components of an awesome organization.

BEHAVIORAL INTERVIEWING—A job candidate interviewing technique based on the premise that people will behave in the future as they have in the past. With behavioral interviewing, you ask job candidates for real-life examples of how they handled specific situations in the past.

BRAINSTORMING—Generating a wide variety of ideas or alternatives in a short period of time by following specific ground rules (see appendix D, "Model for Creative Problem Solving").

CONSENSUS—A process that involves hearing, discussing, considering, and understanding each team member's perspectives, ideas, and solutions concerning an issue. In most cases each person in the group will arrive at the same decision, and there will be consensus around a specific decision. However, sometimes there is no consensus, and the CEO or leader will need to make a decision. In either case, all team members must commit to support the decision that's been made, and help communicate and implement it (even if they previously preferred another solution).

CREATIVE REACTION FEEDBACK (CRF)—A technique for responding creatively to new information or ideas and developing raw ideas into solutions by (1) clarifying (without judging) the meaning, intentions, and implications of the idea; (2) identifying at least three things that are most valuable about the idea; and (3) determining what needs to be changed or added to the idea to make it a workable solution.

CREATIVITY—Generating new ideas that have the potential to be turned into new products, services, processes, or ways of doing business.

CROSS-FUNCTIONAL—Teams and/or interactions involving people from different functional areas of a company. Effective and synergistic cross-functional communication and interaction are key requirements for an awesome organization.

CULTURE—The supportive environment and intangibles that enable the mission, vision, strategy, and structure to have an impact on a company. Values are the foundation of culture. The cultural environment empowers people on a daily basis to achieve maximum potential. The seven critical factors (the 7 C's) of an organization's culture include: customer and market focus, communication, collaboration, creativity, continuous learning, constructive leadership, and change management.

EXECUTIVE SPONSOR—An Executive Team member who acts as coach for a team whose leader is not a member of the Executive Team. The sponsor (1) closely monitors the team's analysis of issues, ideas, solutions, and recommendations for change; (2) removes organizational barriers to enable the team to work more effectively; (3) is accountable for helping the team be successful; (4) keeps the Executive Team informed of the team's work; and (5) provides the Executive Team's input and feedback to the team.

FUNCTIONS/FUNCTIONAL AREAS—Often referred to as departments, they include product development, customer service, sales, marketing, human resources, finance, operations, manufacturing, business development, facilities management, management information systems, and research and development.

GOALS—The operating objectives and measures that define specific results to be achieved. They create a focus and direction for collective actions that, in turn, lead to the implementation of Strategic Growth Initiatives. Goals are first stated at the overall company level and then defined at the functional and cross-functional team levels.

INFRASTRUCTURE—The combination of the organizational structure and processes that enables work to flow and tasks to be accomplished most efficiently. Organizational structure and processes support the vision, strategy, culture, and the achievement of all goals.

INNOVATION—The development and implementation of a creative idea for a new product, service, process, or method of working. Incremental innovation involves making small, evolutionary improvements; radical innovation involves achieving a breakthrough that completely alters a market or creates a new one.

JOB PROFILE—A tool used in hiring to define the roles, responsibilities, interdependencies with other positions, skills, and educational and cultural requirements (including values) for a job.

KEY ASSUMPTIONS—See *Market and customer focus.*

LEADERSHIP—Guiding the organization in managing growth and change by setting direction, aligning people to a shared vision, and providing an environment that motivates and inspires them to peak performance.

Leadership produces useful change by building an organization that enables people to continually expand their ability to contribute to a shared vision of the company's future and achieve its desired results.

MARKET AND CUSTOMER FOCUS—An understanding of target markets, target customer needs and their competitive issues, drivers of growth, and your competitors' products and/or substitute products. Includes agreed-upon key assumptions about the future of external forces, trends, and factors in the environment. Examples include: predictions for critical market growth, capital, market and technology trends, and competitive scenarios. Because key assumptions provide the base for planning, if those assumptions change, then the plan will need to be revisited and probably changed.

METRICS—Specific, quantifiable, time-based performance measurements that answer the question "How do we know that we are succeeding?" Metrics help maintain a clear focus and commitment to accomplishing goals and action plans.

MISSION—The organization's statement of a clear, strong, compelling, and enduring purpose. The statement describes what business the company is really in and how it makes a difference for its customers, what the company stands for, its unique contribution to the quality of life, and how the company is different and better than other organizations.

ORGANIZATIONAL STRUCTURE—A clear definition of individual roles, responsibilities and accountabilities, and an understanding of how that structure contributes to and aligns with the organization's mission, values, vision, and strategy. The ideal structure is flat, simple, efficient, and allows for cross-functional interaction.

PARTNERSHIP CHART—A tool that helps build teamwork by having team members commit to writing (1) what they think their goals as team members are; (2) the goals they believe other team members have; (3) what they need from each person on the team to achieve their goals; and (4) what they believe the other people on the team need from them to accomplish their goals.

PERFORMANCE GOALS—The specific objectives for each individual or team that implements the tactics outlined in an action plan.

PROCESS—A defined methodology, procedure, or sequence of steps that enable work to flow smoothly and to be accomplished in an effective and efficient manner. When processes are clearly defined, policies are established to reinforce them, and people are trained to use the processes consistently, the organization becomes more efficient and effective. It is especially critical to define handoffs between departments and functions. It is also important to keep improving and fine-tuning the processes as the company grows.

PROFIT SPIRAL™—A model for successful growth and effective management of a growing company. The model is used as the basis for planning and features a spiral that loops five critical business elements — market and customer focus, mission and values, vision and objectives, strategies and plans, and structure and processes — around a sixth element, a supporting core of culture.

RED FLAGS—Warning signs that indicate all is not right with an organization and changes are needed.

SILOS—A description of what occurs in an organization when departments focus only on their work and their own needs. When people work in silos, they are not aware of or do not consider their interdependencies with other functional areas, and seldom understand how their work fits with the overall strategy of the company. Operating in silos (also known as stove pipes) is a very serious problem that stifles innovation and growth, and inhibits collaboration and synergy among groups and functional areas.

SPOT AWARDS—An informal method of instantly recognizing superior performance with prizes that are given out on the spot.

STRATEGIC GROWTH INITIATIVES—See *Strategy*.

STRATEGY—Specific, broad, and actionable statements that link the mission and vision to reality by defining how the company will implement the vision. The CEO and an executive or top team sets the strategy. A good plan includes three to seven key strategy statements, called Strategic Growth Initiatives, for the current year, with goals and action steps for each initiative, which, when accomplished, position the company to achieve its two- to three-year vision.

STRUCTURE—See *Organizational structure*.

SYNERGY—The interaction of elements that, when combined, produce a total effect that is greater than the sum of the individual elements or contributions. Synergy is achieved in an ideal team whose members come up with innovative and workable solutions by building on each other's perspectives and ideas.

TACTICS—The organization's coordinated efforts and actions in leveraging its strengths and resources to bring about the specific results stated in the Strategic Growth Initiatives and directed and measured by the goals.

TEAM—A group of people who are committed to common goals, concrete deliverables, timelines, and successful metrics. Effective teams achieve synergy by managing differences and working effectively together with full participation, goal setting, balanced decision making, and creative problem solving (see appendix B, "Stages of Growth and the Leader's Roles"). Good teams exchange feedback, learn from successes and failures, run effective meetings, and develop mechanisms to resolve healthy conflicts.

TEAM HUDDLES—A 15-minute team meeting scheduled for the same time each day or each week in which (1) each team member reports on what's happening; (2) the team discusses what it can do to improve its critical metric; and (3) the team talks about how to remove bottlenecks or get their message out to others in the organization.

TEAM LEADER—The individual who is responsible and accountable for enabling his or her team to accomplish its specific goals and to operate as an effective, synergistic team. Team leadership can be assigned to a member of the top team or to another appropriately skilled individual — or the team can appoint its own leader.

VALUES—The specific attitudes, beliefs, and behaviors that are expected and reinforced throughout an organization regarding how to work with customers and with each other to successfully accomplish the mission, vision, and strategy. Values should never be compromised or changed in response to current conditions.

VISION—A series of statements that describe the ideal results to be achieved within a specific time frame (usually 24 to 36 months). These statements are written in the present tense and specify what is new, different, and better in each part of the business (customers, market share, competitive advantage, product/services, sales/marketing growth, financial growth, operations/internal processes, partnerships, people, and culture). Together these statements create a vivid picture, a tangible image of an ambitious, desirable future state that is connected to the customer and better than the current state.

VITAL SIGNS—A tool used in this book to point out fundamental information that is essential to building an awesome organization.

STAGES OF GROWTH AND THE LEADER'S ROLES

In *Leading at the Speed of Growth: Journey from Entrepreneur to CEO,* we highlighted three stages of growth beyond Start-up: Initial Growth, Rapid Growth, and Continuous Growth.

Start-up: During this stage, you're trying to figure out what product or service to offer that will meet the needs of the market and ways your company can provide value to its customers. Your roles as leader are doer and decision maker.

Initial Growth: In this first stage of growth, your company is very sales driven as it tries to launch a new or different product, capture market share, and grow revenues. Company operations are fast paced, highly flexible, and even chaotic. People do whatever is necessary to be successful. Your leadership roles are delegator and direction setter.

Rapid Growth: In the second growth stage, your company is trying to achieve widespread use of its products or services, gain a significant share of its chosen markets, ward off advances from competitors, and move into a market leadership position. Lots of new people need to be hired — rounds and rounds of them. Integrating them and aligning their efforts can be a daunting, never-ending task. Your leadership roles are team builder, coach, planner, and communicator.

Continuous Growth: This final stage is comprised of successive rounds of turbulence and periodic "reinventions" of the company. Rapid Growth has led to many more customers and market opportunities, a much larger employee base, a more complex organization, and the potential to dominate the industry. But, more of everything also includes more potential to go out of control.

In Continuous Growth, the company tries to dominate the industry by finding new markets and growing new niches in the current market, expanding the product lines, providing more total solutions to help customers, and branding itself and its people as thought leaders. Growth strategies include new product development, strategic alliances, acquisitions and mergers, spinning off subsidiaries, lining up corporate partnerships to provide funding, and even an initial public offering (IPO). Your leadership roles in this stage must be strategic innovator, change catalyst, organization builder, and chief of culture.

Note that as the company changes, so do your roles and responsibilities. You'll need to make those changes to successfully lead your company through all stages of growth, as shown in the following figure.

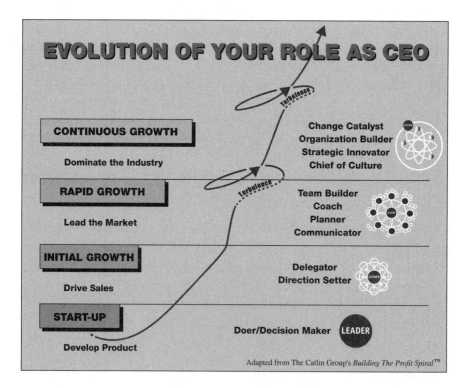

Adapted from The Catlin Group's *Building The Profit Spiral*™

APPENDIX C

CREATING A CORE VALUES STATEMENT FOR GROWTH

PURPOSE OF THE PROCESS

To strengthen the company's culture to support its strategies for profitable growth by creating a Core Values Statement that articulates its operating values, style, and commitments to customers and employees.

Values are beliefs about working for success that members of an organization care most deeply about. They must be the benchmarks that shape how a company deals with both its customers and with one another, and will collectively define the corporate culture. These can't be platitudes and apple pie, but rather, must be real influences on day-to-day actions, reactions, and decisions. They will be guiding principles describing *how* a company will operate to successfully fulfill its mission, vision, and strategies.

GOALS OF THE PROCESS

- Define the cultural values and operating principles that are critical to supporting the mission, vision, and strategy for growth.

- Ensure that these values and principles are understood and followed.

- Involve all people in creating and using them.

- Design and use effective systems to ensure accountability for using them.

BENEFITS

- Clarifies the company's identity, image, and differentiation from any other company.

- Ensures consistent behaviors and decisions across all locations.

- Guides decision making, problem solving, goal achievement at all levels — also hiring, performance review, and professional development.

- Provides motivation, inspiration, energy, and excitement.

PROCESS

1. Set goals for the purpose and outcomes of the process with the top team.

2. Gather input from all managers and staff (using the following Team Exercise in groups of 8 to 10). Top team also analyzes what values are implicit in the company's current operations, plans, activities, and programs — and the CEO's belief system.

3. Top team uses the Team Exercise themselves and then uses input from all other groups to create a draft and plan for next steps.

4. Get feedback on the top team's draft from key managers and staff and refine; consider using a values communication team to help.

5. Roll out final version to everyone with training in how to use it.

6. Establish systems, processes, and programs to ensure "Values in Action" and monitor regularly.

TEAM EXERCISE TO DEFINE CORE VALUES STATEMENT

20 min.: Brainstorm — Using the Brainstorming Rules (see appendix D, "Model for Creative Problem Solving"), fill one page on a flip chart for each question (approximately 5 to 10 min. each).

10 min.: Prioritize — Each individual chooses the 3 "most critical to success" and "fundamental to what the company stands for" for each question.

10 min.: Summarize — Write the team's list of 4 to 6 core values/operating principles to live by.

30 min.: Describe — Write descriptions for each value of the visible, observable behaviors that exemplify that value. These descriptions should define specifically what people should be held accountable for.

1. From the customers' (and future customers') points of view, what is the company's "hallmark"?

   Thought starters:

   - What do you want the company to stand for in customers' minds that makes it unique?

   - How is the company distinguished from all others?

   - What is it known for?

   - What is it admired for?

2. From the employees' point of view, what is the company's "hallmark"?

   Thought starters:

   - How does the company inspire its people?

   - What do you want the company to stand for (in employees' minds) that makes it unique?

   - How is the company distinguished from all others?

   - What is it known for?

   - What is it admired for?

3. What values are most important to you, personally, in accomplishing your best work?

Thought starters:

- What values make you most proud to be a part of this company?

- What values do you care most deeply about?

- What values are critically important to the company's success?

- How are these values being visibly demonstrated in the future?

4. What behaviors or commitments must be *consistent* in every part of the company to fulfill the company's mission and vision — and help it successfully overcome its challenges?

Thought starter:

- What should people be *doing* on a daily basis when they are living up to these values? (Use verbs in your lists.)

APPENDIX **D**

MODEL FOR CREATIVE PROBLEM SOLVING

This is a useful tool to spur creative thinking and innovation that can be used by either teams or individuals to solve problems, plan new initiatives, or create new opportunities. Encourage continuous innovation and improvement by making sure everyone in the company learns how to use this 8-step model.

1. **Discovery:** Gather facts, feedback, and ideas from appropriate sources on the issue.

2. **Opportunity Statement:** Complete this sentence — "How might we . . .?" (Fill in the blank with a clear goal that states the compelling opportunity for the company.)

3. **Future State:** List all the best outcomes when the Opportunity Statement ("How might we . . . ?") is answered.

4. **Present State:** List all barriers or gaps in current situation standing in your way, and then prioritize the most significant.

Model for Creative Problem Solving, © 2001, The Catlin Group.

5. Brainstorm Alternatives: List ideas to overcome each of the high-priority barriers and gaps using these Brainstorming Rules:

- Establish a time limit.

- Request free flow of ideas from all participants.

- List every idea.

- Do not judge.

- *Do not discuss.*

- Think far out.

- Build on others' ideas.

When the time is up, stretch for more ideas — an additional 20 percent. Then choose the most interesting alternatives and use Creative Reaction Feedback to further develop them.

6. Solutions: Select the most promising potential solutions and test with criteria:

- Fit with Future State, as defined earlier in Step 3.

- Fit with the company's mission, values, vision, and plan.

- Feasibility; can you see the next step?

Then use the Creative Reaction Feedback to develop these potential solutions into viable strategic objectives and initiatives.

7. Action Plan: Set goals, identify resources required, action steps, time frames, who is responsible, metrics of success, and accountability.

8. Communicate and Track: Communicate to all who are affected by the plan to get their agreement and commitment, and then monitor progress until results are achieved.

EXAMPLES OF MISSION, VALUES, AND VISION STATEMENTS

The mission, values, and vision are the bedrock of a company's plan. Here are examples of mission, values, and vision statements from two companies. Notice that each has a different way of articulating these fundamental parts of their plans, but that they both follow the definitions of mission, values, and vision used in this book as well as in the Building the Profit Spiral™ model. You may think these statements are not specific enough — or too specific — but each company's top team chose every word carefully and reached consensus on the statements. These statements now guide everyone in the company to make good decisions and take effective action. Sometimes the statements and the specific words are not as significant as the process by which the words were chosen and statements developed. The process of discussion and development of these statements creates the buy-in and full commitment of everyone in the company. The vision statements are supported by one-year Strategic Growth Initiatives required to achieve the vision. You can use these examples as you create your own mission, values, and vision statements, and strategic growth initiatives (SGIs).

Example #1: *From an electronic marketing company*

MISSION STATEMENT

To help our clients win by building high value electronic dialogs with their customers through innovative technology, extreme service, and strategic creativity.

CORE VALUES

Excellence

- Build knowledge
- Demonstrate thought leadership
- Be accountable
- Have a sense of urgency
- Seek efficiencies

Innovation

- Invent
- Be creative
- Embrace change
- Build on success
- Learn from failure

Teamwork

- Commit to the success of others
- Share expertise
- Respect differences
- Have a sense of humor
- Celebrate victory

Passion and integrity drive everything we do.

THREE-YEAR VISION

- We generate $100 million in revenue and $20 million in operating income with 70 percent gross margins.
- We have 100 percent client satisfaction.
- Our clients are leading companies with whom we have established strategic long-term relationships.
- We solve our clients' strategic business needs through solutions that combine electronic marketing services with automated client-facing tools.

- We receive 50 percent of our revenues via third-party sales channels that provide high sales and operating leverage.

- Technology pervades everything we do, which leads to increased efficiency and cutting edge electronic marketing capabilities.

- Our company's name is synonymous with electronic dialog marketing excellence.

- We have an entrepreneurial culture that attracts, develops, and retains world-class employees.

Example #2: *From a telecommunications equipment company*

MISSION

Our computing solutions enable remote workers to connect to their companies' networks easily and efficiently. We give our customers a clear competitive advantage with our high-quality products and services. We continuously strengthen our values-based, leadership-centered culture, with outstanding people and an environment that nurtures trust, and where all employees participate in the company's success. We strive for growth and profit to provide a healthy return for our shareholders and to give us the flexibility and independence to execute our Mission.

OUR CORE VALUES

To state our values is nothing. Only by our actions do we make them real.

INTEGRITY

To earn the trust of our customers, our peers, and ourselves, we will do more than simply state our values — we will live them as well. We are accountable for our words, for our commitments, and for our actions.

COMMUNICATION

We proactively communicate goals, decisions, and other important information. We value an environment of open and honest communications, trust, respect for others' opinions, and commitment to positive conflict resolution.

CUSTOMER FOCUS AND PASSION

The purpose of our business is to obtain and retain satisfied customers. We deliver high-quality products that meet our customers' needs. We provide exceptional service and support for those products. We measure success by our customers' perceptions of our quality and responsiveness. Above all, we take individual ownership of customer issues.

FOCUS ON RESULTS

We value people and organizations that produce results. We strive for simplicity and encourage people to challenge the status quo to arrive at more effective ways of accomplishing results. We reward outstanding accomplishments.

OUR PEOPLE ARE IMPORTANT

Our people are our most important asset. We respect our employees' right to balance their personal and professional lives, and we value the diversity of our people. We treat each other with respect and dignity. We invest in the growth and development of our employees.

TEAMWORK

We meet diverse challenges with a team-centered culture in which winning teams thrive. We build and support teams that understand each team member's requirements, set objectives, make effective team decisions, and execute as one.

PURPOSE BEFORE ACTION

We are both decisive and steadfast in an environment of constant change. We establish purpose before making decisions and taking action. We stand by each other's decisions and actions. We encourage innovation and risk taking. We search for education in our mistakes.

WINNING

Winning makes teamwork fun. We win by satisfying our customers' needs, by beating our competitors, and by providing a high-performance environment for our employees. We recognize and generously reward winners.

GREAT PEOPLE — GREAT LEADERSHIP

We hire outstanding people and devote ourselves to their success. We establish win-win agreements with all employees. As managers and leaders, we are first and foremost agents for our employees' success.

VISION — WHAT DEFINES SUCCESS IN TWO YEARS?

If we achieve the following, we are a straight A student, graduated at the top of our class, scored 800s on our SATs, and can achieve anything we darn well please with the rest of our lives. We expect no less of ourselves.

MARKET

- We have 70 percent market share of products in our category.

- We record at least 50 percent of our revenue outside North America.

- Our market is defined in our company's terms.

- We are universally recognized by customers, competitors, and the industry in general as the leader in our computing solutions.

PRODUCTS

- Our products are strategically important to customers and meet their needs.

- Our products solve real application needs instead of providing only technological building blocks.

- We always win comparative reviews.

- We have combined our expertise in client software and our understanding of desktop computer applications to build an insurmountable barrier to our competitors.

- We sell a complete family of products that solve the whole gamut of users' needs, using all-important applications on all-important platforms over all-important media.

- We are a model user of our own products.

QUALITY

- Customers universally recognize the quality of our products, sales, service, and support as the highest in our entire industry.

CUSTOMERS

- We completely understand the structure and needs of our top 150 customers.

- Our top 150 customers completely understand our plans and are part of our planning process.

- We have "win-win" agreements with our customers.

- We habitually make decisions from a customer point of view.

PARTNERSHIPS

- Our technology is a component of the majority of companies providing computing solutions for our users' needs.

- We form technology partnerships as needed to build comprehensive solutions for our customers.

- Almost all of our sales are leveraged — selling and supporting our products is good business for our channel partners.

CULTURE AND LEADERSHIP

- We can honestly state that we live by our shared mission, vision, and values.

- We attract, motivate, and retain great people.

- Our people are trusted, empowered, and perform at high levels.

FINANCE AND GROWTH

- More than 95 percent of our revenue comes from our core products.

- Our stock is traded publicly at a market capitalization-to-revenue ratio that is higher than average in our industry.

HELPING BUILD YOUR COMPANY'S PROFIT SPIRAL™

This appendix contains information and tools to help you and your top team during planning.*

CREATING A GOOD MISSION STATEMENT

The organization's mission is a statement of its clear, strong, compelling, and enduring purpose. The statement describes what business the company is really in and how it makes a difference for its customers, what the company stands for, its unique contribution to the quality of life, and how the company is different and better than other organizations.

A good mission starts with customer focus and tells how your company will change their world. It defines the problems you help customers solve and tells specifically how you do that better than anyone else does. Your mission should make people feel involved in something that matters. Here are tips on how to write a good mission statement:

- A mission is customer-focused if it:
  - States how your company will solve an important problem for customers.
  - States clearly what your products and services enable customers to do.

All exercises for Building the Profit Spiral™ are copyrighted by The Catlin Group, 2001.

- Focuses your people on knowing what customers value most and in exceeding customer needs and expectations.

- A good mission does not begin with a general statement such as "We're the world's leading provider of (fill in the blank)." By defining what problems you solve for customers and how you enable them to succeed, you create a far more compelling mission than just talking about what you produce. (For example, "We enable people to improve their _____.")

- A mission needs to be broad enough to allow you to pursue new opportunities but narrow enough to keep the organization focused on what its real purpose is. Thus, a well-crafted mission helps people avoid wasting time and resources on opportunities that don't fit with the business you're in as defined by the mission.

- Don't worry about making it something that will fit on a coffee mug or on the back of a T-shirt. A mission needs to describe the uniqueness of who the company is and its reason for being; it's much more than a tag line.

- You know you have a good mission that expresses your company's uniqueness when it's something that your competitors couldn't use as their mission.

AN EXERCISE TO HELP CREATE YOUR VISION

After the Discovery phase of your planning cycle, have your top team use the brainstorming guidelines in appendix D, "Model for Creative Problem Solving," to generate ideas around this scenario: Imagine your company has been named *Fortune* magazine's "Company of the Year" two or three years from now. The magazine asks you to write about what you did to deserve this honor, and asks you to consider these questions:

- What did your organization accomplish? Why is it "Company of the Year?"

- What products and/or services does your company deliver? To what markets and to which customers? How do customers react to your products and services?

- What is your company's size?

- How is the competition responding to your company?

- What image does your company have?

- What is going on inside your company — how is it organized, what are its core values, and what special contributions are your people making?

- What is being done to strengthen the culture as an awesome organization?

- What key partnerships has your company built?

- What does your company feel most satisfied about?

- What are your company's most significant accomplishments in giving customers a competitive advantage in their markets or in improving their lives?

- What absolutely critical success factors brought your company to this level?

- What was particularly innovative?

- How did the CEO and executive team provide the right leadership?

Generate a lot of ideas for each question, listing them in present tense, and then prioritize the most exciting and compelling options for the business. Combine the priorities to create a one- or two-page vision that consists of headline statements of the ideal achievements for each area of the business (customers, market share, competitive advantage, product/services, sales/marketing growth, financial growth, operations/internal processes, partnerships, people, and culture) with three or four supporting bullets for each headline that describe specifically what will be new, different, or better when the headline is achieved. These bullets in the vision statement become your company's set of objectives to be accomplished in a two- to three-year time frame. The vision statement will be updated each year to keep the company continuously focused on a two- to three-year horizon.

CREATIVE REACTION FEEDBACK (CRF)

A key objective throughout the planning process is to assure alignment — to make certain that there is an organization-wide understanding of — and commitment to — the company's direction and goals. Throughout the process, when new plans and ideas are being proposed and described, it is critical to make sure people learn about and get involved in each of the elements of the Profit Spiral that have been developed by the top team. Rather than simply tell everyone what the plan is, you can get a deeper involvement through a process called Creative Reaction Feedback, which is facilitated in three steps:

- Ask people to listen for understanding, without judging. To do this, have people ask clarifying questions and play back what they think the intentions and implications are of what they're hearing.

- Ask people to tell you what's really exciting and valuable about the mission, values, vision, plan, and/or proposed ideas — and why.

- Finally, have people identify concerns they have and their suggestions for changes to the ideas. Then solicit their help in brainstorming to further develop ideas for successful implementation.

This sequence is important in leading people through a thought process that enables them to internalize the information, identify its benefits, and find creative solutions to any issues raised. Using CRF in situations every day is a great way to acknowledge and empower people and encourage innovation.

TIPS FOR A MORE EFFECTIVE PLANNING PROCESS

Tip #1: Use a trained facilitator. No matter how skilled you are as a facilitator or as a planner, it is generally more effective to bring in an outside facilitator to lead planning meetings. Using a facilitator frees you from having to play the difficult dual role as facilitator of the process and participant with your own ideas, priorities, and contributions to make. This helps assure that you won't be so busy facilitating that you don't have time to get your own good ideas up on the board. Also, it eliminates the possibility that you will dominate the meeting just because you're the one standing up front. Using another member of the top team, such as a Human Resources person who is trained in facilitating, is also problematic because it means this person is unable to bring the full value that he or she would bring as a participating team member, and you might miss out on some great feedback and ideas.

Tip #2: Let people throughout the organization participate at key points. The first time you can involve people is during the Discovery phase. Seek people's feedback about your organization's SWOT (strengths, weaknesses, opportunities, and threats), and ask them what they think the company's mission and vision should be. Use the *BAO SCANs* included in this book to gather such input. Use this information in the first off-site during the Visioning and Planning phase.

The next chance for involving people is in cross-functional teams to propose and implement strategies for the company plan. Also, during the creation of the departmental plans, everyone should participate in a process that mirrors the one used by the executive team to create the company plan. A side benefit of having people participate in the planning process is that it builds skills in strategic thinking and creative problem solving, effective meeting management, and listening.

By seeking input and participation at these key times, as well as during the companywide meeting where you share the growth plan, you can create a spirit of commitment and consensus throughout the organization. Also, quarterly meetings for tracking progress and solving emerging issues offer an opportunity to involve people.

Tip #3: Involve your awesome people in special ways. Be sure to put your awesome people on the cross-functional teams that are addressing issues that involve more than one department. You may want the best-of-the-best to lead these teams.

Another idea for getting awesome employees involved in planning is to form a Strategic Advisory Team (SAT). This group includes a nonmanagement representative from each functional area, with people rotating in and out of the group on a 6- to 12-month basis. Having received a thorough briefing on the plan and its importance, the SAT meets regularly with employees to gather ideas about how the plan can be met, what problems are emerging, and how morale is being maintained throughout the organization. The SAT reports what it has learned to management, serving an important role as strategic advisors. As your organization grows, such a group can help management keep in touch with employees and vice versa. It's an honor to serve on the SAT, and it becomes a great way to recognize awesome people by enabling them to participate in this way.

Tip #4: Build accountability into the plan. For many organizations, this is the hardest job of all. You want to hold people's feet to the fire, but when you're not getting great performance, it's easy to let it slide because you want to avoid unpleasant confrontations. The key for overcoming this difficulty is to have a clear definition of success in the plan, as well as having incentives in place so that people know what they will gain by succeeding. But, you also need to make the consequences of failure clear, too. Having everybody in the company clear on what will happen to the company if the plan's goals are not achieved and having them involved in tracking progress builds support for the plan.

INDEX